BIOSCIENTIFIC
DLOGY

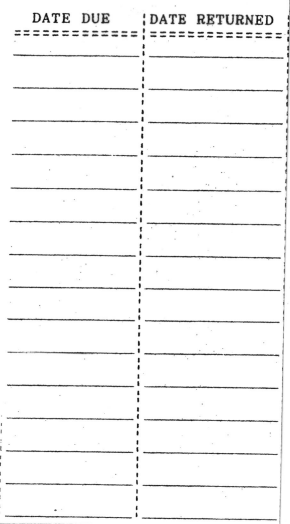

DATE DUE	DATE RETURNED

BIOSCIENTIFIC TERMINOLOGY

Words From Latin and Greek Stems

DONALD M. AYERS

THE UNIVERSITY OF ARIZONA PRESS
Tucson

This book includes, in part, many definitions drawn from the following specialized dictionaries:

Blakiston's New Gould Medical Dictionary. Copyright ©1956 by McGraw-Hill, Inc. Used with permission of McGraw-Hill Book Company.

A Dictionary of Biological Terms by Henderson and Kenneth, by permission of Litton Educational Publishing, Inc.

The University of Arizona Press
© 1972 The Arizona Board of Regents

Library of Congress Control Number 74-163010
ISBN 978-0-8165-0305-6

Manufactured in the United States of America
on acid-free, archival-quality paper.

12 11 10 09 08 07   18 17 16 15 14 13

CONTENTS

FOREWORD

Students of the biological sciences*—especially beginners—are often dismayed at the large number of "new" words they encounter in their studies. They frequently ask, "Why can't I learn biology without learning all those words I'll never use?" In response, some instructors, especially those teaching courses designed for non-science majors, have tried to develop courses containing only a minimum number of "new" words without completely obscuring the bioscientific concepts meant to be taught. Most such attempts have had only limited success.

Unfortunately for those who dislike learning "new" words, meaningful dialogues on any subject depend upon the utilization of words that have precise meanings—precise meanings which are known to both parties! Everyone, at one time or another, has been involved in discussions wherein apparent differences of opinion have vanished as soon as the words being used were adequately defined.

In science, where precision of meaning is all important, knowledge of a large number of words, each with a very exact meaning, is essential to the learning process. In fact, the preface to the twenty-fourth edition of Dorland's *Illustrated Medical Dictionary* states, "All learning in science is based on education in vocabulary, for the imagery of words and symbols is the only means of expression of scientific data and concepts. For the continuing successful interchange of ideas, the words and ideographs of science must have precise and specific meanings. . . ." Dorland's dictionary consists of 1,724 pages of definitions of terms, with some fifty to sixty different terms on each page—all words judged to be of importance to a medical doctor in communicating precisely (holding "meaningful dialogue") with his peers on the many facets of modern medical science. Obviously other fields of biological science utilize still other words!

---

*The term "biological sciences" is used here in the broad sense to include not only the classical divisions, such as botany, microbiology and zoology (together with their subdivisions) but also the many applied fields, such as agriculture, agronomy, medicine and wildlife management.

If each of these words is viewed as simply another "new" word to be "memorized"—then you as a user have reason to be dismayed. Fortunately, most of these "new" words of the bioscientific vocabulary are the result of the combining of relatively few prefixes, stems and suffixes of Greek and Latin origin. Mastery of even only a few of these gives an immediate insight into the precise meaning of a large number of "new" words.

Answering the probable query, "Why Greek and Latin?", we turn to a twofold answer. First, English, as we know it today, has evolved from an Indo-European parent language. Classical Greek and Latin are other branches from the same origin. A general reference on the origin and development of the English language, such as that on pages 1–14 in Donald M. Ayers's *English Words from Latin and Greek Elements* (Tucson: University of Arizona Press, 1965) will establish more about this relationship.

Second, for many centuries in our Western civilization, the educated man—whether a native speaker of English, French, German, Swedish or some other language—was traditionally a student of both classical Greek and Latin. Logically, early scientists utilized these two "common" languages to communicate with other scientists. As new facts, ideas and concepts emerged, "new" words were coined, utilizing appropriate stems, prefixes and suffixes of Greek or Latin origin.

This practice continues today. As a result, bioscientific words are more or less identical in many languages other than English. Most scientists realize that the scientific name of a plant or animal consists of two Latin or Latinized words and is written *in the Latin alphabet,* no matter what language is being used. Thus, even if we were using Sanskrit, Chinese or Japanese, the scientific name of man is still *Homo sapiens,* and is so written.

As noted by Donald M. Ayers, most books in the past written as aids to the student wishing to become familiar with bioscientific terminology ". . . attempt to impart some knowledge of the Latin and Greek languages . . ., consequently they tend to be written more from the standpoint of Latin and Greek than of English and give considerable attention to Latin and Greek grammar, a matter of which . . . the student who is primarily trying to improve his vocabulary regards as extraneous."

As a result of Dr. Ayers's many years of teaching a course in scientific terminology to English-speaking students, he developed the following set of guides. Unlike most previous presentations, they are written from the point of view of the speaker of English. Stems or bases (e.g., DUC-, NOMIN-) are given rather than actual Latin and Greek words (e.g., *ducere, nomen, nominis*), and the meanings attached to them are not necessarily those of the Latin but rather those which they have when used in English derivatives. Suffixes are treated not so much with regard to their origin as to their present form and meaning. Thus, for example, no distinction has been made between the English adjectival suffixes *-ary,* derived from Latin *-aris* (as in military), and *-ary,* derived from *-arius* (as in arbitrary). For the same reason the discussion of grammatical points has been kept to a minimum.

Each lesson consists of four parts: an explanatory section, frequently including new prefixes or suffixes; a list of new bases with examples of their uses; an exercise which requires use of all new material; and a list of additional words for further work or for tests.

Careful attention to these lessons will give you not only a relatively painless and highly interesting familiarity with the many words presented but also equip you to make logical deductions about the precise meaning of most other "new" words you may encounter in your particular specialty within the biological sciences.

E. LENDELL COCKRUM
Professor of Biological Science
University of Arizona

PART I
BIOSCIENTIFIC WORDS
DERIVED FROM GREEK

LESSON 1.   Introduction to Greek Bases and Prefixes

The words which we shall be studying are long, complicated scientific terms derived from Greek and Latin. Such words can usually be divided into elements of three types—*bases* (sometimes called *roots* or *stems*), *prefixes* and *suffixes*. Throughout this book bases will be printed in capitals followed by a hyphen. Variant forms of the bases rarely used to build English words will appear in parenthesis. Prefixes and suffixes will be printed in italics. Thus the word *amphibious* is made up of the following elements:

amphi-, "both" + BI-, "life" + *-ous,* "pertaining to"

Synthesis is composed of:

syn-, "together" + THE-, "to put" + *-sis,* "act of"

Energy is made up of:

en-, "in" + ERG-, "work" + *-y,* "state of"

These three elements have been used over and over again in the formation of English biological terminology. In *Gould's Medical Dictionary,* for example, entries containing the base ACR-, "highest," or "the extremities," occupy two full pages as follows:

acroagnosis, acroanesthesia, acroarthritis, acroasphyxia, acroataxia, acroblast, acrocephalopagus, acrocephalosyndactylia, acrocephaly, acrochordoma, acrochordon, acrocinesis, acrocontracture, acrocyanosis, acrodermatitis, acrodigitalin, acrodolichomelia, acrodont, acrodynia, acroedema, acroesthesia, acrogeria, acrognosis, acrohyperhidrosis, acrohypothermy, acrokeratosis, acromacria, acromania, acromastitis, acromegaloidism, acromegaly, acromelalgia, acrometagenesis, acromicria, acromioclavicular, acromiocoracoid, acromiohumeral, acromion, acromiothoracic, acromphalous, acromyotonia, acronarcotic, acroneuropathy, acroneurosis, acronychous, acronyx, acropachy, acropachyderma, acroparalysis, acroparesthesia, acropathology, acropathy, acropetal, acrophobia, acropigmentation, acroposthitis, acroscleroderma, acrosclerosis, acrosome, acrosphenosyndactylia, acrostealgia, acroteric, acrotrophoneurosis.

First of all, let us consider Greek bases. These were originally Greek words, but through time the characteristic endings (such as *-a, -on, -os*) have been removed. Thus, from *ergon,* "work," comes the English base ERG- (as in *allergy*); from the Greek *bios,* "life," has come the base BI- (as in biology and biochemistry). Most dictionaries, in describing the origin of a term of Greek ancestry give the Greek word from which it has been derived (e.g., *ergon* or *bios*) rather than the base, but if one keeps the English word in mind, he will generally have no trouble determining the base that has been used.

Of course, in some instances actual Greek words which have not been anglicized appear in English with their original endings retained, as, for instance, *psyche, criterion, pleura, phenomenon.* But usually only the base is used.

Sometimes a base appears by itself, without the addition of prefixes or suffixes. Occasionally a final silent *e* is added.

CRYPT-, "hidden"   —crypt
ERG-, "work"   —erg (a unit of work or energy)
CYCL-, "circle," "wheel"   —cycle
PYR-, "fire"   —pyre

Much more often, however, two or more bases are combined, or prefixes and suffixes are added, as in the following:

CHOLE-, "bile" + CYST-, "bladder" + ENTER (o)-, "intestine" + STOM-, "mouth" + -*y*, "state of"–cholecystenterostomy, "the surgical formation of a communication between the gall bladder and the intestine"

anti-, "against" + PYR-, "fire" + -*(e)tic*, "pertaining to"–antipyretic, "an agent that reduces fever"

When two or more bases are combined, frequently an *o* appears between them as a connective. For example:

PSYCH(o)-, "mind" + SOMAT-, "body"   + -*ic*
    psychosomatic
THERM(o)-, "heat" + DYNAM-, "power" + -*ics*
    thermodynamics

Some dictionaries, in listing such word elements as separate entries, which they call "combining forms," include the *o*, giving PSYCHO-, THERMO-, and so forth. There are numerous words, however, in which this *o* does not appear, such as *psychiatry, thermal* and *diathermy.*

Frequently prefixes are attached to bases. Prefixes were originally Greek prepositions or adverbs but now are found as elements which never occur by themselves but which are placed in front of a base to modify the meaning of the base. Examples are *en-*, as in *energy;* *amphi-*, as in *amphibious;* and *syn-*, as in *synthesis*, all listed previously.

Most Greek prefixes end in a vowel, which usually disappears before an initial vowel or *h* in a base.

para-graph and *para-site*, but *par-ody*

cata-strophe and *cata-logue*, but *cat-holic*

hypo-dermic and *hypo-thesis*, but *hyp-hen*

A base may be preceded by more than one prefix.

a-, "not" + *syn-*, "together" + CHRON-, "time" + *ous*
    asynchronous

par-, "beside" + *en-*, "in" + THE-, "to place" + *-sis*
    parenthesis

Learn the following prefixes and their meanings.

1. *a-* (*an-* before vowels or *h*), "not," "without"

    examples: atheist, atypical, amoral
                anarchy, anesthetic

2. *amphi-, ampho-*, "both," "on both sides of," "around"

    examples: amphibious, amphitheater
                amphogenic   (producing   approximately
                    equal numbers of male and female
                    offspring)

3. *ana-* (*an-* before vowels or *h*), "up," "back," "again"

    examples: analysis, anatomy, anachronism
                anode, aneurysm

4. *anti-* (*ant-* before vowels or *h*), "against," "opposite"

    examples: antidote, antitoxin, antiseptic
                antagonist, antarctic

5. *apo-* (*ap-* before vowels or *h*), "from," "off," "away"

    examples: apology, apostle
                aphorism, apheliotropism (tendency to
                    turn away from light)

6. *cata-* (*cat-* before vowels or *h*), "down," "against," "according
        to," "very"

    In many English words it is difficult to see the force of this prefix.

examples: catalyst, catastrophe
category, cathode, catholic

7.   *dia-* (*di-* before vowels or *h*), "through," "across," "between"

examples: diameter, diagnosis
diocese, diopter (unit of measurement of the refractive power of a lens)

NEW BASES

Learn the following bases and their meanings.

1.   ALG-, "pain" (-*algesia*, "sense of pain")
(gen.) nostalgia

analgesic—remedy for relieving pain

neuralgia—pain along the course of a nerve

algolagnia—sexual pleasure derived from the experiencing or inflicting of pain

algedonic—pertaining to the pleasantness-unpleasantness dimension in experience

causalgia—burning pain sometimes present in injuries to the nerves

2.   ARTHR-, "joint," "speech sound," "articulation"

arthritis—inflammation of a joint

dysarthria—impairment of speech articulation

arthropod—a member of the phylum Arthropoda, including crustaceans, insects and spiders

enarthrosis—a ball-and-socket joint, as, for instance, the hip

arthrobranchial—joint gills

arthropterous—having jointed fin-rays, as fishes

diarthrosis—a freely movable articulation

nearthrosis—a new and abnormally produced articulation in the sequence of a fracture, dislocation or disease of the bone

stereoarthrolysis—loosening stiff joints by operation or manipulation in cases of ankylosis

synarthrophysis—progressive ankylosis of a joint

3.   BI-, "life"
(gen.) biography, autobiography, amphibious

biomorphic—related to the forms of living beings; often used of primitive art

symbiosis—a condition in which two organisms live together for mutual benefit

diplobiont—a plant flowering or bearing fruit twice in a season

biopsy—the examination of living tissue

abiogenesis—the theory of the production of living matter from nonliving matter

biochrome—a pigment synthesized in the metabolic process of living organisms

biotherapy—the treatment of diseases by means of substances secreted by living organisms, as serums

dermatobiasis—infection with Dermatobia (botflies); larvae are obligatory sarcobionts

geobios—terrestrial life

metabiosis—a relationship between two organisms in which only one of the partners benefits

photobiotic—living in light exclusively

psychobiology—psychology in relation to biology

4. BALL-, BOL-, -BLE, "to throw," "to put"

(gen.) ballistics, symbol, parable (literally, a comparison), diabolic, hyperbole (literally, an exaggeration), problem, discobolus (discus-thrower)

xeriobole—a plant that scatters its seeds by dehiscence through dryness

metabolism—the process by which assimilated food is built up into protoplasm and by which protoplasm is broken down into waste matter with the release of energy

embolism—the destruction of a blood vessel by foreign matter lodged in it

hemiballismus—a condition characterized by violent spasmodic movements of the extremities on one side of the body

embololalia—the insertion of meaningless words into speech in some schizophrenic states

epiboly—a process of overgrowth in gastrulation in telolecithal eggs

periblem—layers of ground or fundamental tissue between dermatogen and plerome of growing points

Sporobolus—genus of grasses to which dropseed belongs

5. BRADY-, "slow"

bradycarpic—fruiting after the winter in the second season after flowering

bradycardia—abnormal slowness of the heart (pulse rate less than sixty beats a minute)

bradylexia—abnormal slowness in reading

6. CRYPT-, "hidden"

(gen.) crypt, cryptography, cryptanalysis, cryptic, crypto-communist

crypt—various recesses, glandular cavities, etc. in the body, as tonsillar crypts

cryptogam—a plant that does not have apparent reproductive organs

cryptorchism—a condition in which the testes fail to descend

cryptesthesia—the power of perceiving without sensory mechanism; clairvoyance

cryptoclastic—made up of minute fragmental particles, often used to designate a type of rock

cryptogenic—of unknown or obscure cause

cryptophyte—a plant that produces its buds underwater or underground

cryptovolcanic—produced by completely concealed volcanic action

cryptozoic—fauna dwelling in darkness or under rocks

syncryptic—pertaining to protective resemblance between diverse species

7. DROM-, "running," "course"

(gen.) dromedary (a camel trained for running), airdrome, hippodrome

acrodromous—pertaining to a leaf in which the veins converge at the point

syndrome—a number of symptoms that occur at the same time, characterizing a particular disease

heterodromia—a condition in which a nerve conducts impulses better in one direction than in the other

dromomania—a pathological desire to wander

anadromous—pertaining to fishes migrating annually from salt to fresh water

adromia—a complete failure of impulse conduction in muscles or nerves

dromography—process of registering by instrument the velocity of blood current

photodromy—the movement of particles suspended in a fluid toward light or away from it

8. GE-, "earth"

    (gen.) geology, geometry, geography, George, geophysics

    geomancy—divination by examining the figures formed on the ground when a handful of earth is thrown

    geocarpy—the ripening of fruits underground, as with the peanut

    geophagy—the practice of eating earth

    geophilous—living in or on the earth

    amphigean—native around the world

    geophyte—a land plant; a plant with dormant parts underground

    geotaxis—locomotor response to gravity

    hypogeous—growing or maturing under the earth's surface

9. HOD-, OD-, "road," "way"

    (gen.) period, episode, exodus, synod, method, cathode

    anode—a positive electrode

    hodophobia—abnormal fear of travel

    esodic—afferent nerve conducting impulses to the central nervous system

    prosodus—a canal in sponges

    urodeum—the portion of the cloaca into which the urogenital ducts open

10. MNE-, "to remember"

    (gen.) mnemonic, amnesty

    amnesia—loss of memory

    pseudomnesia—a condition in which events seem to be remembered which have not been actually experienced

    acousmatamnesia—inability to remember sounds

    autoanamnesia—a history related by the patient

catamnesis—the medical history of a patient following illness or behavior disorder

ecmnesia—loss of memory of recent happenings but retention of events occurring in a remote period

mnemodermia—pruritis and discomfort of the skin hours and days after the cause of symptoms has been removed

11.   MORPH-, "form"

(gen.) morphine, metamorphosis, anthropomorphic, amorphous

theriomorphic—pertaining to a divinity represented in the form of an animal

morphology—the study of structure and form

polymorphonuclear—having a nucleus with several lobes

dysmorphophobia—abnormal fear of deformity

actinomorphous—radially symmetrical

enantiomorph—one of a pair of isometric substances that are mirror images with asymmetrical structure

gynandromorphy—the degree or prominence of feminine characteristics in male physique and vice versa

mesomorphic—characterized by a predominance of structures such as bone and muscle, which are developed from the mesodermal layer of the embryo; athletic build

morpheme—a word or part of a word that conveys meaning and can't be broken down any further and still convey meaning

phyllomorphosis—variation of leaves at different seasons

12.   ODONT-, "tooth"

(gen.) mastodon, orthodontist

exodontist—a dentist who specializes in the extraction of teeth

prosthodontia—the branch of dentistry which deals with the replacement of teeth by artificial means

pleurodont—having the teeth fastened to the side of the bone, as with some lizards

homodont—having teeth all alike

polyphyodont—having many successive sets of teeth

rhizodontotropy—pivoting an artificial crown on the root of a tooth

tetraselenodont—having four crescentic ridges on molar teeth *xanthodont*—having yellow-colored incisors, as certain rodents

13. PHOR-, PHER-, "to bear," "to go"
(gen.) semaphore, periphery, phosphorus, metaphor
gynophore—a stalk that supports an ovary
oophorectomy—the surgical removal of an ovary
heterophoria—a tendency of the eyes to turn away from the correct position
euphoria—an exaggerated feeling of well-being
chromatophore—a pigment-bearing cell
aerophore—a device for inflating the lungs with air in the case of a still-born child or asphyxia
metaphery—the displacement of organs
odontophore—the tooth-bearing organ in molluscs
osmodysphoria—intolerance of certain odors
photophore—luminous organs of certain crustaceans

14. PLEX-, "stroke"; PLEG-, "paralysis"
paraplegia—paralysis of the lower half of the body
laryngoplegia—paralysis of the larynx
apoplexy—sudden paralysis with loss of consciousness, caused by the breaking or blocking of a blood vessel in the brain
diplegia—paralysis of similar parts on two sides of the body
quadriplegia—the four extremities of the body paralyzed

15. POD-, -PUS, "foot"
(gen.) tripod, podium, antipodes, octopus
podiatrist—one who treats minor disorders of the feet
micropus—congenital abnormal smallness of the feet
cephalopod—molluscs with sucker-bearing arms on the region of the head, such as the octopus
adenopodous—bearing glands on peduncles or petioles
cynopodous—with nonretractile claws
metapodium—posterior portion of the molluscan foot
podotheca—a foot-covering, as of birds or reptiles

16. PROCT-, "anus," "rectum"
proctology—the medical specialty concerned with the anus, rectum and sigmoid colon

cytoproct—the point at which waste is discharged from a cell

periproct—the surface immediately surrounding the anus of echinoids

proctostasis—constipation due to nonresponse of rectum to the defecation stimulus

17. STOL-, STAL-, -STLE, "to send," "to contract"
(gen.) epistle, apostolic

systole—the contraction of the heart

peristalsis—the rhythmic contraction of the alimentary canal that moves its contents onward

anastalsis—antiperistalsis

catastalsis—the downward-moving wave of contraction occurring in the stomach during digestion

hemisystole—contracting of the left ventricle after every second atrial contraction

telediastolic—relating to the last phase of a diastole

thermosystaltic—contracting under the influence of heat; pertaining to muscular contraction due to heat

18. STOM-, STOMAT-, "mouth," "opening"
(gen.) stomach

gymnostomatous—referring to mosses having a naked mouth, i.e., without a peristome

enterostomy—an operation to form an artificial opening into the intestine

stomatitis—inflammation of the mouth

odontostomatous—having tooth-bearing jaws

actinostome—five-rayed oral apperture of starfish

microstome—a small opening or orifice

nephrostome—the opening of a nephridial tubule into the body cavity

19. TROP-, TREP-, "to turn," "response to stimulus"
(gen.) tropic (literally, pertaining to the sun turning at the solstice), heliotrope (literally, that which turns toward the sun)

apotropaic—intended to avert evil, as a ritual

apheliotropism—the turning away from the sun

phototropic—responding to the stimulus of light

esotropia—a condition in which one eye deviates inward while the other fixes upon an object; convergent concomitant strabismus

anisotropia—the quality of being doubly refractive or unequally refractive in different directions

autotropism—tending to grow in a straight line, applies to plants unaffected by external stimulus

barotropic—response to pressure stimulus

orthotropism—growth in a vertical line

stereotropism—growth or movement toward a solid body

Treponema—genus of spiral organisms; *Treponema pallidum* causes syphilis

treponemiasis—infection with treponema; syphilis

20. UR-, "urine," "urinary system" (URE-, "to urinate")

ureter—a tube carrying the urine from the kidney to the bladder

uremic—pertaining to the presence of urine in the blood

albuminuria—the presence of albumin in the urine

hippuric acid—an acid found in high concentration in urine of herbivorous animals

urocyanosis—blue discoloration of the urine

urolithiasis—the formation of urinary calculi

EXERCISE

List the prefixes and bases and give their meanings.

1. *anatropia*—a tendency of the eyes to turn upward when at rest; anaphoria

2. *antibiotic*—pertaining to antibiosis, an association between two or more organisms which is harmful to one of them; tending to destroy life

3. *amphipodous*—having feet for walking and feet for swimming

4. *anamorphosis*—evolution from one type to another through a series of gradual changes

5. *anticryptic coloration*—protective coloration facilitating attack

6. *anabolism*—synthetic or constructive metabolism, the conversion of nutritive material into more complex living matter

7. *cataphoresis*—the movement of suspended particles through a fluid under the action of applied electromotive force

8. *arthralgia*—pain in a joint

9. *aphodal*—applied to a type of canal system in sponges

10. *apoplexy*—the symptom complex resulting from hemorrhage into or upon the brain, or from embolism or thrombosis of the cerebral vessels

11. *cataplexy*—a sudden and overwhelming emotion, fright or shock causing muscular rigidity in some animals; in man, the sudden loss of muscle tone provoked by exaggerated emotion

12. *diaphoresis*—perspiration, especially perceptible perspiration

13. *apogee*—point of an orbit of a satellite farthest from the earth

14. *diageotropism*—tendency of certain parts of plants to assume position at right angles to direction of gravity

15. *proctodaeum*—the latter part of the embryonic alimentary canal, formed by anal invagination

16. *antidromic*—contrary to the normal direction; applied to conduction of an impulse along an axon toward the body of nerve cell

17. *diuretic*—an agent that increases the volume of urine

18. *amphistomous*—having a sucker at each end of the body, as certain worms

19. *diastole*—the rhythmic period of relaxation and dilatation of a chamber of the heart during which it fills with blood

20. *bradydiastolic*—pertaining to a prolongation of the diastolic interval

21. *anastomosis*—the intercommunication of blood vessels by the natural anatomic arrangement which provides alternate pathways for blood supply to a peripheral part

22. *cryptanamnesia*—subconscious memory; the recall to mind of a forgotten episode which seems entirely new to the patient

23. *antiodontalgic* or *antodontalgic*—relieving a toothache

24. *bradyarthria*—slow speech due to organic disturbance of the speech apparatus

25. *anamnesis*—faculty of memory; information gained from the patient and others regarding past history of a case

MORE WORDS TO WORK WITH

acephalostomia
acetonuria
aeroembolism
algesimeter
algophobia
anaerobic
anarthria
arachnordureterostomy
arthropod
arthrostomy
asymbolia
atelopodia
ballistophobia
barodontalgia
blepharoplegia
brachystomatous
bradyacusia
bradygenesis
bradykinesia
bradylogia
bradyphrenic
cephalalgia
cheilostomatoplasty
chemotropism
cryalgesia
cryptococcosis
cryptomenorrhea

cryptomere
diastalsis
dimorphism
distomous
dromic
dromophobia
dysuria
ectodynamorphia
gastralgocenosis
gastropod
geobios
glossoplegia
halobios
helicopod
hemiplegia
heterodromy
hyperalgesia
hypermnesia
hyperuricemia
ideometabolism
labrinthodont
laloplegia
lipometabolism
melangeophilous
melanphore
mogiarthria
mryiapod

nycturia
odontoblastoma
odontoclast
onycgocryptosis
parallelodromous
paramnesia
paroophoritis
pedodontia
phytogeography
pneumoarthrography
podagra
podobromhidrosis
proctalgia
proctoscope
prodrome
pygamorphous
rhizodontropy
siderodromophobia
sporophore
stenostomatous
stomatalgia
stomatomycosis
taurobolium
trepopnea
trophophyte
urozanthin
zoophorous

LESSON 2.   The Greek Alphabet

Though the letters of the Greek alphabet in their original form are used to some extent in scientific terminology, as in the words *sigmoid* and *deltoid*, and are frequently employed as symbols, we are interested in the Greek alphabet here primarily from the standpoint of transliteration. We will focus upon the way in which transliterated Greek words have come to appear in English, for often there is a difference between the original Greek word as it is transliterated in dictionaries and its English derivatives. *Cycle*, for example, comes from the Greek word *kyklos* and *sphere* is derived from *sphaira*.

Most of the letters of Greek words remain the same in their English derivatives, but there are some important exceptions, and, in consulting a dictionary, it will be useful to keep these exceptions in mind.

1.   Greek *k* normally becomes *c*, but occasionally remains *k*.

Greek	*English*
konos	cone
krisis	crisis
kinein	cinema, but kinetic
leukos	leucoma, but leukemia

2.   Greek *ai* becomes *e* or *ae*.

haima	hemorrhage (haemorrhage in British usage)
aisthein	anesthetic, aesthetic

3.   Greek *ei* usually becomes *i*, but sometimes remains *ei*.

cheilos	chiloplasty (or cheiloplasty)
cheir	chiropodist

4.   Greek *oi* becomes *oe* or *e*.

amoibe	amoeba (or ameba)
oikos	economy, ecology, monoecious

Exceptions are *poikilothermic* and *homoiothermic*.

5.   Greek *ou* generally become *u*, but occasionally remains *ou*.

ouron	urine, urogenital
akouein	acoustic, amblyacusia
boule	abulia (or aboulia)

6.   Greek *r* normally appears as *rh* at the beginning of a word or *rrh* within a word.

rhinos	rhinoceros, platyrrhine
rheos	rheostat, catarrh

Learn the following prefixes and their meanings.

1.   *dys-*, "bad," "disordered," "difficult"

examples: dysfunction, dysentery, dystrophy

2.   *es-, eis-*, "inward," "into"

examples: esoteric, esodic (or eisodic)

3. *ec-* (*ex-* before vowels or *h*), "out," "out of," "outside"

        examples: eccentric, ecstasy, eclipse
                      exodus, exodontist

4. *en-* (*em-*, *el-*), "in," "into," "inward"

        examples: energy, enthusiasm
                      embryo, emphatic
                      elliptical

5. *en-* + *anti-*, "opposite"

        examples: enantiopathic (causing opposite feelings),
                      enantiolalia (a disturbance in which the patient says the opposite of what is intended)

6. *endo-*, *ento-* (*end-*, *ent-* before vowels or *h*), "within," "inner"

        examples: endocrine, endoderm, endoparasite
                      entophyte, entozoa (internal animal parasites),
                      endamoeba (or entamoeba), endarteritis (inflammation of the inside of the arteries), entoptic (lying within the eyeball)

7. *epi-* (*ep-* before vowels or *h*), "upon," "on," "to," "in addition to"

        examples: epidemic, epidermis, epitaph
                      eponym, ephemeral

8. *eu-*, "well," "good," "normal"

        examples: eugenics, eulogy

9. *exo-*, *ecto-*, "outside," "external"

        examples: exotic, exoskeleton
                      ectoparasite, ectoderm

NEW BASES

Learn the following bases and their meanings.

1. BUL- (BOUL-), "will"
    paraboulia—abnormality of volitional action
    abulia or *aboulia*—loss of ability to make decisions
    hyperbulia—exaggerated willfulness

2. CARDI-, "heart"
   acardiacus—omphalosite completely lacking a heart
   cardioblast—one of the embryonic cells designed to form the
   walls of the heart
   diplocardiac—having a double heart, or one in which the two
   sides are more or less separate, as in birds and mammals
   hydropericardium—a collection of a serous effusion in the
   pericardial cavity
   myocardial—pertaining to the muscular tissue of the heart
   orthocardiac—dilatation of the right side of the heart which
   occurs when the upright position of the body is
   assumed

3. CEPHAL-, "head" (enCEPHAL-, "brain")
   acanthocephaliasis—infestation with parasitic worms of the
   phylum Acanthocephala
   acrocephaly—deformity of the head in which the top is more
   or less pointed
   cephalopod—marine mollusc with muscular, sucker-bearing
   arms on head region, as the cuttlefish and octopus
   cynocephalous—with the head shaped like a dog's
   encephalodysplasia—maldevelopment of the tissues of the
   central nervous system
   prosencephalon—the forebrain or anterior brain vesicle of the
   embryo

4. CHONDR-, CHONDRI-, "cartilage," "granule"
   (gen.) hypochondriac
   chondriosome or *mitochrondria*—granular, rod-shaped or filamentous organelle in cytoplasm
   chondriokinesis—the division of the chondriosome in mitosis
   and meiosis
   perichondrium—the fibrous connective tissue covering cartilage
   synchondrosis—a joint in which the surfaces are connected by
   a plate of cartilage

5. DEM-, "people," "country"
   (gen.) democracy, demagogue, demographer, epidemic
   apodemialgia—wanderlust, a morbid dislike of homelife with
   desire to wander

ecdemic—not endemic; of foreign origin

pandemic—occurring over a wide geographic area and affecting a large proportion of the people

6. DERM-, DERMAT-, "skin"
(gen.) taxidermy, pachyderm

dermatophyte—one of a group of fungi which invade the superficial skin

dermographia—a condition in which the skin is particularly susceptible to irritation; characterized by elevations or wheals caused by tracing the fingernail or blunt instrument over the skin

mesoderm—the third germ layer, lying between the ectoderm and entoderm, which gives rise to the connective tissue, muscles, urogenital system, etc.

pododerm—dermal layer of a hoof, within the horny layer

7. GAM-, "marriage," "union"
(gen.) bigamy, monogamy, misogamy, polygamy

agamogenesis—asexual reproduction

gamete—sexual cell; a minute reproductive body which is capable of uniting with another of like origin to form a new individual, or zygote; in higher animals, sperms and eggs

aplanogamete—a nonmotile, conjugating germ cell

autogamy—self-fertilization

cytogamy—cell conjugation

gamophyllous—with united perianth leaves

gamostele—stele formed from fusion of several steles

oogamy—the union of a nonmotile female gamete or egg cell with a male gamete

8. LECITH-, "yolk"

centrolecithal—with yolk aggregated in the center

lecithin—a colorless to yellow-brown, waxy solid widely distributed in the body; also found in the yolk of eggs

lecithocoel—segmentation cavity of holoblastic eggs

lysolecithin—a substance having strong hemolytic properties produced from lecithin by the action of snake venom

9. OPHTHALM-, "eye"

megalophthalmus or *megophthalmus*—excessive largeness of the eyes

ophthalmogyric—pertaining to or causing movements of the
eye

photophthalmia—inflammation of the eyes due to excessively
strong light, as welder's arc light or sunlight on snow

podophthalmite—in crustaceans, eye-stalk segment farthest
from the head

xerophthalmia—a dry and thickened condition of the conjunctiva

10.   OST(E)-, "bone"
(gen.) osteopath

actinost—basal bone of fin-rays in teleosts

angiosteosis—ossification of blood vessels

dysostosis—defective formation of bone

heteroosteoplasty—the grafting, by operation, of bone taken
from another animal

osteanagenesis—regeneration of bone

osteodermia—bony formations in the skin

periosteophyte—a morbid, osseous formation upon or proceed-
ing from the periosteum

synostosis—a union of originally separate bones by osseous
material

11.   PHYLL-, "leaf"

adenophyllous—bearing glands or leaves

autophyllogeny—growth of one leaf upon or out of another

lithophyll—a fossil leaf or leaf impression

phylloclade—any flattened stem performing the functions of
leaves, as the joints of cacti

phyllopodous—having leaflike swimming feet, as in Branchio-
poda

phyllotaxy—the arrangement of leaves on an axis or stem

12.   PHYT-, "plant," "growth"
(gen.) neophyte

autophyte—a self-nourished plant

entophyte or *endophyte*—a plant growing within another, either
as a parasite or otherwise

epidermophytosis—term commonly used to indicate any fungus infection of the feet producing scaliness and vesicles with pruritus

gametophyte—in the alternation of generations in plants, the individual or generation which bears sex organs

hematophyte—a vegetable organism, such as a bacterium, living in the blood

zoophyte—an animal resembling a plant in appearance and growth, as sponges

13. PLAS(T)-, "to form," "to mold"
(gen.) plastic, plaster

alloplasty—a plastic operation in which material from outside the human body, such as ivory or animal bone, is utilized

amyloplast or *amyloplastid*—a leucoplast or colorless, starch-forming granule in plants

cytoplasm—substance of the cell body exclusive of the nucleus

hyperplasia—excessive formation of tissue; an increase in the size of a tissue or organ owing to an increase in the number of cells

metaplasia—transformation of one form of adult tissue to another

ooplasm—the cytoplasm of the egg

protoplasm—the viscid material constituting the essential substance of living cells, upon which all vital functions, such as nutrition, secretion and growth, depend

somatoplasm—the protoplasm of the body cells, as distinct from germ plasm, which composes reproductive cells

14. SOM-, SOMAT-, "body"

acrosome—a body at apex of the spermatozoon

dermatosome—one of the vital units forming a cell membrane

gymnosomatous—having no shell or mantle, as certain molluscs

karyomicrosome—a nuclear granule

meromicrosomia—abnormal smallness of some part of the body

somatotopagnosia—inability to identify or orient the body or its parts, usually the result of a brain lesion

somesthesia—sensibility to bodily sensations

somite—a segment of the body of an embryo

15. THEC(A)-, "case," "sheath"
(gen.) apothecary, bibliotheca

apothecium—a cup-shaped ascocarp

cephalotheca—head integument in insect pupa

exotheca—the extracapsular tissue of a coral

hydrotheca—cuplike structure into which the polyp may with-
　　draw in many coelenterates

podotheca—a foot-covering, as of birds or reptiles

theca—spore or pollen case

thecaphore—a structure on which a theca is borne

thecium—the part of a fungus or lichen containing the sporules

thecodont—having teeth in sockets

16. THERM-, "heat"
    (gen.) thermometer, thermite, thermal, thermostat

    adiathermancy—imperviousness to heat waves

    hyperthermalgesia—abnormal sensitivity to heat

    hypothermia—subnormal temperature of the body

    thermophagy—the habit of swallowing very hot food

    thermophyte—a heat-tolerant plant

    thermotropism—curvature in plants in response to a tempera-
    　　ture stimulus

17. TOM-, "to cut," "section" (enTOM-, "insect")
    (gen.) anatomy, tome, atom, appendectomy, epitome

    diatomaceous—microscopic algae divided into halves

    dermatome—the areas of skin supplied with sensory fibers; an
    　　instrument for cutting skin

    lithotomous—stone-boring, as certain molluscs

    myotome—an instrument for performing myotomy; that part
    　　of a somite which differentiates into skeletal muscle;
    　　a muscle group innervated by a single spinal nerve

    somatome—a transverse segment of an organized body, a
    　　somite; an embryotome

18. TOP-, "place"
    (gen.) topography, topical, isotope

    atopognosia—lack of ability to locate a sensation accurately

    ostectopy—displacement of bone

    topotype—a specimen from locality of original type

19. TROPH-, "nourishment," "development"

    autotroph—organism capable of self-nourishment, especially
    　　by using a chemical element, such as carbon or nitro-

gen, for food; a bacterium able to grow in an inorganic environment by using CO_2 as its sole source of carbon

hypertrophy—an increase in size of an organ independent of natural growth

metatrophic—living on both nitrogenous and carbonaceous organic matter

monotrophic—existing on one kind of food

trophobiotic—pertaining to a relationship in which an organism of one kind aids and protects an organism of another kind in return for some food products

trophonemata—uterine villi or hairlike projections which transfer nourishment to the embryo

trophoneurosis—a functional disease of a part due to failure of nutrition from defective nerve action in involved parts

trophotropism—tendency of an organism to turn toward its food supply

20.   ZO-, "animal," "living being"
(gen.) zoology, zodiac

cryptozoic—applicable to fauna dwelling in darkness, or under stones, bark, etc.

epizootic—a disease of animals which is widely prevalent in contiguous areas

hemocytozoon—a protozoan parasite inhabiting the red blood cells

metazoan—pertinent to a group that comprises all animals having the adult body composed of numerous cells differentiated into tissues and organs

phyllozooid—a shield-shaped medusoid of protective function

protozoon—a unicellular or noncellular animal organism

zoogamy—sexual reproduction in animals

EXERCISE

List the prefixes and bases and give their meanings.

1.   *dystrophy*—defective nutrition; defective or abnormal development or degeneration

2.   *dysbulia*—impairment of willpower

3. *esotropic*—exhibiting a situation in which one eye fixes upon an object and the other deviates inward

4. *exostosis*—the most common benign tumor of bone

5. *exophthalmic*—pertaining to abnormal protrusion of the eyeball from the orbit

6. *endogamy*—the custom or requirement of marriage within the tribe, caste or social group; inbreeding

7. *enuresis*—incontinence of urine

8. *endoderm* or *entoderm*—the innermost of the three primary germ layers, which forms the lining of the gut

9. *enantiomorph*—a form which is similar to another, but not transposable; forms related to each other as a right-handed to a left-handed glove; said of certain hemihedral crystals and of certain molecules and compounds

10. *epitheca*—an external layer surrounding the theca, or covering, in corals

11. *entomogamous*—insect-pollinated

12. *epicardium*—the visceral layer of the pericardium

13. *epiphyte*—plant which lives on the surface of other plants

14. *exocardiac*—originating or situated outside the heart

15. *eucephalous*—with a well-developed head; applicable to certain insect larvae

16. *endemic*—peculiar to a certain region, said of a disease which occurs more or less constantly in any locality

17. *dyschondroplasia*—a disease of unknown etiology attacking the bones of the hand; characterized by cartilaginous tissue developing regularly but ossifying very slowly

18. *ectozoon*—an external animal parasite; ectoparasite

19. *gamophyllous*—with united perianth leaves

20. *ectolecithal*—having yolk surrounding formative protoplasm

21. *osteotome*—an instrument somewhat similar to a chisel used for cutting bone

22. *phyllophorous*—bearing or producing leaves

23. *ectosome*—an enveloping portion of a sponge containing no flagellated chambers

24. *ectotrophic*—finding nourishment from outside; applicable to fungi which surround roots of host with hyphae

25. *exothermic*—relating to the giving out of energy, especially heat energy

26. *entochondrostosis*—ossification from within outward

MORE WORDS TO WORK WITH

arthroplasty	encephalitis	ophthalmoplegia
atrophy	endemic	ophthalmoscope
brachycephalic	endocarditis	osteoclast
cardiomegaly	epidermis	Paleozoic
chlorophyll	exogamy	pericardiocentesis
chondroblast	geothermal	pericardium
chondroclast	halophyte	phylloerythrin
chondroma	homoiothermal	phytotoxin
chromosome	hydrocephaly	poikilothermic
dermatitis	hypodermic	polylecithal
dermatology	microcephaly	psychosomatic
dextrocardia	microtome	rhizophyllous
diathermy	neoplasm	spermotheca
dolichocephalic	neurothecitis	stenophyllous
ectopic	ophthalmology	thermopolypnea
electroencephalogram	ophthalmomycosis	zoophobia

LESSON 3.   More Greek Prefixes

Learn the following prefixes and their meanings.

> *hyper-*, "over," "excessive," "more than normal"
>> examples: hypercritical, hypertension, hypertropia

> *hypo-* (*hyp-* before vowels or *h*), "below," "deficient," "less than normal," "somewhat"
>> examples: hypodermic, hypothesis
>> hyphen, hypesthesia

> *meta-*, (*met-* before vowels or *h*), "after," "change," "transfer"
>> examples: metabolism, metamorphosis
>> method, metencephalon

para-, (*par-* before vowels or *h*), "beside," "resembling," "disordered," "associated"

    examples: parasite, paratyphoid, paralysis, paramedical
              parenthesis, parody

peri-, "around," "near"

    examples: periscope, perimeter

pro-, "before," "in front of," "forward"

    examples: program, prologue, prostate

pros-, "toward," "in addition to," "fronting"

    examples: proselyte, prosthetic, prosencephalon

syn-, (*sym-*, *syl-*, *sy-*, *sys-*), "with," "together"

    examples: synonym, synthetic
              sympathy, symphony
              syllable
              systole, system
              syssarcosis (connection by means of muscle)

NEW BASES

Learn the following bases and their meanings.

1. ACOU- (ACU-), "to hear"
   (gen.) acoustic
   acousmatagnosis—inability to recognize sounds or understand spoken words; mind-deafness
   anacusia—complete deafness
   diplacusis—hearing the same sound differently by the two ears
   odynacousis—pain caused by noises

2. AMBLY-, "dull"
   Amblycephalidae—a genus of broad-headed, nonpoisonous snakes, formerly considered the type of a family, Amblycephalidae, called bluntheads
   amblychromasia—in bacteriology, a deficiency in nuclear chromatin which causes the cell to stain faintly

3. ANTH-, "flower"
   (gen.) anthology, chrysanthemum

anther—the part of the stamen which produces pollen

anthophilous—attracted by flowers; feeding on flowers

chloranthy—reversion of floral leaves back into ordinary green leaves

cladanthous—having terminal archegonia on short, lateral branches

exanthema—an eruption upon the skin

gymnanthous—with no floral envelope

Haemanthus—genus of bulbous herbs comprising the blood lily

4. CHROM-, CHROMAT-, CHRO-, "color"
   (gen.) monochrome, panchromatic, chromatic, chromium

   achroacytosis—an increase in the number of colorless or lymphatic cells in the blood

   achromodermia—a deficiency or lack of pigment in the skin

   chromatin—the protoplasmic substance in the nuclei of cells which is readily stainable

   chromophobe—a cell not stainable

   dichromatism—a condition in which an individual can perceive only two of the three basic hues

   dyschromatodermia or *dyschroa*—discoloration of the skin

   metachrosis—the change or play of colors seen in the squid, chameleon, etc.

   pseudochromesthesia—a condition in which each of the vowels of a word seems to have a distinct sound

5. DACTYL-, "finger," "toe"
   (gen.) dactylic

   dactylolysis—a tropical disease in which a toe is slowly and spontaneously amputated by a fibrous ring

   dactylopodite—the distal joint in certain limbs of Crustacea; the metatarsus and tarsus of spiders

   dactylopterous—with anterior rays of pectoral fins more or less free

   orthodactylous—having straight digits

   oxydactyl—having slender, tapering digits

6. DE-, "to bind"; DESM-, "ligament"
   (gen.) diadem, asyndeton

   adesmy—a break or a division in an organ, usually entire

allosyndesis—pairing of homologous chromosomes from opposite parents

amphidesmic—furnished with a double ligament

arthrodesis—fusion of a joint by removing the articular surfaces and securing bone union

asyndesis—incoherency in syntax or sentence construction

desmocyte—any kind of supporting tissue cell

desmoplasia—the formation and proliferation of connective tissue; the formation of adhesions

syndesmology—the study of ligaments

syndesmosis—a form of articulation in which the bones are connected by fibrous connective tissue

7. ENTER-, "intestine"

anenterous—having no alimentary tract

enterolysis—removal of adhesions binding the intestine

myenteric—relating to the muscular coat of the intestine

8. ERG-, "work"
(gen.) energy, allergy, georgic, surgeon

adrenergic—liberating adrenaline; activated by adrenaline

endoergic or *endothermic*—relating to the absorption of heat

ergatandromorph—an ant or other social insect in which the worker and male characters are blended

ergology—the study of artifacts made for use rather than trade

hyperergia or *hypergia*—increased functional activity

hyperergy—hypersensitivity to an allergen

9. ESTHE- (AESTHE-), "to feel," "to perceive"
(gen.) aesthete, aesthetics

acanthesthesia—a sensation as of pricking with a needle

aesthacyte—a sensory cell of primitive animals

akinesthesia—loss of muscular sense or sense of movement

caumesthesia—the experience of a sense of heat when the temperature is not high

synesthesia—a secondary sensation or subjective impression accompanying an actual perception, as a sensation of color or sound aroused by a sensation of taste

10. GER-, GERONT-, "old person," "old age"

acrogeria—premature aging of skin of hands and feet

gerontophobia—morbid fear of old age

gerodontia—dentistry for the aged

11. GNATH-, "jaw"

dysgnathic—pertaining to jaws which are improperly developed and in poor relation to one another

gnathopod—any crustacean limb in oral region modified to assist with food

gnathotheca—the horny outer covering of a bird's lower jaw

hypognathous—having the lower jaw abnormally small

opisthognathism—recession of the lower jaw

12. GNO-, "to know"

(gen.) diagnosis, prognosticate, agnostic, Gnosticism

acroagnosis—loss of sense perception in a limb

astereognosis—inability to recognize objects by sense of touch

autotopagnosia—loss of ability to orient parts of one's own body

baragnosis—loss of perception of weight

pharmacognosy—the science of crude drugs

13. GRAPH-, "to write"; -GRAM, "thing written"

(gen.) graph, graphite, biography, paragraph, telegram, monograph, monogram, epigram, epigraphy, orthography, diagram, ideograph, geography, photography

dromograph—instrument for registering the velocity of blood current

dysantiographia—inability to perform copywriting or to print

engram—the hypothetical impression or trace left upon the neuron by psychic experience; a latent memory picture

14. HEPAT-, HEPAR-, "liver"

heparin—a substance or mixture of substances occurring in liver and other tissues having the property of prolonging the clotting time of blood

hepaticoenterostomy—surgical establishment of communication between the hepatic duct and the intestine

hepatolysin—a cytolysin acting especially on liver cells

15. KINE- (CINE-), "to move"

(gen.) cinema, kinetic

akinesthesia—loss of muscle sense or sense of movement

eukinesia—normal power of movement

heterokinesis—movement resulting from external stimulus

heterokinesia—the execution of bodily movements exactly the opposite of those ordered

hyperanakinesia—excessive activity of a part

hyperkinemia—a condition marked by a greater cardiac output of blood than normal

kinesiology—the science of the anatomy, physiology, and mechanics of purposeful muscle movement in man

ookinesis—the mitotic phenomena in an egg during maturation and fertilization

thrombokinase—a substance activating prothrombin to thrombin

telekinesis—the power claimed by some people of causing objects to move without touching them

16. LEX-, "to read"

bradylexia—abnormal slowness in reading

alexia—visual aphasia or word blindness

dyslexia—impairment of the ability to read

17. MY-, MYS-, MYOS-, "muscle"

acromyotonus—tonic muscular spasm of the extremities usually causing deformity to the hands and feet

amyostasia—a tremor of the muscles causing difficulty in standing

endomysium—the connective tissue between the fibers of a muscle bundle

myochrome—any muscle pigment

myosin—one of the principal proteins in muscle

18. NEPHR-, "kidney"

nephridium—an excretory organ, usually that of invertebrates; embryonic kidney tubule of vertebrates

nephrocystanastomosis—surgical formation of an opening between the renal pelvis and the urinary bladder

nephrocyte—cells in sponges and insects which secrete waste and then migrate to the surface of the body to discharge

nephrotome—the section of the embryo from which kidney structures develop

perinephrium—the connective or adipose tissue surrounding a kidney

19. OSM-, "smell"

anosmia—absence of the sense of smell

macrosmatic—possessing a highly developed sense of smell

osmeterium—protrusible organ borne on first thoracic segment of larvae of some butterflies which emits a smell

20. THE-, "to put," "to place"

(gen.) thesis, antithesis, hypothesis, synthetic, epithet, parenthesis

allenthesis—introduction of foreign substance into the body

athetosis—nervous disorder marked by recurrent, slow, continual change of position of fingers, toes, hands, etc.

epithem—an excrescence on the beak of birds; a plant tissue forming a hydathode; the secretory layer in nectaries

metathesis—a chemical reaction in which there is an exchange of radicals

EXERCISE

List the prefixes and bases and give their meanings.

1. *amblyacusia*—dullness of hearing

2. *hyperacusia*—abnormal acuteness of the sense of hearing; auditory hyperesthesia

3. *metachromy*—change in color, as of flowers

4. *hyperesthesia*—excessive sensibility

5. *paragraphia*—perverted writing, a form of aphasia in which letters or words are misplaced or improperly used; a loss of ability to express ideas in writing, usually the result of a brain lesion

6. *hypokinesia*—abnormally decreased muscular movement

7. *paralexia*—a condition in which the patient misreads words because of brain injury

8. *metenteron*—the enteron modified in any manner from the primitive archenteron; one of the radial digestive

chambers of an anthozoon as distinguished from the mesenteron

9. *peridontium*—the supporting and investing tissue surrounding a tooth; namely, the periodontal membrane, the gingiva and the alveolar bone

10. *paracusia*—any perversion of the sense of hearing

11. *perimysium*—the connective tissue enveloping bundles of muscle fibers

12. *parosmia*—a perversion of the sense of smell; may be present in organic brain disease, in schizophrenia (olfactory hallucinations) or in psychoneurotic conditions

13. *perianth*—the floral envelope; external floral whorls including calyx and corolla; the external envelope of a flower; the floral leaves collectively

14. *perihepatitis*—inflammation of the peritoneum surrounding the liver

15. *progeria*—premature senility

16. *prognosis*—a prediction of the duration, course and termination of a disease, based on all information available in the individual case and knowledge of how the disease behaves generally

17. *prognathous*—having projecting jaws

18. *pronephros*—one of the anterior of the three pairs of embryonic renal organs of typical vertebrates

19. *prosodus*—a delicate canalicule between chamber and incurrent canal in some sponges

20. *prosthetic*—replacing or substituting; pertaining to an artificial substitute for a missing part, as denture, hand, leg, eye

21. *syndactylism*—adhesion of fingers or toes; webbed fingers or webbed toes

22. *syndesis*—the state of being bound together

23. *syndesmectopia*—ligamentous displacement

24. *synanthy*—adhesion of flowers usually separate

25. *synanthesis*—condition in which stamens and pistils mature simultaneously

26. *synergistic*—pertaining to cooperative action of discrete agen-

cies such that the total effect is greater than the sum of the two effects taken individually, as drugs; cooperating, as muscles

MORE WORDS TO WORK WITH

acoumetry	desmognathous	hyposmia
acroparesthesia	didactylism	lexicography
aerenterectasia	dysentery	megalohepatia
agnathocephalus	dyssynergia	micrergate
agraphia	electrocardiograph	myalgia
ambylycephalus	enteromyiasis	myenteron
amblyopia	enteroptosis	myocarditis
anesthetic	epinephrine	myositis
anisognathous	erg	nephritis
anthophobia	ergophobia	nephrolith
arachnodactyly	eurygnathic	nephrolytic
archenteron	gastroenteritis	nyctanthous
archinephron	geromorphism	parachromatopsia
baresthesia	gerontophilia	periodontist
blepharodyschroia	gnathalgia	photosynthesis
brachydactylia	graphomania	physiognomy
bradykinesis	heparinemia	pneumoarthrography
cholecystogram	hepatitis	polydactyly
chromhidrosis	hepatization	polygraph
chromosome	hepatoma	proanthesis
dermographia	hepatopexy	thermoanesthesia
	hyperesthesia	

LESSON 4.   Greek Adjective-Forming Suffixes

Elements called suffixes frequently are found attached to bases, appearing at the end of a word. In addition to their position, suffixes differ from prefixes in that they not only modify the meaning of a base, but also determine the part of speech of the word thus formed. As with prefixes, individual suffixes can be found listed as separate entries in any good abridged dictionary, where their meanings are discussed more thoroughly than is possible here.

More than one suffix may be found in a single word.

LOG-, "reason" + -ic, "pertaining to" + -al, "pertaining to"   logical
COLL-, "glue" + -oid, "like"   + -al, "pertaining to"   colloidal

Learn the following suffixes and their meanings. The first three suffixes are actually of Latin origin, but are found attached to Greek bases so frequently that it will be useful to learn them at this time.

1. *-al,* "pertaining to," "like," "belonging to," "having the character of"

dia-	+ GON-, "angle"	+ *-al*	diagonal
BI(o)-, "life"	+ *-logy,* "science of" + *-ic* + *-al*		biological
ana-	+ TOM-, "to cut"	+ *-ic* + *-al*	anatomical

2. *-an (-ian),* "pertaining to," "like," "one connected with"

amphi-	+ BI-, "life"	+ *-an*	amphibian
PROT(o)-, "first"	+ ZO-, "life"	+ *-an*	protozoan
THE-, "god"	+ *-logy,* "study of"	+ *-an*	theologian

3. *-ous (-ious),* "full of," "pertaining to," "like"

amphi-	+ BI-, "life"	+ *-ous*	amphibious
syn-	+ ONYM-, "name"	+ *-ous*	synonymous
HOM(o)-, "same"	+ GENE-, "kind"	+ *-ous*	homogeneous

4. *-ic, -tic (-ac* after *i),* "pertaining to," "like"

epi-	+ DEM-, "people" + *-ic*	epidemic
GASTR-, "stomach"	+ *-ic*	gastric
STA-, "to stand"	+ *-tic*	static
CARDI-, "heart"	+ *-ac*	cardiac

5. *-ics, -tics,* "art, science, or study of"
   Originally the latter suffix was the plural form of the previous suffix, but now it is treated as a singular.

PHYS-, "nature"	+ *-ics*		physics
GENE-, "to be produced"		+ *-tics*	genetics
EC(o)-, "house"	+ *-nomy,* "study of" + *-ics*		economics

6. *-oid, -ode,* "like," "having the shape of"

SPHER-, "sphere"	+ *-oid*	spheroid
ADEN-, "gland"	+ *-oid*	adenoid
NEMAT-, "thread"	+ *-ode*	nematode
PHYLL-, "leaf"	+ *-ode*	phyllode

NEW BASES

Learn the following bases and their meanings.

1. AMYGDAL-, "almond," "tonsil"
   amygdalin—a glycoside occurring in bitter almonds
   amygdalolith—tonsillar calculus

amygdalitis—inflammation of the tonsils

2. ANDR-, "man," "male"

(gen.) philander

androgynary—having flowers with stamens and pistils developing into petals

androgyny—hermaphroditism

andromonoecious—having male and hermaphrodite flowers on the same plant

andromorphous—having the form of a man

androphore—stalk that carries male gonophores in Siphonophora

ergatandrous—having workerlike males

protandrism or *protandry*—condition in hermaphrodite plants and animals where male elements mature and are shed before female elements mature

3. ANTHROP-, "man," "human being"

(gen.) anthropology, philanthropy, misanthrope, anthropomorphic, lycanthropy

anthropopathy—ascription of human feelings to God, a god or an object in nature

anthropophilic—showing a preference for human beings over animals

Sinanthropus—a genus of fossil men that includes Peking Man

4. CHRON-, "time"

(gen.) chronic, chronological, chronicle, synchronize, chronometer, anachronism

chronaxie—the duration of time that a current must flow in order to excite muscle tissue

heterochronism—departure from typical sequence in time of formation of organs

sphygmochronography—the registration of the extent and oscillations of the pulse wave

5. CLAD-, "branch"

cladode—branch arising from axil of leaf or green, flattened stem resembling a foliage leaf

cladodont—having teeth with prominent central and small lateral cusps

heterocladic—describing a communication between branches of different arteries *neurocladic*—pertaining to a theoretical phenomenon in which regeneration of injured neuraxons is considered to occur by production of collateral or terminal branches

phylloclade, cladophyll or *cladode*—a green, flattened or rounded stem which functions as a leaf, as in cactus

6. DYNAM-, DYN-, "power"
(gen.) dynamic, dynamite, dynamo, dynasty

adynamia—loss of vital strength or muscular power, weakness

dynamometer—an instrument for the measurement of muscular strength

hemodynamics—the study of how the physical properties of the blood and its circulation through the vessels affect blood flow and pressure

hyperdynamic—showing excessive strength or exaggeration of function, as of nerves or muscles

7. EME-, "to vomit"

autemesia—functional or idiopathic vomiting

hyperemesis—excessive vomiting

emetic—having the power to evoke vomiting

8. GYMN-, "naked," "uncovered"
(gen.) gymnasium, gymnosophist

gymnocarpous—with naked fruit; applicable to lichens with uncovered apothecia

gymnopterous—having bare wings without scales, applicable to insects

gymnorhinal—having nostril region not covered by feathers, as some birds

gymnosomatous—having no shell or mantle

gymnospore—a naked spore or germ not enclosed in a protective envelope

9. GYN(E)-, GYNEC- (GYNAEC-), "female"
(gen.) misogynist

digynous—having two carpels

ergatogyne—a female ant resembling a worker

gynandrous—having stamens fused with pistils, as some orchids

gynecomastia—enlargement of the mammary gland in the male

gynodioecious—plants producing female or hermaphrodite flowers only

10. HELIC-, HELIX, "spiral"
(gen.) helicopter, helical
helix—the rounded, convex margin of the ear
anthelix—the curved ridge of the pinna just anterior to the helix
helicine—ascending by spiral; pertaining to the helix
helicopepsin—a proteolytic enzyme found in snails
helicorubin—a respiratory pigment found in the gut and liver of snails

11. HYDR-, "water," "fluid"
(gen.) hydrant, hydraulic, hydrogen, hydro-electric, hydrophobia
hydrarthrosis—an accumulation of fluid in a joint
hydrocarpic—said of aquatic plants whose flowers are pollenated above water but withdrawn below water for development
hydropericarditis—pericarditis accompanied by serious effusion into the pericardium
hydrophyllium—one of leaflike bodies arising above and partly covering the sporosacs in a siphonophore
hydrostome—the mouth of a hydroid polyp
hydrotheca—cuplike structure into which a polyp may withdraw in many coelenterates
hydrotropism—response to stimulus of water
prohydrotropism—positive hydrotropism

12. IATR-, "physician," "medical treatment"
(gen.) psychiatry
amblyopiatrics—treatment of amblyopia
cyniatria—branch of medicine dealing with dogs
iatrogenic—induced by a physician; effect of physician's words or actions upon a patient

13. MELAN-, "black," "dark"
(gen.) melancholy, Melanesia
melanin—a dark brown or black animal or plant pigment
melanidrosis—a form of chromhidrosis in which the sweat is dark colored or black
melanism—abnormal deposit of dark pigment in tissue, organs and the skin
melanoderma—black pigmentation of the skin

melanophore—a dendritic cell containing melanin in its cyto-plasm

melanophyllous—having leaves of a dark color

melanotrichous—black-haired

14.   NECR-, "corpse," "dead tissue"
(gen.) necrology, necromancy, necropolis

necrocytotoxin—a toxin produced by the death of cells

necromimesis—a delusional state in which the patient believes himself to be dead; simulation of death by a deluded person

necrophagous—eating carrion

necrophilia—sexual perversion in which dead bodies are vio-lated; insane sexual desire for a corpse

osteoradionecrosis—bone necrosis due to irradiation by roent-gen or radium rays

15.   OLIG-, "few," "scanty"
(gen.) oligarchy, oligopoly

oligandrous—having few stamens

oligochromemia—deficiency of hemoglobin in the blood

oligohydruria—urine with a relative diminution of water; highly concentrated urine

ologopod—furnished with few feet or legs

oligotrichia—scantiness or thinness of hair

oligotrophic—providing inadequate nutrition

16.   PED- (PAED-), "child" (-*pedia*, "instruction")
(gen.) encyclopedia, pedagogical, hypnopaedia

orthopedic—pertaining to the branch of surgery concerned with corrective treatment of deformities, diseases and ailments of the locomotor apparatus, especially those affecting limbs, bones, muscles and joints; formerly devoted to correction and treatment of deformities in children

paedogamy—type of autogamy in protozoa where gametes are formed after multiple division of the nucleus; con-jugation of two protozoa originating from division of same individual

pedarthrocace—necrotic ulceration or caries of the joints of children *pedomorphic*—pertaining to retention in the adult of youthful and juvenile characteristics

pteropaedes—birds able to fly when newly hatched

17. PHAG-, "to eat"
(gen.) sarcophagus

autophagia—self-consumption; emaciation; biting one's own flesh, as in dementia

autophagus—applicable to birds capable of running about and securing food for themselves when newly hatched

dysphagia—difficulty in swallowing or inability to swallow

glossophagine—securing food by means of the tongue

lithophagous—stone-eating, as birds; rock-burrowing, as some molluscs

phagocyte—colorless blood corpuscle which tends to ingest foreign particles

phyllophagous—feeding on leaves

trichophagia—the eating of hair

18. PHIL-, "to love," "have an affinity for"
(gen.) philanthropy, Philadelphia, Philip, bibliophile, philosophy, Anglophile, philology

cryophilic or *crymophilic*—thriving at a low temperature

dichromophilism—capacity for double-staining

geophilous—living in or on the earth

lithophilous—growing on stones or rocks; saxicoline

polychromatophilism—capacity to be stained with more than one dye

19. POLY-, "many," "much"
(gen.) polygamy, Polynesian, polytheism, polygon, polyglot

polyantha—any of several hybrid garden roses

polyesthesia—an abnormality of sensation in which a single touch is felt in two or more places at the same time

polymer—the product resulting when two or more molecules of the same substance combine

polyphagous—eating various kinds of food

polyphyodont—having many successive sets of teeth

polyp—a pedunculated mass composed of neoplastic tissue or other structure found on mucous membranes

polypod—furnished with many feet or legs

polytrophia—abundant or excessive nutrition

polyuria—the passage of an excessive amount of urine

20.   TARS-, "instep," "edge of the eye"

hypotarsus—the calcaneum of a bird; process on metatarsus of birds

tarsalgia—pain, especially of neuralgic character, in the tarsus of the foot

tarsoplasty—plastic surgery of the eyelid

tarsoptosia—flat foot

EXERCISE

List the prefixes, bases and suffixes and give their meanings.

1. *anthropoid*—pertaining to or resembling the primates—man, the apes and the monkeys

2. *android*—resembling the male

3. *cladanthous*—having terminal archegonia on short lateral branches; opposed to acrocarpous

4. *amygdaloid*—almond-shaped; pertaining to or of the nature of the rock amygdaloid, i.e., any igneous rock that contains small cavities produced, before solidification, by expansion of steam and afterward filled by deposits of different minerals; a structure in the brain

5. *emetomania*—morbid desire to vomit

6. *androgynous*—having the characteristics of both sexes; being in nature both male and female; hermaphroditic; bearing both staminate and pistillate flowers in the same cluster

7. *parenteral*—outside the intestines; not via the alimentary tract

8. *pediatrics*—the branch of medicine dealing with children's diseases

9. *helicopod*—circumduction; movement of the leg in a lateral arc as it scrapes the floor; the gait seen in spastic hemiplegia

10. *metatarsal*—pertaining to the portion of the foot between the tarsus and the phalanges, containing fives bones of the foot

11. *gymnanthous*—with no floral envelope; achlamydeous

12. *helical*—spiral

13. *gynandromorph*—an individual of a bisexual species which exhibits the character of each sex in certain parts of the body

14. *dyschronous*—not agreeing as to time

15. *polymorphic*—having or occurring in several forms, as a substance which crystallizes in several forms; in reference to the symptomatology of a disease process, polysymptomatic, i.e. having manifold symptoms which may not all occur simultaneously or in the same patient

16. *thermodynamics*—the science which treats of the relation of heat and other forms of energy

17. *hydrodynamics*—that branch of the science of mechanics which relates to the laws of motion and actions of liquids

18. *anhydrous*—denoting the absence of water, especially the water of crystallization

19. *melangeophilous*—dwelling in loam

20. *oligolecithal*—having little yolk

21. *necrophilic*—subsisting on dead matter

22. *necrotic*—pertaining to the pathological death of a cell or group of cells in contact with living cells

23. *geophagous*—eating earth or clay

24. *phytophagous*—plant-eating; vegetarian

25. *anthophilous*—attracted by flowers; feeding on flowers

MORE WORDS TO WORK WITH

acanthocladous	asynchronous	emetocatharsis
aerophagia	blennemesis	emetophobia
amygdaloidectomy	carpophagous	emetatrophia
anacrogynous	cheiropterophilous	euchlorhydria
androgalactozemia	cholemesis	geodendrochronology
anemophilous	chromophil	geriatrics
anthropometry	cladoptosis	gymnophobia
anthropophagy	cynanthropy	gynecology

MORE WORDS TO WORK WITH *(Continued)*

gynephobia	melanoma	plastodynamia
helicotrema	misopedia	polyandry
hemophilia	olighidria	polychromatic
hydrocephaly	oligophyllous	polygyny
hyperemesis	oliguresis	stomatonecrosis
lithopedion	ologacanthous	tarsectomy
melanoglossia	pedodontia	tarsophyma
	philodendron	

LESSON 5. Greek Compound Suffixes I

In many cases a suffix is combined with a particular base so frequently that it is more useful to treat these two elements together as a suffix than to take them separately. These combinations are usually distinguished from regular suffixes, however, by the term "compound suffixes." Thus LOG-, "word," "reasoning" + *-y*, "state of" gives us the compound suffix *-logy*, "science of," as in *biology;* and from PHOB-, "to fear" + *-ia*, "state of" we have *-phobia*, "abnormal fear of," as in *claustrophobia.*

Various alterations are made in the form of compound suffixes if additional elements are attached.

AUTO(o)-	+	*-nomy*	+	*-ic*	autonomic
BI(o)-	+	*-logy*	+	*-ist*	biologist
POLY-	+	*-hedron*	+	*-al*	polyhedral

Learn the following compound suffixes and their meanings.

1. *-emia (-hemia),* "condition of the blood," "congestion of blood"

    examples: anemia, leukemia, anoxemia, tularemia

2. *-logy,* "science of," "systematic study of"

    examples: physiology, cardiology, psychology, astrology

3. *-lysis,* "dissolution of or by" ("surgical division or separation")

    examples: hydrolysis, nephrolysis, electrolysis

4. *-mania,* "madness for or about"

    examples: kleptomania, dipsomania, egomania, monomania

5. *-pathy,* "disease of," "treatment of disease of or by"

       examples: osteopathy, neropathy, hydropathy

6. *-phobia,* "abnormal fear of"

       examples: claustrophobia, agoraphobia, hydrophobia

7. *-therapy,* "treatment of or by"

       examples: chemotherapy, psychotherapy, heliotherapy

8. *-tomy,* "surgical operation on," "surgical cutting of"

       examples: glossotomy, gastrotomy, lobotomy

9. *-ectomy,* "surgical removal of"

       examples: appendectomy, tonsillectomy

10. *-uria,* "condition of the urine"

       examples: hematuria, acetonuria, noctalbuminuria

NEW BASES

Learn the following bases and their meanings.

1. ACR-, "extremity," "summit"
   (gen.) acropolis, acrobat, acrostic, acronym

   acrodontism—the condition whereby teeth are attached to the summit of a parapet of bone, as in lizards

   acromicria—underdevelopment of the extremities and of the skull as contrasted with visceral development

   anacromyoidian—with syringeal muscles attached at dorsal ends of bronchial semi-rings, as in birds

   acropodium—digits, as fingers or toes

   acroscopic—facing toward the apex

   acrospore—the spore at the end of a sporophore

2. AMYL-, "starch"

   amyloid—a starchlike chemical

   achrooamyloid—a recently deposited amyloid which does not form a blue color with iodine

   amylase—an amylolytic enzyme which hydrolyzes starch to sugar

   amylolysis—the digestion of starch or its conversion to maltose

   amyloplast—a leucoplast or colorless, starch-forming granule

3. BAR-, "weight," "pressure"; BARY-, "heavy"
    (gen.) barometer, isobar, barium, baritone
    abarognosis—loss or lack of ability to estimate weight
    baresthesia—perception of weight or pressure
    barodontalgia—dental pain occurring in individuals exposed to
    decreased barometric pressures such as occur in high
    altitude flying; also called aerodontalgia
    baryphonia—a heavy or deep quality of the voice
    dysbarism—a condition of the body resulting from the exis-
    tence of a pressure differential between the total
    ambient barometric pressure and the total pressure
    of dissolved and free gases within the body tissues,
    fluids and cavities
    eurybaric—applicable to animals adaptable to great differences
    in altitude

4. BLENN-, "mucus"
    blennophthalmia—catarrhal conjunctivitis
    blennorrhagia—excessive mucous discharge
    oligoblennia—a deficient secretion of mucus

5. CYT-, "cell"
    achroacytosis—an increase in the number of colorless or lym-
    phocytic cells in the blood; lymphocythemia
    chromocyte—any colored cell
    cytoderm—in botany, a cell wall
    cytolysis—the disintegration or dissolution of cells
    cytoplasm—the protoplasm of a cell other than that of the
    nucleus
    cytosome—a cell body exclusive of the nucleus
    cytostome—the oral aperture of a unicellular organism
    cytozoon—a protozoan parasite inhabiting a cell or having the
    structure of a simple cell
    erythrocythemia or *erythrocytous*—increased erythrocyte count
    oligocythemia—a reduction in the total quantity of erythro-
    cytes in the body
    syncytium—a mass of cytoplasm which has numerous nuclei
    but which is not divided into cells by cell walls

6. DIPS-, "thirst"
    adipsia—absence of thirst; avoidance of drinking

dipsophobia—a morbid fear of drinking

Haemadipsa—a genus of terrestrial leeches, one species of which produce external hirudiniasis

polydipsia or *anadipsia*—excessive thirst

7. DREPAN-, "sickle"

Drepanidae—a family of small, slender moths usually with forewings hooked; the species are called hooktips

drepanium—a helicoid cyme with secondary axes developed in a plane parallel to that of the main peduncle and its first branch

drepanocyte—a crescent-shaped cell

8. ERYTHR-, "red"

anerythroblepsia or *anerythropsia*—impaired color perception of red; red blindness

erythremia or *erythrocytosis*—primary polycythemia

erythrochloropsia—a form of subnormal color perception in which green and red are the only colors correctly distinguished

erythroderma or *erythrodermia*—a dermatosis characterized by an abnormal redness of the skin

erythrophilous—referring to red-staining nuclear substance of cells; having an affinity for red dye

erythrophyll—a red coloring matter in some leaves and red algae

hemoerythrin—a red pigment found in the blood of worms and other invertebrates

photerythrous—of heightened sensitivity to the red end of the spectrum

zooerythrin—a red pigment found in plumage of various birds

9. GLYC-, "sugar"; GLYCOS-, "sugar," "glucose"

glycogen—a carbohydrate found in liver cells and many other tissues; it is formed from carbohydrates and stored in the liver, where it is converted, as the system requires, into glucose

glycolysis—the process of conversion of carbohydrate in tissue into pyruvic acid or lactic acid

glycophyte—a plant unable to thrive on substratum containing more than 0.5% sodium chloride in solution, opposite to halophyte

hyperglycosuria—the presence of deficient amounts of sugar in the urine

10. HIST-, HISTI-, "tissue"

histiocyte or *histocyte*—fixed macrophagy of the loose connective tissue

histokinesis—movement that takes place in the minute structural elements of the body

histometaplastic—causing the transformation of one tissue into another type

histotrophic—pertaining to or connected with tissue formation or repair; connected with nourishment of fetus

histozoic—living on or within the tissues, denoting certain protozoon parasites

11. HYSTER-, "uterus," "hysteria"

hysterics—colloquial term for a hysterical attack

hysteria—a psychoneurotic disorder characterized by extreme emotionalism

hysterography—roentgenological examination of the uterus

hysterolaparotomy—abdominal hysterectomy

hysterotomy—incision of the uterus; a caesarian section

12. ICHTHY-, "fish"

ichthyismus—poisoning due to the absorption of mytilotoxin in muscles or from eating spoiled fish

ichthyodont—a fossil fish tooth

Ichthyol—trade name for a mild antiseptic prepared from shales containing fossil fish remains

ichthyotoxismus—food poisoning from fish

13. IRID-, IRIS, "iris," "rainbow"

iridization—the appearance of an iridescent halo, seen by persons affected by glaucoma

iridocyte—a special cell responsible for the beautiful iridescence of many fishes

iridodialysis—the separation of the iris from its attachments

iridokinesia—any movement of the iris

iridoplegia—paralysis of the sphincter pupillae of the iris

14. ISCH-, "to suppress"

ischesis—retention of a discharge or secretion

ischomenia—suppression of the menstrual flow

ischuria—retention or suppression of the urine

15. LAPAR-, "abdomen," "soft part of the body between the ribs and hip"

thoracolaparotomy—obsolete term for an operation in which both thorax and abdomen are opened

laparotrachelotomy—low caesarian section

laparorrhapy—suture of the abdominal wall

16. LIP-, "fat"

lipochrome or *chromolipoid*—any one of the group of fatlike substances containing a pigment or coloring matter and occurring in natural fats such as egg yolks

lipodystrophy—a disturbance of the fat metabolism in which the subcutaneous fat disappears over large areas of the body but is unaffected in others

lipase—a fat-splitting enzyme

17. MAST-, MAZ-, "breast"
(gen.) mastodon

acromastitis—inflammation of a nipple

hypermastia—overgrowth of the mammary gland

amastia or *amazia*—congenital absence of the mammae

18. PHREN-, "mind," "diaphragm"

phrenic—pertaining to the mind or the diaphragm

gastrophrenic—pertaining to the stomach and the diaphragm, as the gastrophrenic ligament

hebephrenia—a type of schizophrenia marked by silliness and extreme mannerisms, often caricaturing certain adolescent behavior

hypophrenia—feeblemindedness

phrenemphraxis—crushing of the phrenic nerve with a hemostat to produce temporary paralysis of the diaphragm, a form of collapse therapy used in the treatment of pulmonary tuberculosis

19. PY-, "pus"

hydropyonephrosis—distention of the pelvis of the kidney with urine and pus

pyophthalmia—purulent ophthalmia

pyorrhea—a purulent discharge

20.   THANAT-, "death"
thanatoid—resembling death
thanatology—the study of the phenomenon of organic death
thanatophobia—a morbid fear of death

EXERCISE

List the prefixes, bases and suffixes and give their meanings.

1. *hyperglycemia*—excess of sugar in the blood
2. *amyluria*—presence of starch in the urine
3. *mastectomy*—excision or amputation of the breast
4. *ichthyology*—the branch of biology dealing with the study of fish
5. *ecdemomania*—obsolete word for a morbid desire to wander
6. *erythrophobia*—a morbid intolerance or fear of red cŏlors, may be associated with the fear of blood; fear of blushing
7. *gymnophobia*—a morbid fear of a naked person or a naked part of the body
8. *drepanocythemia*—sickle-cell anemia characterized by sickling of erythrocytes when deoxygenated; hereditary, familial, chronic hemolytic anemia.
9. *acrophobia*—a morbid fear of being at a great height
10. *zoophobia*—a morbid fear of animals
11. *hypobaropathy*—chronic mountain sickness
12. *blennuria*—the presence of mucus in the urine
13. *enterolysis*—removal of adhesions binding the intestines
14. *histolysis*—disintegration and dissolution of organic tissue
15. *phrenicotomy*—surgical division of a phrenic nerve in the neck for the purpose of causing a one-sided paralysis of the diaphragm, with consequent immobilization and compression of a diseased lung
16. *melanuria*—the presence of black pigment in the urine
17. *hysterectomy*—total or partial removal of the uterus

18. *dipsotherapy*—treatment of certain diseases by reducing the amount of fluid allowed the patient

19. *ischemia*—local diminution in the blood supply due to obstruction of inflow of arterial blood; local anemia

20. *laparotomy*—generally, an incision through the abdominal wall; celiotomy, i.e., the operation of cutting into the abdominal cavity through the loin or flank

21. *lipemia* or *lipidemia*—the presence of a fine emulsion of fatty substances in the blood

22. *lipolysis*—the decomposition of fat

23. *thanatomania*—death by autosuggestion, as in individuals who believe they are under the spell of a sorcerer

24. *pyuria*—the presence of pus in the urine

25. *iridemia*—hemorrhage of the eye

MORE WORDS TO WORK WITH

acanthozooid
acroasphyxia
acrolith
acromegaly
acroparesthesia
aglycemic
amylodyspepsia
aniridia
antihistamine
arthroempyesis
barotropism
blennemesis
blennorrhea
bradyphrenia
cytology

dipsomania
drepanocytosis
erythrocytolysis
galactischia
glycerin
glycorrhiza
gynecomastia
histology
hyperamylasemia
hyperglycistia
hystero-epilepsy
hystero-oophorectomy
ichthyolite
ichthyomancy
ichthyophagous

iridescent
laparocolostomy
lipasuria
lipohemarthrosis
lipoma
lipuria
mastoid
mastoidectomy
mazalgia
oligophrenia
polymastia
pyemia
pyogenic
schizophrenia

LESSON 6.   Greek Compound Suffixes II

Learn the following compound suffixes and their meanings.

1. *-genous, -genic,* "producing," "produced"

examples: photogenic, endogenous, cytogenous (having to do with the production of cells)

2. *-hedron*, "solid figure having a (specified) number of faces"

examples: icosohedron, dodecahedron

3. *-iasis*, "diseased condition"; often refers to an infestation by parasites

examples: psoriasis, amebiasis, elephantiasis, bilharziasis

4. *-meter*, "instrument for measuring," "measure"

-metry, "art or science of measuring"

examples: thermometer, anemometer, perimeter
telemetry, optometry, photometry

5. *-nomy*, "science of," "system of laws governing"

examples: agronomy, astronomy, economy, autonomy

6. *-oecious*, "having a house or dwelling"

examples: monoecious (having male and female sex organs in same individual), androdioecious (having perfect and staminate flowers on different plants)

7. *-philous, -philic*, "loving," "thriving in," "pollinated by the agency of"

examples: necrophilic, anemophilous

8. *-plasty*, "formation," "plastic surgical operation"

examples: arthroplasty, anaplasty, hysteroplasty

9. *-rrhea*, "abnormal flow or discharge of"

examples: diarrhea, gonorrhea, logorrhea

10. *-stomy*, "the making of a surgical opening"

examples: gastrostomy, arthrostomy, hepaticoenterostomy

NEW BASES

Learn the following bases and their meanings.

1. ACANTH-, "thorn," "prickle"
(gen.) pyracantha

acanthesthesia—a sensation as of pricking with needles

acanthocladous—having spiny branches

acanthocyst—a sac containing lateral or reserve stylets in Nemertea

acantholysis—any skin disease in which there is an atrophy of the prickle-cell layer

acanthophore—a conical mass, the basis of the median stylet in Nemertea; a tubular spine in some bryozoons

acanthosis—a benign overgrowth of the prickle cell layer of the skin

heteracanthous—having the spines in the dorsal fin asymmetrical

hexacanth—having six hooks; applicable to embryos of certain flat worms

paracanthosis—a process characterized by some anomaly in the prickle cell layer of the epidermis

2. AER-, "air," "gas"
    (gen.) aerate, aeroplane

aerocele—a tumor caused by the escape of air into an adventitious pouch usually connected with the trachea or larynx

aerocyst—an air vesicle of algae

aerocystoscopy—examination of the interior of the urinary bladder with a cystoscope, the bladder being distended with air

aeropathy—any pathologic condition brought about by a change in atmospheric pressure, as caisson disease or aeroembolism

aerophyte—a plant which grows attached to an aerial portion of another plant

3. AUT-, "self"
    (gen.) autopsy, autograph, autonomy, automobile, autobiography, autemesia

autism—a tendency to morbid concentration on oneself

autocytotoxin—a cell toxin produced against the cells of one's own body

autodont—designating or pertaining to teeth not directly attached to jaws, as in cartilaginous fish

autophagia—self-consumption, emaciation; biting of one's own flesh, as in dementia *autophyllogeny*—growth of one leaf upon or out of another

autotomy—mechanism by means of which many organisms are able to cast off parts of their bodies; self-division; a surgical operation performed on one's own body; in psychiatry, the act of scratching away some part of the body, as in catatonia

autotroph—a bacterium able to grow in an inorganic environment by using CO_2 as its sole source of carbon

4. BLEPHAR-, "eyelid"

ablephary—congenital absence of the eyelids

blepharoplasty—operation for restoration of the eyelid

symblepharosis—adhesion of the eyelids to the globe of the eye or to each other

5. CARCIN-, "cancer"

carcinogen—any cancer-producing substance.

carcinoid—a tumor derived from argentaffin, usually benign

mastocarcinoma—mammary tumor which is malignant

6. CHEIL- (CHIL-), "lip"

acheilary—having labellum undeveloped, as some orchids

chilidium—a shelly plate covering deltidial fissure in dorsal valve of certain Brachiopoda

acheilia—congenital absence of the lips

7. COL-, "colon"
   (gen.) colic

coloproctostomy—formation of a new passage between the colon and the rectum

paracolitis—inflammation of the tissue adjacent to the colon, not covered by peritoneum

phrenicocolic or *phrenocolic*—pertaining to the diaphragm and the colon

8. COPR-, "excrement"

coprodaeum—the division of the cloaca which receives the rectum

coprolite—petrified feces

coprolith—a hard mass of fecal matter in the bowels

coprophrasia—the abnormal interjection of obscene words into speech

9. CRY-, CRYM-, "cold," "ice"
    (gen.) crystal
    cryesthesia—abnormal sensitiveness to cold

10. CYST-, "bladder," "cyst," "sac"
    acrocyst—the spherical, gelatinous cyst formed by gonophores at maturation of generative cells
    cystitis—inflammation of the urinary bladder
    cytocyst—the envelope formed by remains of a host cell within which a protozoon parasite multiplies
    gametocyst—cyst surrounding two associated free forms in sexual reproduction of gregarines
    hematocyst—a cyst containing blood
    nematocyst—a stinging cell
    nephrocystanastomosis—renal pelvis and urinary bladder
    oocyst—cyst formed around two conjugating gametes in Sporozoa
    polycystic—containing many cysts

11. DACRY-, "tear"
    Dacrydium—a genus of shrubs, named from resinous gum exuded
    dacryocystitis—inflammation of the lacrimal sac

12. GASTR- (GASTER-), "stomach," "belly of a muscle"
    (gen.) gastronomic
    gamogastrous—a pistil formed by union of ovaries
    gastropod or *gasteropod*—a mollusc with ventral muscular disc adapted for creeping
    gastrozooid—in coelenterate colonies, the nutrient member with mouth and tentacles
    metagastric—pertaining to posterior gastric region
    progastrin—precursor of gastric secretion in mucus membrane of stomach

13. HELMINTH-, "worm"
    anthelmintic—destructive to worms
    helminthology—the study of parasitic worms
    helminthoma—a tumor caused by the presence of a parasitic worm

14. HETER-, "other," "different"

(gen.) heterodox, heterogeneous

heterochromia—a difference in coloration in two parts of a structure, or in two structures that are normally alike, as the irises of the eyes

heterodont—having teeth of more than one shape, as in man

heterogamy—the conjugation of gametes of unlike size and structure, as in higher plants and animals

heterokinesis—movement resulting from external stimuli

heterokinesia—the execution of body movements opposite those ordered

heterophoria—any tendency of the eyes to turn away from the position correct for binocular vision

heterophoralgia—pain caused by heterophoria

15. HYGR-, "moisture"

hygrokinesis—movement in response to changes in humidity

hygroma—a cystic cavity derived from distended lymphatics and filled with lymph

hygroplasm—the more liquid part of protoplasm; opposite of stereoplasm

hygroscopic—readily absorbing moisture

hygrostomia—chronic salivation

16. MEN-, "moon," "menstruation"

meniscectomy—the surgical excision of a meniscus or semilunar cartilage

meniscocyte—a sickle-shaped erythrocyte

meniscus—a crescent or crescentic body, especially an interarticular fibrocartilage; a concavoconvex lens or convexoconcave lens; curved surface of a column of liquid

17. OT-, "ear"

diotic—binaural; pertaining to both ears

otocyst—in invertebrates, an auditory vesicle, otocell or otidium; in vertebrates, an embryonic auditory vesicle

otolith—calcareous particles or platelike structures found in auditory organ of many animals

18. PSYCH-, "mind," "soul"
(gen.) metempsychosis

psyche—the mind as a functional entity, serving to adjust the total organism to the needs and demands of its environment

psychokinesis—the direct action of mind on matter, i.e., on objects discrete from the subject's body

psychopathic—pertaining to a morally irresponsible person

Psychozoic—of or relating to the period beginning with the appearance of man on the earth

19. RHIN-, -RRHIN-, "nose"
(gen.) rhinoceros

amphirhinal—having or pertaining to two nostrils

catarrhine—having a narrow or slender nose

gymnorhinal—with nostril region not covered by feathers, as in some birds

rhinencephalon—that portion of the cerebrum concerned with reception and integration of olfactory impulses; the anterior inferior part of the forebrain that is chiefly concerned with olfaction

rhinophonia—a nasal tone in the speaking voice

rhinophore—a process on the aboral side of the eye of certain molluscs, with supposed olfactory function

rhinotheca—the sheath of the upper jaw of a bird

20. TAC-, TAX-, "to arrange," "to put in order"
(gen.) tactics, taxidermy, syntax

amyotaxia—muscular ataxia or incoordination of spinal or cerebellar origin

anthotaxis—arrangement of flowers on an axis

asyntaxia—failure of the neural tube to close

cytotaxis—rearrangement of cells on stimulation

phototaxis—response to stimulus of light

phyllotaxy—the arrangement of leaves on an axis or stem

taxeopodous—having proximal and distal tarsal bones in straight lines parallel to the limb axis

taxon—a taxonomic group or entity; the name applied to a taxonomic group in a formal system of nomenclature

EXERCISE

List the prefixes, bases and suffixes and give their meanings.

1. *iatrogenic*—induced by a physician; referring to the effect of a

physician's words or actions on a patient

2. *crymophilic* or *psychrophilic*—pertaining to cold-loving organisms; applied to microorganisms which develop best from 15° to 20° C

3. *cryogenics* (formerly *cryogeny*)—the branch of physics that relates to the production and effects of very low temperatures

4. *polyhedron*—a solid figure having many surfaces

5. *coprophilic*—growing on fecal matter, said of certain bacteria; fond of pornography

6. *carcinogenic*—pertaining to a substance or agent causing development of a carcinoma or epithelioma; loosely, pertaining to a substance or agent causing development of a malignancy of any sort

7. *acanthocephaliasis*—infestation by Acanthocephala (Acanthocephala—round worms with hooked proboscises)

8. *hygrophilic*—inhabiting moist or marshy places

9. *heteroecious*—passing different stages of life history in different hosts; metoecious; metoxenous

10. *helminthiasis*—a disease condition produced by the presence of parasitic worms in the body

11. *rhinoplasty*—a plastic operation upon the nose

12. *psychometry*—the branch of clinical or applied psychology dealing with the use and application of mental measurement

13. *dysmenorrhea*—difficult or painful menstruation

14. *aerogenous*—forming gas

15. *chromodacryorrhea*—the flow of colored tears from the Harderian glands in rats

16. *taxonomy*—the laws of classification as applied to natural history

17. *graphorrhea*—uncontrollable desire to write, in which pages are covered with usually unconnected and meaningless words

18. *heteroplasty*—the operation of grafting parts taken from another species

19. *colocolostomy*—an anastomosis between two noncontinuous segments of the colon in order to short-circuit the lumen around inoperable obstructing tumors or to prepare for later resection

20. *cheiloplasty*—a plastic operation on the lip

21. *gastroenterostomy*—the formation of a communication between the stomach and the small intestine

22. *otopyorrhea*—a purulent discharge from the ear

23. *hygroblepharic*—serving to moisten the eyelid

24. *dacryocystotomy*—incision of the lacrimal sac

25. *autoplasty*—repair of a defect by grafting tissue taken from another area of the patient's body

26. *homoplasty*—repair of a defect by grafting tissue from the same species

27. *alloplasty*—repair of a defect with non-organic substances such as gold or ivory

MORE WORDS TO WORK WITH

aerendocardia
aeroembolism
aerophagia
amenorrhea
anaerobic
anotus
aremia
autogamy
barotalgia
blepharodyschroia
blepharoplegia
blepharopyorrhea
carcinoma
cheilitis
cholecystectomy
colitis
copremesis

copremia
crymotherapy
cryophyte
dacryoblennorrhea
dacryorrhea
dermatoheteroplasty
digastric
encopresis
euryhygric
gastralgia
gastroenteritis
gastrula
helminthemesis
heteromorphous
heterosexual
hygrophyte
hypercryalgesia
ischomenia

macrocheilia
melanogaster
menarche
menopause
microrrhinia
osteocarcinoma
otalgia
pachycheilia
parotid
Platyhelminthes
psychogenic
psychology
psychosomatic
psychotherapy
rhinitis
syncheilia
thermotactic

LESSON 7.   Greek Noun-Forming Suffixes I

Learn the following suffixes and their meanings.

1. *-ter,* "means of," "place for"

URE-, "to urinate"	+ *-ter*	ureter
SCEP(T)-, "to support oneself"	+ *-ter*	scepter
SPHING-, "to bind"	+ *-ter*	sphincter
CRA-, "to mix"	+ *-ter*	crater
THEA-, "to view"	+ *-ter*	theater

2. *-ist, ast,* "one who"

ant- + AGON-, "struggle"	+ *-ist*	antagonist
GYMN-, "naked"	+ *-ast*	gymnast
PSYCH-, "mind" + IATR-, "physician"	+ *-ist*	psychiatrist
BACTER-, "bacterium" + *-logy*	+ *-ist*	bacteriologist

3. *-te, -t,* "one who," "that which" *(-tes)*

ATHLE-, "to contend"	+ *-te*	athlete
pro- + PHE-, "to speak"	+ *-t*	prophet
GAME-, "to marry"	+ *-te*	gamete
anti- + DO-, "to give"	+ *-te*	antidote
THERMO(o)-, "heat" + STA-, "to stand"	+ *-t*	thermostat
dia- + BE-, "to go"	+ *-tes*	diabetes

4. *-ician,* "specialist in," "practitioner of"

PED-, "child" + IATR-, "physician"	+ *-ician*	pediatrician
DIET-, "way of life"	+ *-ician*	dietician
MUS-, "music"	+ *-ician*	musician

NEW BASES

Learn the following bases and their meanings.

1. ACTIN-, "ray"

actinic—pertaining to, or designating, the rays of the spectrum which produce chemical change

actiniform—exhibiting radiate form or structure, such as the ray fungus or sea anemone *actinogenic*—producing radiation

actinost—basal bone of fin-rays in teleosts

actinostome—mouth of the sea anemone; five-rayed oral aperture of the starfish

adiactinic—impervious to, or not penetrated by, actinic rays

hexactinal—with six rays

2. ARGYR-, "silver"

argyria—the dusty gray or bluish discoloration of skin and mucous membrane produced by the prolonged administration or application of silver preparations

Argyrotaenia—genus of moths

hydrargyrophthalmia—ophthalmia due to mercurial poisoning

3. BA-, "to step," "to go," "to walk"
(gen.) base, basis, acrobat, anabasis

basidium—a special cell or row of cells of certain fungi, forming spores by abstriction

basidiophore—a sporophore which carries basidia

basiophthalmite—the proximal joint of the eye stalk in crustaceans

basophobia—morbid fear of walking or standing erect

gynobase—a gynoecium-bearing receptacle of certain plants, such as the pistils and ovaries

4. BROM-, "stench," "bromine"
(gen.) bromide

bromoderma—skin eruption due to ingestion of bromides

brominism—bromine poisoning; the diseased state caused by prolonged administration of bromides

bromopnea—fetid breath

5. CHOL(E)-, "bile," "gall"
(gen.) choleric, cholera, melancholy

cholagogue—agent which stimulates flow of bile from liver

cholochrome—any bile pigment

eucholia—normal condition of the bile

6. CLAS-, "to break"
(gen.) iconoclast

arthroclasia—breaking down of ankylosis of joint

cardioclasis—rupture of the heart

odontoclast—a multinucleated cell found associated with absorption of the roots of a deciduous tooth

7. CRANI-, "cranium"

amphicrania—headache affecting both sides of head, as opposed to hemicrania

chondrocranium—the embryonic cartilaginous cranium

craniosynostosis—premature closing of the cranial sutures, resulting in a small skull

pericranium—the periosteum on the outer surface of the cranial bones

8. CRI-, "to separate," "to distinguish"; CRIN-, "to secrete" (gen.) critic, criterion, crisis, hypocrite

apocrine—designating a type of secretion in which the secretion-filled free end of a gland is pinched off, leaving the nucleus and most of the cytoplasm to recover and repeat the process

chromocrinia—the secretion or excretion of colored material

cytocrinia—the transfer of pigment from melanoblasts to other cells or melanin from basal to intermediate cells of the epidermis, as in sunburn

endocrine—secreting internally

enterocrinin—a hormone produced by the intestinal mucosa which stimulates the glands of the small intestine

epicritic—pertaining to sensory nerve fibers which enable one to make very fine distinctions of temperature and touch

exocrine—secreting to an epithelial surface, either directly or by ducts

neurocrine—pertaining to secretory function of new cells

9. EURY(S)-, "wide"

euryphagous—subsisting on a wide variety of foods

eurysome—short and stout

procteurynter—an instrument for dilating the anus or rectum

10. HEM-, HEMAT- (HAEM-, HAEMAT-), "blood"

acardiohemia—lack of blood in the heart

haematobic—living in blood

hematophagous—pertaining to a blood-sucking insect

haemin—a blood substance

histohaematin—an intracellular haemin compound

11. HIDRO(S)-, "sweat"

synhidrosis—concurrent sweating; the association of perspiration with some other condition

acrohyperhidrosis—increased perspiration of the hands and feet

chromhidrosis—a rare condition in which the sweat is colored

12. LITH-, -LITE, "stone"
(gen.) lithograph, monolithic, neolithic

cryolite—sodium-aluminum fluoride, named from its icy appearance

dacryolith—a calcareous concretion in the lacrimal passages

lithodialysis—the solution of calculi in the urinary bladder; the breaking of a vesicle calculus previous to its removal

lithophyll—a fossil leaf or leaf impression

otolith—a calcareous particle or platelike structure found in auditory organs of certain animals

13. MYI-, "fly"

Anthomyia—a genus of flies laying eggs in food and causing enteromyiasis

myiasis—disease caused by the invasion of the larvae of flies

ophthalmomyiasis—disease due to the presence of the larvae of flies in the eye

14. OP-, OPT-, "eye," "to see"; PROSOP-, "face"
(gen.) autopsy, thanatopsis, synopsis, optic

chromatopseudopsis—color blindness

emmetropia—normal or perfect vision; the condition in which parallel rays are focused exactly on the retina without effort of accommodation

hemianopsia—blindness in half the visual field; may be bilateral or unilateral

hypermetropia—focus of light behind the retina

myiodeopsia—condition in which muscae volitantes appear (muscae volitantes—floating specks in the field of vision due to opacities in the media of the eye)

myopia—nearsightedness

15. ORTH-, "straight," "correct"

(gen.) orthodox, orthography

anorthite—feldspar not at right angles in cleavage; oblique cleavage

orthochromatic—originating in photography, denoting correctness in rendering of colors

orthoenteric—having alimentary canal along internal ventral body surface

orthopsychiatry—prevention and treatment of behavioral disorders; mental hygiene and preventive methods are the main areas of interest

orthoptic—pertaining to normal binocular vision

16. PHA-, PHAN-, "to appear," "to show"
(gen.) diaphanous, epiphany, phantom, phase

chromophane—the pigment of the inner segments of the retinal cones of certain animals

diaphane—transparent investing membrane of an organ or a cell

menophania—first appearance of the menses

metaphase—middle stage of meiosis

myophan—musclelike; applies to striation of protozoa

thermophase—first developmental stage in some plants which can be partially or entirely completed during seed ripening if temperature and humidity are favorable

17. RHE-, -RRH, "to flow," "current"
(gen.) catarrh, rheumatism

cryptorhetic—secreting internally; endocrine

rheobase—the minimum electric potential necessary for stimulation

rheocardiography—recording of differences of electrical conductivity of the body synchronous with the cardiac cycle

rheophore—an electrode

rheotaxis or *rheotropism*—locomotor response to stimulus of current, usually water

18. SCOP-, "to view"
(gen.) scope, episcopal, telescope, microscopic

cryoscope—device for determining the freezing point of any liquid *scopophobia*—morbid dread of being seen

endoscope—instrument used to examine an internal body cavity or viscus through its natural opening

19. STA-, "to stand," "to stop," "to fix," "to regulate"
(gen.) static, ecstasy, apostasy, thermostat, Anastasia

acatastasia—irregularity, nonconforming to type

amyostasia—a tremor of the muscles causing difficulty in standing, often seen in locomotor ataxia

ananastasia—abulic inability to rise from a sitting posture

blepharodiastasis—excessive separation of the eyelids; inability to close the eyelids completely

craniostat—a device for holding the skull during craniometric study

hemostasia—stagnation of the blood; arrest of flow of blood

orthostatic—pertaining to or caused by standing upright, as albuminuria

20. STYL-, "pillar"
(gen.) stiletto

cephalostyle—the anterior end of the notochord enclosed in a sheath

style—the slender upper part of a pistil

systylous—in botany, with coherent styles

styloid—processes of the temporal bone, fibula, etc.

stylomastoid—pertaining to styloid and mastoid processes

stylopodium—a conical swelling surrounding bases of divaricating styles of Umbelliferac

EXERCISE

List the prefixes, bases and suffixes and give their meanings.

1. *hematocrit*—a small centrifuge used to separate blood cells

2. *diopter*—unit of measurement of refractive power of an optic lens

3. *optician*—a maker of optical instruments and lenses

4. *ophthalmologist*—one who specializes in the anatomy, physiology and treatment of the eye

5. *optometrist*—one who measures the degrees of visual powers,

without the aid of a cycloplegic or mydriatic; a refractionist

6. *orthodontist*—one who specializes in the branch of dentistry concerned with the treatment of malocclusion

7. *hemostat*—an agent or instrument which arrests the flow of blood

8. *rheostat*—an instrument introduced into an electric current and offering a known resistance, for the purpose of altering the intensity of the current

9. *osteoclast*—a powerful surgical apparatus or instrument for fracturing a bone; one of the large multinuclear cells found in association with the resorption of bone

10. *heterostyly*—in botany, having unlike or uneven styles

11. *hydrargyriasis*—chronic mercurial poisoning

12. *cranioclast*—heavy forceps for crushing the fetal head

13. *hydrophanous*—made transparent by immersion in water

14. *euryhygric*—adaptable to a wide range of atmospheric humidity

15. *diaphanoscope*—a device for lighting an interior body cavity so as to render it visible from the exterior

16. *actinotherapy*—therapeutic use of chemical rays or radiant energy, including sunlight, ultraviolet light, x-rays and emanations of radium or other radioactive material

17. *eurybaric*—adaptable to great differences in altitude

18. *cholecystenterostomy*—the establishment of a communication between the gall bladder and the small intestine

19. *bromhidrosiphobia*—a morbid dread of offensive personal smells, with hallucinations as to the perception of them

20. *lithemia*—a condition in which, owing to defective metabolism of the nitrogenous elements, the blood becomes charged with uric acid

21. *enteromyiasis*—disease due to the presence of the larvae of flies in the intestine

22. *stylet*—a wire inserted into a soft catheter or cannula for securing rigidity; a wire inserted into a hypodermic or other needle to ensure potency

23. *nephrolithiasis*—the formation of renal calculi, or the diseased state that leads to their formation

24. *actinolyte* or *actinolite*—an apparatus designed for use in actinotherapy; a device which generates ultraviolet rays; any substance which undergoes a rather marked change when exposed to light

25. *orthoclase*—common or potash feldspar, which is orthoclastic

MORE WORDS TO WORK WITH

acrania
actinodermatitis
amblyopia
amphiprostyle
anerythropsia
aneurysm
anorthopia
argyrophile
arthroendoscopy
biopsy
bromomania
bromomenorrhea
cholangitis
cholecystogram
cholelithiasis
cholemesis
cholemia
chondroclast
coprolith
cystolithotomy
dermamyiasis

dichromatism
dysbasis
dysendocriniasis
erythropsia
eurycephalic
eurygnathous
euryprosopic
eurythermal
gastrodiaphanoscope
gonybatia
hemarthrosis
hemathidrosis
hematite
hematolite
hematologist
hematoma
hematuria
hemophilia
hemorrhage
hemorrhoid
histoclastic

hyphidrosis
ichthyolite
ischidrosis
lithopedion
lithophagous
lithuresis
metastasis
oligocholia
orthognathic
orthopedic
peristyle
phanerogam
phonolite
podobromhidrosis
prosopalgia
prostate
rhinoscope
scopophilia
stylobate
stylus

LESSON 8.   Greek Noun-Forming Suffixes II

Learn the following suffixes and their meanings.

1. *-ia, -y,* "state of," "condition of," "quality of"
   HYSTER-, "uterus," "hysteria"   + *-ia*   hysteria
   NEUR-, "nerve" + ALG-, "pain"   + *-ia*   neuralgia
   AGON-, "struggle"   + *-y*   agony
   PHIL-, "loving" + SOPH-, "wise" + *-y*   philosophy

2. *-ism, -ismus,* "condition of" ("belief in")

ALCOHOL	+ *-ism*	alcoholism
BOTUL-, "sausage"	+ *-ism*	botulism
meta- + BOL-, "to put"	+ *-ism*	metabolism
LARYNG-, "larynx"	+ *-ismus*	laryngismus
STRAB-, "to squint"	+ *-ismus*	strabismus

3. *-sis, -sia, -sy, -se,* "act of," "process of" (sometimes "result of the act of")

Note that the adjectival form of this suffix is *-tic, -stic,* "pertaining to the act or process of."

syn- + THE-, "to put"	+ *-sis*	synthesis
ana- + LY-, "to loosen"	+ *-sis*	analysis
dia- + GNO-, "to know"	+ *-sis*	diagnosis
a- + MNE-, "to remember"	+ *-sia*	amnesia
an- + ESTHE-, "to feel"	+ *-sia*	anesthesia
ec- + STA-, "to stand"	+ *-sy*	ecstasy
IDI(o)-, "own" + *syn-* + CRA-, "to mix"	+ *-sy*	idiosyncrasy
DO-, "to give"	+ *-se*	dose
an- + ESTHE-, "to feel"	+ *-tic*	anesthetic
syn- + THE-, "to place"	+ *-tic*	synthetic
dia- + GNO-, "to know"	+ *-stic*	diagnostic
SPA-, "to stretch"	+ *-stic*	spastic

4. *-ma, -m, -me,* "result of the act of"

Note that when additional elements are added to this suffix it appears as *-mat-;* e.g., dramatic, stigmatic, schizmatic, thematic.

CINE- (KINE-), "to move"	+ *-ma*	cinema
DRA-, "to act"	+ *-ma*	drama
STIG-, "to brand"	+ *-ma*	stigma
SCHIZ-, "to split"	+ *-m*	schism
THE-, "to place"	+ *-me*	theme

NEW BASES

Learn the following bases and their meanings.

1. BLEP-, "to see"

ablepsia—loss or absence of vision

monoblepsia—a condition in which either eye has a better visual power than both together; a form of color blindness in which only one color can be perceived

parablepsis—false or perverted vision

parachromatoblepsia or *parachromatism*—false, or incorrect perception of color, not true color blindness

2. COR(E)-, "pupil of the eye"

corediastasis— dilatation of the pupil

corelysis—the detachment of iritic adhesions to the lens or cornea

polycoria—the existence of more than one pupil in an iris

3. CRA-, "to mix"

(gen.) crater (from Latin, "mixing bowl")

crasis—constitution, make up

hematodyscrasia—diseased state of the blood

hypocrateriform—saucer-shaped

4. CYAN-, "blue"

(gen.) cyanide

cyanochrous—having a blue skin

cyanophyll—a bluish-green coloring matter in plants

cyanopia or *cyanopsia*—a perverted sense of vision rending all objects blue

oxyhaemocyanin—haemocyanin combined with oxygen

5. CYE-, "to be pregnant"

cyophoria—pregnancy, gestation

metacyesis—extrauterine gestation

paracyesis—extrauterine pregnancy

6. GALACT-, GALA-, "milk"

(gen.) galaxy

galactase—a soluble proteolytic enzyme normally present in milk

galactin—an amorphous substance derived from milk; a potent hormone stimulating lactation

galactophorous—lactiferous; applies to ducts of the mammary glands

galactorrhea—excessive flow of milk

galactose—a type of sugar

galactotropic—stimulating milk secretion; applicable to the hormone prolactin

galactostasis—suppression of milk secretion; an abnormal collection of milk in a breast

7. GEU-, "to taste"

dysgeusia—morbidity or perversion of the sense of taste

psychogeusic—pertaining to perception of taste

hypergeusia—abnormal acuteness of the sense of taste

8. GLOSS-, GLOT(T)-, "tongue," "language"
    (gen.) polyglot, glossary

aglossostomia—with tongue lacking and mouth imperforate

bradyglossia—slow speech due to difficulty in tongue movement

epiglottis—an elastic cartilage covered by mucous membrane forming that superior part of the larynx which guards the glottis during swallowing

glossotheca—the proboscis-covering part of the pupal integument of insects

glottochronology—the study of the time during which two or more languages have evolved separately from a common source

phrenoglottismus—spasm of the glottis caused by disease of the diaphragm

styloglossal—pertaining to a muscle arising from the styloid process of the temporal bone and inserted into the tongue

9. IDI-, "one's own," "peculiar," "distinct"
    (gen.) idiot, idiom

idioandrosporous—bearing androspores and oogonia on separate filaments

idiobiology—the branch of biology concerned with the study of organisms as individuals

idiochromatic—having a distinctive and constant coloration, used especially of minerals

idiogamist—one who is capable of coitus only with his marital partner or with a few women, being impotent with women in general

idiotype—individual genotype

10. IS-, "equal," "same"

anisochromia—a variation in the color of erythrocytes in which only the peripheral zone of the cell is colored

isohemolysis—the lysis of red blood cells of one individual of a species by specific antibodies in the serum of another

isometric—pertaining to equality of measure; taking place against resistance without significant shortening of muscle fibers

isozoic—inhabited by similar forms of animal life

11. LAL-, "to talk"

barylalia—an indistinct, thick speech; occurs in patients with organic brain disease; common in advanced general paresis

bradylalia—slowness of utterance

enantiolalia—talking contrariwise; a disturbance in mental and speech function which prompts ideas and words opposite those presented as stimuli

heterolalia—unconscious saying of one thing while another is intended; heterophemy

rhinolalia—a nasal tone in the voice due to undue closure or patulousness of the choanae

12. MEGA-, MEGAL-, "large," "one million"
(gen.) megaphone, omega, megaton, megacyle

hydromegatherm—a plant which must have much heat and moisture to develop fully

megalaesthete—sensory organs, sometimes in the form of eyes, as in Placophora

megalopic—belonging to the megalops stage, i.e., a larval stage of certain crustaceans, conspicuous by large, stalked eyes

megaphyllous—having relatively large leaves

Megarhinus—a genus of large, nonbiting American mosquitoes with curved beaks

13. MOGI-, "difficult"

mogilalia—difficulty in speech, such as stuttering or stammering

mogigraphia—writer's cramp

14. NE-, "new," "new and different form of"

(gen.) neon, neologism, neoclassic, neophyte

glyconeogenesis—the formation of carbohydrates from substances which are not carbohydrates

nearthrosis—a new and abnormally produced articulation in the sequence of a fracture, dislocation or disease of a bone

neoanthropic—belonging to the same species as recent man

neogamous—applicable to forms of protozoa exhibiting precocious association of gametocytes

neolalia—speech, especially of psychotics, that includes words that are new and meaningless

neophobia—dread of new scenes or novelties

15. ODYN-, "pain"
(gen.) anodyne

odynophobia—morbid dread of pain; algophobia

glossodynia—pain in the tongue

myodynia—muscular pain

16. ONYCH-, "finger or toenail," "claw"

acronychous—having claws, nails and hoofs

eponychium—a horny condition of the epidermis; the horny layer

neonychium—a soft pad enclosing each claw of an embryo

onychoheterotopia—an anomaly consisting of the presence of abnormally situated nails, as on the lateral aspect of the terminal phalanges

17. PATH-, "disease," "suffering," "feeling"
(gen.) sympathy, pathetic, apathy, antipathy

apopathetic—behavior not overtly directed toward others but clearly influenced by their presence; showing off

hyperpathia—a disagreeable or painful sensation in a region which is really hyperesthetic

idiopathic—pertaining to a primary disease, i.e., one not the result of any other disease, but of spontaneous origin; a disease for which no cause is known

pathomimesis—imitation of the symptoms and signs of a disease; occurs in hysteria and in malingering

18. PEP(S)-, PEPT-, "to digest"

pepsin—a substance containing a proteolytic enzyme obtained from the glandular layer of a hog's stomach *peptic*—pertaining to pepsin; pertaining to digestion, as peptic ulcer

peptonephridia—the anterior nephridia which function as digestive glands in some Oligochaeta

19. PSEUD-, "false"
(gen.) pseudoscientist, pseudonym

chromatopseudopsis—color blindness; chromatelopsia

pseudacusis—a disturbance of hearing in which a person's own voice sounds strange or peculiar, being altered in pitch and quality

pseudoblepsia—a visual hallucination; a distorted visual image

pseudocyst—a saclike space containing liquid, etc., which has no definite lining membrane

pseudoisochromatic—pertaining to the different colors which appear alike to the color-blind

pseudonychium—a lobe or process between the claws of insects

pseudopod—a footlike body-wall process of certain larvae

20. TELE-, "afar," "operating at a distance"
(gen.) telegraph, telephone

teleopsia—a disorder in visual perception of space

telegnosis—knowledge of distant happenings obtained by occult or unknown means; clairvoyance

teletherapy—treatment in absentia; suggestive therapeutics

EXERCISE

List the prefixes, bases and suffixes and give their meanings.

1. *acyanopsia, acyanoblepsia* or *acyoblepsia*—inability to see blue colors

2. *anerythroblepsia* or *anerythropsia*—impaired color perception of red; red blindness

3. *dyscrasia*—an abnormal state of the body

4. *glossolalia*—unintelligible jabbering; talk in a strange or unknown tongue; jargon

5. *idioglossia*—any form of speech or utterance invented by an individual and unique with him, usually incomprehensible to others; in a very young child, a transitional stage toward normal speech

6. *aneurysm*—a dilatation of the wall of an artery forming a blood-containing tumor

7. *ichthyismus*—poisoning due to the absorption of mytilotoxin in muscles or eating spoiled fish

8. *neoplasm*—any new growth, usually applied to a tumor; an aberrant new growth

9. *megalocardia*—hypertrophy of the heart

10. *anisocoria*—inequality in the diameter of the pupils

11. *mogiarthria*—a form of dysarthria involving defective coordination of the muscles

12. *pseudocyesis*—phantom pregnancy; the belief on the part of a woman in the existence of pregnancy when none exists

13. *telepathy*—the direct awareness of what is taking place in another person's mind

14. *embololalia*—the insertion of meaningless words into speech, occurring in some aphasic or schizophrenic states

15. *telekinesis*—the power claimed by some people of causing objects to move without touching them

16. *mastodynia*—a condition affecting females, usually of low fertility, between the ages of twenty-five and forty, clinically characterized by pain in one or both breasts

17. *galactacrasia*—deficiency of or abnormality in mother's milk

18. *melanonychia*—a condition in which the fingernails or toenails turn black

19. *parageusia*—perversion of the sense of taste

20. *melanoglossia*—the disease known as blacktongue or Stuttgart disease

21. *pathogenic*—pertaining to the capacity to produce disease

22. *amylodyspepsia*—inability to digest starchy foods

23. *paronychia*—a suppurative inflammation about the margin of a nail

24. *barodontalgia* or *aerodontalgia*—dental pain occurring in individuals exposed to decreased barometric pressures such as occur in high-altitude flying

MORE WORDS TO WORK WITH

acrocyanosis
acromegaly
acyanoblepsia
acyesis
amblygeustia
androgalactozemia
anisognathous
anisogynecomastia
anisometropia
anonychia
anthocyanin
anthropopathism
chionablepsia
cholecyanin
corectopia
coreplasty
cyanephidrosis
cyanophil
cyesiology

cyesiognosis
diplocoria
dyslalia
dyspepsia
eccyesia
entocyemate
empathy
eupeptic
galactischia
galactosemia
glossophagine
helicopepsin
hemiglossoplegia
hemigeusia
hepatomegaly
hypoglossal
idiosome
idiosyncrasy
isiodactylism
isothermal

orchidectomy
orchiodynia
laloplegia
lalorrhea
megalith
megalomania
mogiphonia
neolithic
odynacousia
onychocryptosis
onychophagist
otodynia
pathology
pathophobia
pseudogeusia
pseudomnesia
telelectrocardiogram
telemeter
xenoglossophobia

LESSON 9.   Greek Noun-Forming Suffixes III

Learn the following suffixes and their meanings.

1. -*oma*, usually "tumor arising in or composed of," occasionally "swelling containing," rarely "diseased condition," "result of" (related to -*ma* in Lesson 8)

MELAN-, "black," "dark"	+ -*oma*	melanoma
CARCIN-, "cancer"	+ -*oma*	carcinoma
OSTE-, "bone"	+ -*oma*	osteoma
HEMAT-, "blood"	+ -*oma*	hematoma
GLAUC-, "silvery white"	+ -*oma*	glaucoma

Note that, if -*oma* is followed by an additional element, it becomes -*omat-*:

CARCIN-, "cancer" + -*omat*	+ -*ous*	carcinomatous

MELAN-, "black," "dark"

+ -*omat*	+ -*ous*	melanomatous

2. -*osis*, "diseased condition of," "act of," "process of" (related to -*sis* in Lesson 8)

PSYCH-, "mind"	+ -*osis*	psychosis
NEUR-, "nerve"	+ -*osis*	neurosis
HYPN-, "sleep"	+ -*osis*	hypnosis
OSM-, "impulse"	+ -*osis*	osmosis

3. -*itis*, "inflammation of," "inflammatory disease of"

APPENDIC-, "appendix"	+ -*itis*	appendicitis
ARTHR-, "joint"	+ -*itis*	arthritis
TONSILL-, "tonsil"	+ -*itis*	tonsillitis

4. -*in*, -*ine*, "chemical substance"

This suffix is of Latin derivation.

anti- + TOX-, "poison"	+ -*in*	antitoxin
INSUL-, "island"	+ -*in*	insulin
epi- + NEPHR-, "kidney"	+ -*ine*	epinephrine

5. -*ium*, "part," "lining or enveloping tissue," "region"

peri- + NEPHR-, "kidney"	+ -*ium*	perinephrium
epi- + GASTR-, "stomach"	+ -*ium*	epigastrium

NEW BASES

Learn the following bases and their meanings.

1. ADEN-, "gland"

   adenodactyli or *adenocheiri*—elaborate accessory copulatory organs which are outgrowths of the atrial walls in Turbellaria

   adenophore—the stalk of a nectar gland

   adenopodous—bearing glands on peduncles or petioles

   ectadenia—ectodermal accessory genital glands in insects

   heteradenia—an abnormality in the formation or location of gland tissue

2. ANGI-, "vessel"

   angiodystrophia—defective nutrition of blood vessels

   angiitis—inflammation of blood or lymph vessel

angiopneumography—radiographic visualization of the pulmonary artery by means of a nontoxic, radiopaque substance

angiostomatous—narrow-mouthed; applicable to molluscs and snakes with nondistensible mouths

gametangium—a structure producing sexual cells

3. ARACHN-, "spider" (occasionally "arachnoid membrane")

Arachnida—a large class of Arthropoda which includes scorpions, spiders and mites

arachnidium—apparatus by which a spider web is produced

arachnoidureterostomy—a one-stage operation for relief of progressive hydrocephaly in infants, in which cerebrospinal fluid is shunted into the urinary tract

4. ASTR-, ASTER-, "star"

(gen.) disaster, asterisk, aster, astrology, astronaut

aster—the radiating structure surrounding the centrosome of a cell, seen at the beginning of mitosis

amphiaster—the achromatic figure in mitosis consisting of two asters connected by a spindle

asteroid—one of the small planets between Jupiter and Mars

Asteroidea—the class of echinoderms comprising starfish

Asterophyllites—a form genus of fossil plants having a starlike arrangement of leaves

cytaster—the starlike system of cytoplasmic radiations surrounding the central body during mitosis

5. BLAST-, "bud," "germ," "embryonic cell"

amphiblastula—the stage in development of certain sponges in which the posterior end of the embryo is composed of granular archaeocytes and the anterior end is composed of flagellate cells

astroblast—a primitive cell which develops into an astrocyte

blastoderm—primitive germ layer or epithelium of a blastula or blastocyst from which primary germ layers are derived

blastokinesis—a process of cephalo-caudal reversal in the eggs of insects and certain cephalopods

blastostyle—in Hydrozoa, a columniform zooid with or without mouth and tentacles, bearing gonophores

erythroblastosis—hemolytic anemia of the newborn, involving an increased number of nucleated red blood cells

lipoblast—a formative fat cell

lipoblastosis—multiple lipomas in subcutaneous and visceral fat deposits

megaloblast—a large erythrocyte, seen in some anemias; an immature megalocyte

6. CHLOR-, "green," "chlorine"

chloroplast—a minute granule or plastid containing chlorophyll

chlorosis—green sickness, a type of anemia seen most frequently in young women

erythrochloropia—color-blind condition whereby green and red are the only colors distinguished

hypochloruria—diminution in the amount of chloride in the urine

zoochlorellae—symbiotic green algae living in various animals

7. COCC-, "berry-shaped organism"

Chlorococcales—an order of unicellular green algae

coccolith—a calcareous spicule in certain Flagellata

Cryptococcus—a genus of yeastlike, budding, imperfect fungi

cocculus—the very poisonous, bean-shaped berry of a woody vine used in the East Indies to stupify fishes and as an ointment to control vermin

cytococcus—nucleus of a fertilized egg

pyococcus—any pus-producing coccus

Streptococcus—a genus of gram-positive, chain-forming bacteria

8. CONI-, "dust"

conidiophore—bearing condia, a fungal spore

hemoconia—minute, highly refractive particles of fat found in the blood

otoconium—one of minute crystals of calcium carbonate found in membranous labyrinth of the inner ear; ear dust

9. EO(S)-, "dawn or early age," "rosy"

Eolithic—relating to earliest period of the Stone Age

eosin—red crystalline fluorescent dye

eosphorite—a kind of mineral; red aluminum manganese phosphate

10. LY-, "to loosen," "to dissolve," "to break up"

dermatolysis—abnormal laxation of the skin

dialystely—a condition in which steles in a stem remain more or less separate

lithodialysis—solution of calculi in urinary bladder; breaking of a vesical calculus previous to its removal

lyophil—solutions which, after evaporation to dryness, go readily into solution again on addition of fluid

lysin—a cell-dissolving substance

lysogenesis—production of lysins

onycholysis—a slow process of loosening a nail from its bed, beginning at the free edge and progressing gradually toward the roots

11. MENING-, "membrane," especially "meninges, the membranes enveloping the brain and spinal cord" (MENINX)

meningosis—union of bones by membranes

meninguria—presence or passage of membranous shreds in the urine

meningitis—inflammation of the membranes of the brain or spinal cord

12. METR-, "uterus"

hematometra—an accumulation of blood or menstrual fluid in the uterus

metremia—congestion of the uterus

metrypercinesis—excessive uterine contraction

13. MYC-, MYCET-, "fungus"

actinomycosis—a parasitic, infectious, inoculable disease affecting cattle, hogs and sometimes man

mycoderm—a bacterial film formed during alcoholic fermentation

neomycin—antibiotic produced by a soil actinomycete

14. MYEL-, "spinal cord," "marrow"

hydromyelia—a dilatation of the central canal of the spinal cord containing an increased quantity of cerebro-spinal fluid

miningoencephalomyelitis—inflammation of the meninges, brain and spinal cord *myelin*—the white, fatty substance forming the sheath of some nerves

myeloblastoma—a tumor composed of precursors of bone marrow cells

myelocyte—any cell concerned with development of granular leucocytes

15. NEUR-, "nerve," "nervous system," "tendon"

acrotrophoneurosis—a trophic disturbance of the extremities caused by a nervous lesion

angioneurosis—a psychoneurosis which partially expresses itself by a disturbance of the vasomotor system

aponeurosis—an expanded tendon serving as a means of attachment for flat muscles at their insertion

argyroneurous—with silver-colored nerves or veins

cryptoneurous—with no definite or distinct nervous system

dialyneury—condition of having pleural ganglia united to opposite visceral nerves in gastropods

neuroanatomy—the nervous system

neurosyphilis—syphilitic infection of the nervous system

neurotomy—the division of a nerve

16. ORCH(I)-, ORCHID-, "testicle"
(gen.) orchid

synorchism—partial or complete fusion of the testes within the abdomen or scrotum

cryptorchism—failure of the testes to descend

orchidectomy—surgical removal of the testes; castration

17. PAN-, PANT-, "all," "complete"
(gen.) pantomime, pantheism, panacea, pandemonium, Pan-American, pantheon

pangamic—indiscriminate mating

panmnesia—a potential remembrance of all impressions

panzootic—in veterinary medicine, affecting many kinds of animals

18. PNEUMON-, PNEUM-, "lung"

autopneumonectomy—one lung being sequestrated by a pathological process, such as inflammation or injury, so it becomes useless

parapneumonia—a disease presenting the symptoms of lobar

pneumonia but not caused by the pneumococcus

pneumolith—a calculus or concretion occurring in a lung

19. POLI-, "gray"

polioencephalomyelitis—inflammation of the gray matter of the brain and spinal cord

polioencephalalopathy—any disease of the gray matter of the brain

polioplasm—granular cytoplasm

20. THROMB-, "clot"

thrombocyte—blood platelet

thrombocytocrit—a glass tube for counting blood platelets

thrombokinase—a complex protein substance with the capacity to activate prothrombin to thrombin

thromboplastin—extracts which promote clotting

EXERCISE

List the prefixes, bases and suffixes and give their meanings.

1. *cholecystokinin*—a hormone having the property of causing or promoting gall bladder contraction

2. *hidradenitis*—inflammation of the sweat glands

3. *hemangiomatosis*—widespread dissemination of a tumor made up of blood vessels

4. *astrocytoma*—one of the commonest glial tumors of the central nervous system formed of protoplasmic or fibrillary astrocytes (fibrillary astrocytes—the many-processed stellate cells of the neuroglia, attached to the blood vessels of the brain and spinal cord)

5. *arachnolysin*—a substance contained in the spider *Epeira diadema* which reacts strongly with the blood of the rabbit and man but not with the blood of the horse or guinea pig

6. *pneumoconiosis*—chronic inflammation of the lungs caused by the inhalation of dust

7. *eosin*—a rose-colored dye

8. *eosinophil*—having an affinity for eosin

9. *otomycosis*—the growth of fungi in the ear or the diseased condition caused thereby

10. *othematoma*—hematoma of the external ear

11. *hemolytic*—pertaining to the destruction of red blood cells and the resulting escape of hemoglobin

12. *prothrombinemia*—an excess of prothrombin in the blood, the protein precursor in plasma of thrombin, which induces clotting

13. *orchitis*—inflammation of the testes

14. *neuroblastoma*—a tumor composed of neuroblasts, the formative cells of neurons; also called sympathicoblastoma

15. *chloroma*—multiple tumors of marrow and soft tissue near bones; grossly, the nodules are green

16. *endometriosis*—the presence of endometrial tissue in abnormal locations

17. *parametritis*—inflammation of the tissues about the uterus

18. *chondroblastoma*—a rare benign tumor derived from cartilage cells or cartilage-forming connective tissue

19. *panarthritis*—inflammation of many joints

20. *meningococcus*—the bacterium that causes cerebrospinal meningitis

21. *meningococcemia*—the presence of meningococci in the blood

22. *poliosis*—a condition characterized by the absence of pigment in the hair

23. *arachnodactyly*—spider fingers; a condition in which the fingers and sometimes toes are abnormally long

24. *poliomyelitis*—a common virus disease of man which in the acute form may involve the central nervous system; formerly, any inflammation of the gray matter of the spinal cord

25. *osteomyelitis*—inflammation of the marrow of the bone

26. *pericardium*—the closed, membranous sac enveloping the heart

27. *phylloerythrin*—a red pigment derived from chlorophyll and occurring in bile of herbivorous mammals

28. *perineurium*—the connective tissue sheath investing a fasciculus or primary bundle of nerve fibers

MORE WORDS TO WORK WITH

achlorhydria
achloropsia
adenitis
adenoid
adenoma
adenopathy
androconia
angioblast
angiology
angiosteosis
anorchism
antithrombin
arachnephobia
arachnidism
arachnitis
arachnoiditis
astrocyte
astroid
catalyst
chloranthy
chloromycetin
chlorophyll
coccidioidomycosis
dyspepsia
dermatoconiosis
electrolyte
endoangiitis
Eoanthropus
gonococcus
hematomyelia

hepatocholangienterostomy
meningoencephalitis
metapneumonic
mycetophagous
mycology
mycophthalmia
mycosis
myelodysplasia
myometritis
neurosurgery
onychomycosis
orchidopathy
orchidoplasty
orchiodynia
panarthritis
panchromatic
pancreas
pandemic
panhysterectomy
pantanencephalia
pantophobia
phytopneumonoconiosis
pneumonia
pneumonoultramicroscopic-
    silicovolcanoconiosis
poliothrix
psychoneurosis
thromboangiitis
thrombosis

LESSON 10.   Greek Noun-Forming Suffixes IV

Learn the following suffixes and their meanings.

1.   *-us,* "individual," "person"

an-	+ OT-, "ear"	+ *-us*	anotus
HYDR(o), "water"	+ CEPHAL-, "head"	+ *-us*	hydrocephalus

2. *-idae, -ida, -id,* "descended from," "related to"
    These suffixes are generally used to indicate rank and classification in zoology and botany.

ACAR-, "mite"	+ *-idae*	Acaridae
ARACHN-, "spider"	+ *-ida*	Arachnida
ARACHN-	+ *-id*	arachnid

NEW BASES

Learn the following bases and their meanings.

1. AGOG(UE)-, "inducing the flow of," "expelling"
    (gen.) demagogue, synagogue, pedagogic
    cholagogue—an agent which promotes the flow of bile
    galactagogue—an agent that promotes the flow of milk
    helminthagogue—an anthelmintic

2. ARCH(E)-, "ancient," "beginning," "primitive"
    (gen.) archeology, archetype
    archaeostomatous—having the blastopore persistent and forming the mouth; channel leading into the archenteron of the gastrula
    archenteron—embryonic alimentary cavity
    archeocyte or *archaeocyte*—cells arising from undifferentiated blastomeres and ultimately giving rise to germ cells and gametes
    archiblastula—typical hollow ball of cells derived from an egg with total and equal segmentation
    adrenarche—the time in the development of the child when an increased output of adrenal cortical hormones occurs

3. AUX(E)-, "increase"
    auxesis—increase in size or bulk
    auxin—a plant hormone which governs cell extension or growth
    auxobaric—increasing pressure, denoting development of pressure in the cardiac ventricle
    auxocardia—normal increase in volume of heart during diastole
    auxochrome—that which increases color; increase in development of color

auxocyte—a spermatocyte, oocyte or sporocyte during its early growth period

heterauxesis—irregular or asymmetrical growth

onychauxesis—hypertrophy of the nail

4. DIDYM-, "twin," "testicle"

anadidymus—inferior duplicity

cryptodidymus—a form of duplicity in which a fetus (or fetal part) is included within the body of an individual

didymolite—a mineral occurring in dark gray, monoclinic, twinned crystals

didymospore—a two-celled spore

didymitis—orchitis

didymous—growing in pairs, or arranged in pairs

perididymis—the fibrous covering of the testes

5. GYR-, "circle," "ring"

(gen.) gyrate

Gyraulus—a genus of snails

gyrencephalate—having the surface of brain convoluted

gyroidal—spiral in arrangement

gyromancy—divination in which one walking in or around a circle falls from dizziness and prognosticates from the place of the fall

gyrose—with undulating lines, sinuous

gyrus—a cerebral convolution

ophthalmogyric—pertaining to or causing movements of the eye

6. HIPP-, "horse"

(gen.) hippopotamus, Philip, hippodrome

ephippium—the pituitary fossa; a saddle-shaped modification of cuticle in certain insects; literally, a saddle cloth

Hippidion—genus of extinct Pleistocene horses

Hipposideros—horseshoe bats

hippuric acid—an acid found in high concentration in the urine of herbivorous animals

7. ISCHI-, "hip"

hypoischium—a small, bony rod passing backward from the ischiadic symphysis *ischioalgia*—sciatica

ischiodidymus or *ischiopagus*—conjoined twins united at the sacral or ischial region

ischiomelus—an individual with an acessory limb attached at the nates

ischiopodite—proximal joint of walking legs of certain crustaceans

Saurischia—an order of class Reptilia distinguished by a pelvis

8. LEP-, "to seize"

analeptic—restoring consciousness; hastening convalescence

narcolepsy—a condition characterized by a transient compulsive tendency to attacks of deep sleep

nympholepsy—ecstacy of an erotic type

9. MACR-, "large," "long"

acromacria—spider fingers

macrandrous—having large male plants or elements

macrocarpous—producing large fruit

macrogamy—syngamy between full-grown individuals of a species (syngamy—sexual reproduction)

macroglossia—enlargement of the tongue

macromania—delusion that things (such as a part of the body) are larger than they really are

macropodous—having a long stalk; long-footed

macropsia—disturbance of vision in which objects seem larger than they are

10. MEL-, "limb"

gastromelus—an individual with an accessory limb attached to the abdomen

melodidymus—obsolete word for presence of an accessory limb or limbs

symmelia or *symelia*—coalescence of the lower extremities

11. MICR-, "small," "one millionth"

(gen.) microcosm, microphone, omicron, microscope

hypomicrognathus—an individual having an abnormally small lower jaw

microaesthetes—the smaller sensory organs of Placophora

microlithiasis—formation of very minute calculi

micromelia—abnormal smallness of the limbs

microsaur—one of an extinct order of amphibians resembling the salamander

12. NARC-, "stupor"

autonarcosis—state of being poisoned, rendered dormant or arrested in growth, owing to self-produced CO_2

Narcacion—genus of electric rays

narcoanalysis or *narcotherapy*—use of sleep-inducing drugs in therapy

narcohypnia—a peculiar state in which the patient feels numbness on awakening

narcohypnosis—a state of deep sleep produced by hypnosis

narcotic—drug which produces a stupor, complete insensibility or sleep

narcous—state of profound stupor, unconsciousness or arrested activity

13. OMPHAL-, "naval"

acromphalus—center of the umbilicus; unusual prominence of the navel

hepatomphalocele—liver contained in a hernia through the umbilical ring

omphalogenesis—development of the yolk sac; development of umbilical vesicle and cord

omphalion—center of the umbilicus

omphaloidium—the scar at the hilum of a seed

omphaloproptosis—abnormal protrusion of the umbilicus

omphalopsychite—one who stares fixedly at his navel to induce a mystical trance

14. PEX-, "to fasten"; PAG-, "united"

craniopagus—conjoined twins united by their heads

hypogastropagus—conjoined twins united at the hypogastric region

prosopopagus—unequal conjoined twins in which parasitic twin is attached to the face

hysteropexy—fixation of the uterus by surgical operation

15. PLATY(S)-, "broad," "flat"

amphiplatyan—flat on both ends; used of vertebrae having both anterior and posterior surfaces of the centrum flat *platycephalic*—characterizing a person with a flat skull

platydactyl—with flattened-out fingers and toes, as certain tailless amphibians

platysma—a subcutaneous muscle in the neck

16. SAPR-, "rotten"

saprobic—living on decaying organic matter

saprolite—disintegrated, somewhat decomposed rock

saprophytic—pertaining to a plant that lives on decaying organic matter

saprozoic—living on decaying or dead organic matter

17. SIAL-, "saliva"

aerosialophagy—the habit of constantly swallowing

glycosialia—presence of glucose in saliva

sialolithiasis—presence of salivary calculi

18. STHEN-, "strength"

(gen.) calisthenics

adenasthenia—functional deficiency of a gland

anisosthenic—not of equal power, said of pairs of muscles

hypersthenia—condition of exalted strength or tone of body

metasthenic—with well-developed posterior part of body

19. TACH(Y)-, "swift"

tachistoscope—instrument for providing a very brief time exposure of visual material

tachyphagia—rapid-eating

Tachinidae—a large family of rapid-flying, two-winged flies

20. UR-, "tail"

uromelus—a deformity in which there is more or less complete fusion of legs with but a single foot

uromere—an abdominal segment in Arthropoda

urosthenic—having tail strongly developed for propulsion

urostyle—posterior part of vertebral column in anurous amphibians

EXERCISE

List the prefixes, bases and suffixes and give their meanings.

1. *Eohippus*—a genus of small, primitive, four-toed horses from

the Lower Eocene of the western U.S.

2. *ischiopagus*—conjoined twins united by their sacral or ischial regions

3. *omphalopagus*—united at the umbilicus

4. *epididymectomy*—surgical removal of the epididymis, the portion of the seminal duct lying posterior to the testes

5. *gastrodidymus*—a malformation consisting of equal conjoined twins united at the epigastric region

6. *amelus*—person minus a limb or limbs

7. *parotid*—situated near the ear, pertaining to the parotid gland

8. *tachyauxesis*—heterauxesis in which the part grows more rapidly than the organ

9. *neurasthenia*—a group of symptoms formerly ascribed to debility or exhaustion of nerve centers

10. *saprophage*—an organism that feeds on decaying organic matter

11. *tachycardia*—excessively rapid heart action

12. *platyhelminth*—a flat worm

13. *hypnolepsy*—narcolepsy

14. *macroscopic*—large enough to be seen by the naked eye

15. *platyrrhine*—having a broad, flat nose; in taxonomy, New World monkeys

16. *macracusia*—a cerebral disorder simulating epilepsy in which sounds are exaggerated

17. *microgyria*—abnormal smallness of the convolutions of the brain

18. *catalepsy*—a state of unconsciousness, usually trancelike, where there is a loss of voluntary motion and a peculiar plastic rigidity

19. *enteropexy*—fixation of a portion of intestines to the abdominal wall

20. *sialagogue*—an agent that promotes the flow of saliva

21. *emmenagogue*—an agent that stimulates the menstrual flow

22. *Archeozoic*—earliest era of geologic time

23. *menarche*—start of the menstrual function

24. *erythromelalgia*—disease of the extremities of the body marked
        by increased skin temperature, redness and burning
        pain

25. *anurous*—tailless

MORE WORDS TO WORK WITH

acromicria	lithagogic	omphalitis
anisomelia	macrocephalia	omphalocele
Archaeohippus	macrocheilia	platybasia
archinephron	macrocytosis	platyonchia
asthenophobia	macrodontia	platymorphia
auxodrome	macrogyne	polymelia
auxometer	mastopexy	pygopagus
cholecystopexy	micrergate	saprogen
craniodidymus	microcurie	Saprolegnia
epididymus	micromastia	sialadenitis
epilepsy	microphonia	sialorrhea
gastrodidymous	myasthenia	tachometer
gyrodyne	narcomania	tachylalia
gyroscope	Narconumal	tachysystole
hippanthropy	narcopepsia	uropod
hippophagy	narcospasm	xiphopagus
	oligosialia	

LESSON 11.   Greek Diminutive Suffixes

Learn the following suffixes and their meanings.

1. *-ium, -ion,* "little" (often difficult to distinguish from *-ium*
    presented in Lesson 9)

    BACTER-, "rod"   + *-ium*   bacterium

    POD-, "foot"   + *-ium*   podium
        (podium—tube foot of echinoderm)

    THEC-, "case"   + *-ium*   thecium
        (thecium—the hymenium or spore-bearing layer in fungi)

    STOM-, "mouth"   + *-ion*   stomion
        (stomion—the midpoint of the oral fissure determined
        with the lips closed)

2. *-idium, -idion,* "little"

    CONI-, "dust"   + *-idium*   conidium
    (conidium—an asexual spore)

    BAS-, "base"   + *-idium*   basidium
    (basidium—a conidrophore characteristic of the class Basidiomycetes, bearing basidiospores)

    STOM-, "mouth"   + *-idium*   stomidium
    (stomidium—terminal pore of degenerated tentacles in Actiniaria)

    PLAST-, "to mold"   + *-idion*   plastidion
    (plastidion—any of various small bodies of specialized protoplasm lying in the cytoplasm of cells; a plastid)

3. *-arium, -arion,* "little"

    CON-, "cone"   + *-arium*   conarium
    (conarium—pineal body)

    HIPP-, "horse"   + *-arion*   Hipparion
    (Hipparion—genus of extinct three-toed mammals related to but not now considered the direct ancestor of horses)

4. *-isk, -iscus,* "little"

    ASTER-, "star"   + *-isk*   asterisk

    LEMN-, "ribbon"   + *-iscus*   lemniscus
    (lemniscus—a secondary sensory pathway of the central nervous system)

    MEN-, "moon"   + *iscus*   meniscus
    (meniscus—a crescent or cresentic body, especially an interarticular fibrocartilage)

NEW BASES

Learn the following bases and their meanings.

1. ASC-, "bag"
    ascus—membranous oval or tubular spore sac in fungi
    ascogenous—producing asci
    Ascomycetes—higher fungi having spores formed in asci
    Ascophyllum—bladder-bearing rockweeds

2. BRANCHI-, "gills"
    arthrobranchial—pertaining to joint gills

branchiocardiac—pertaining to gills and heart, applies to vessels given off ventrally from the ascidian (tunicate) heart; also vessels conveying blood from the gills to the pericardial sinus in certain crustaceans

metabranchial—pertaining to or in the region of the posterior gill region

phyllobranchia—a gill consisting of numbers of lamellae, or thin plates

podobranchiae—foot gills, i.e., gills attached to the basal segment of the throacic limb of crustaceans

3.   CARP-, "fruit"

actinocarpous—plants with flowers and fruit radially arranged

amphicarpous—producing fruit of two kinds

angiocarpic—having or being fruit enclosed within an external covering; opposite of gymnocarpic

carpel—a division of a seed vessel

carpolith—a fossil fruit

dialycarpic—having a fruit composed of distinct carpels

geocarpic—having fruits maturing underground, as the peanut

hypocarpogenous—having flowers and fruit placed underground

syncarp—an aggregate fruit with united carpels

4.   -CELE, "hernia," "swelling"

arthrocele—any swollen joint; hernia of the synovial membrane through a joint capsule

dacryocystocele—protrusion of a lacrimal sac

enterocele—hernia containing a loop of intestine

hydrocele—an accumulation of fluid in the sac of the tunica vaginalis of the testes

galactocele—a cystic tumor in the ducts of the breast; a hydrocele with milky contents

hydromyelocele—excessive accumulation of a fluid in the central canal of the spinal cord

myelomeningocele—spina bifida with protrusion of the meningeal sac

5.   COLP-, "vagina"

aerocolpos—distention of the vagina with air or gas

pyocolpocele—a suppurating cyst of the vagina

endocolpitis—mucous vaginitis

6. GEN(E)-, GON-, "to be produced," "to produce"; GON-, "seed"

(gen.) genesis, eugenics, hydrogen, genealogy, homogeneous, genocide

actinogonidial—having radially arranged genital organs

carpogonium—the flask-shaped, egg-bearing portion of the female reproductive branch in some thallophytes

coccogone—a reproductive cell in certain algae

gonostyle—the sexual palpon of Siphonophora; the clasper of Diptera

gonad—sexual gland; the ovary or testes

gynogonidia—female sexual elements in Mastigophora

polygoneutic—raising more than one brood a season

telegony—the erroneous belief that a male once mated with a female will affect the subsequent progeny of the same female mated to a different sire

7. HELI-, "sun"

(gen.) heliocentric, heliolatry, helium, heliotrope

heliolithic—marked by sun worship and erection of megaliths

heliopsis—a flower resembling the sunflower

heliotaxis—locomotor or other response to stimulus of sunlight

paraheliotropism—the tendency of plants to turn the edges of their leaves toward intense illumination, thus protecting the surface of the leaves

8. MER-, "part"

adenomere—that portion of a developing gland which will be responsible for its functioning

dysmerogenesis—segmentation resulting in unlike parts

eumerism—an aggregation of like parts

merocrine—applicable to glands in which secreting cells are able to function repeatedly; act of secretion leaves cell intact

merogony—development of normal young of small size from part of an egg

merotomy—segmentation or division into parts

myomere—a muscle segment

9. NYCT-, "night"

nyctitropism—tendency of certain leaves to curl upward at night

nyctophonia—hysterical loss of voice during the day in one who is capable of speaking at night

10. ONYM-, "name"

(gen.) anonymous, pseudonym, synonym, homonym, antonym, patronymic

metonym—synonymous name rendered invalid by existence of an earlier, valid name

hyponym—a generic name not based on a type species

11. OO-, "egg"

ooblastoma—egg after fertilization

oocyte—an egg before formation of the first polar body

oogamy—union of a nonmotile female gamete or egg cell with male gamete

oogonium—the female reproductive organ in certain thallophytes; the mother egg cell

ookinete—the motile,worm-shaped stage of the zygote in certain protozoa

oolite—rock consisting of small grains that resemble fish roe

oozoid—any individual which develops from an egg

12. PACHY-, "thick"

(gen.) pachyderm

pachyacria—condition marked by clubbing fingers and toes

pachycladous—thick-branched

pachymeningitis—inflammation of the dura

13. PEN-, "deficiency," "want"

glycopenia—tendency to hypoglycemia

pancytopenia—reduction of all three formed elements of blood

penalgesia—reduction in the number of pain and touch spots in trigeminal neuralgia

14. PHLEB-, "vein"

phlebenterism—a condition of having branches of intestine extending into such other organs as arms or legs

phlebismus—undue prominence or swelling of a vein

metrophlebitis—inflammation of the veins of the uterus

15. PHTHI-, "to waste away"

phthisiogyne—pupal female ant parasitized by an Orasema larva

16. PHYC-, "seaweed," "algae"
    Chlorophyceae—algae having clear, green color
    Drepanophycus—genus of fossil plants
    Phycomycetes—class of lower fungi

17. PTO-, "to fall"
    (gen.) symptom
    proptosis—falling downward, prolapse
    ptomaine—an amino compound which results from decomposition of protein or dead animal matter by microorganisms

18. SALPING-, "tube," specifically "eustachian or fallopian tube"
    pyosalpingitis—inflammation of uterine or auditory tubes
    Salpiglossis—genus of Chilean herbs having a tubular calix
    salpingocyesis—tubal pregnancy

19. SAUR-, "lizard"
    branchiosaur—small, prehistoric amphibian, similar to a salamander
    saurian—resembling a lizard
    saurognathous—with saurian arrangement of jaw bones
    sauroxine—an alkaloid obtained from a lizard

20. XANTH-, "yellow"
    xanthochroi—caucasoids having light hair and fair skin
    xanthomatous—yellow nodules on skin, the result of a disturbance of fat metabolism
    xanthomelanous—having olive or yellow skin and black hair
    xanthopsin—yellow pigment in an insect eye
    Xanthorrhoea—genus including the grass tree, excluding the yellow gum
    zooxanthin—yellow pigment found in plumage of certain birds
    xanthopsia—visual disturbance in which objects look yellow

EXERCISE

List the prefixes, bases and suffixes and give their meanings.

1. *lithopedion*—a retained fetus that has been calcified

2. *gnathion*—the most inferior point on the inferior border of the mandible, in the sagittal plane

3. *asterion*—the meeting point of the lambdoid, parietomastoid and occipitomastoid sutures

4. *ascogonidium*—a portion of the female sex organ in ascomycetous fungi, which, after fertilization, develops into asci, i.e., spore cases

5. *oophoridion*—the megasporangium in certain plants (megasporangium—a macrospore producing the sporangium; an ovule)

6. *panhysterosalpingo-oophorectomy*—excision of uterus, oviducts and ovaries

7. *myelocele*—spina bifida with protrusion of the spinal cord

8. *colpocele*—hernia or tumor of the vagina

9. *heliencephalitis*—encephalitis caused by exposure to the sun's rays

10. *ascocarp*—the developing fruit of ascomycetes

11. *meromorphosis*—regeneration of a part with the new part less than that lost

12. *ascidium*—a pitcher- or flask-shaped organ or appendage of a plant, as a leaf of the pitcher plant; in general usage, a wineskin

13. *branchiomere*—a branchial segment

14. *meroblastic*—ova which undergo only partial segmentation or cleavage in development

15. *phycoxanthin*—buff coloring matter of brown algae

16. *ichthyosaur*—a Mesozoic marine reptile having an ichthyoid body and limbs

17. *panmyelophthisis*—a general wasting of the bone marrow

18. *hysteroptosis*—falling or inversion of the uterus

19. *thromboplastinopenia*—deficiency in thromboplastin in blood

20. *endophlebitis*—inflammation of the intima of a vein

21. *nyctanthous*—flowering at night

22. *eponym*—a named formed or derived from that of a person known or assumed to be the first or one of the first to discover a disease, symptom or complex

23. *exanthematous*—pertaining to an eruption on the skin

24. *pachydermatous*—having a thick skin

25. *ootheca*—an egg case, as in insects

26. *xanthosis*—abnormal yellow discoloration of the skin

MORE WORDS TO WORK WITH

acanthocarpous
actinogen
apheliotropism
ascophore
branchia
branchiogenous
branchioma
cladoptosis
corophthisis
dinosaur
erythropenia
gastrocele
gene
genetics
gonorrhea
gymnocarpous

heliotherapy
hepatoptosis
meroacrania
metroptosis
monogenism
nyctalgia
Nycteris
nyctophobia
oocephalus
pachycheilia
pachyonchia
pancolpohysterectomy
paroophoritis
phlebitis
phlebotomy
phthisis
phycocyanin

polymer
pyocolpos
salpingocatheterism
salpingolysis
salpingo-oophorectomy
salpingoothecitis
salpingopharyngeal
Sauropsida
saururine
tyrannosaurus
uroxanthin
xanthophore
xanthophyll
xanthopupurin
Xanthoria
xanthoproteic

LESSON 12.   Greek Verb-Forming Suffixes

Learn the following suffixes and their meanings.

1. *-ize,* "to make," "to treat," "to do something with"

CARBON-, "coal," "charcoal"	+ *-ize*	carbonize
syn- + CHRON-, "time"	+ *-ize*	synchronize
anti(i)- + AGON-, "struggle"	+ *-ize*	antagonize

2. *-ate,* "to make," "to treat," "to do something with"
   This suffix is of Latin origin.

CARBON-, "coal," "charcoal"	+ *-ate*	carbonate
GYR-, "circle"	+ *-ate*	gyrate

| AER-, "air" | + -*ate* | aerate |
| *de-*   + HYDR-, "water" | + -*ate* | dehydrate |

NEW BASES

Learn the following bases and their meanings.

1. -AGRA, "painful seizure"
   ischiagra—obsolete word for gout in hip
   melagra—muscular pain in extremities
   arthragra—muscular pain in the joints

2. BRACHI-, "arm"
   brachiopod—member of a subclass of marine molluscs having
       many foliaceous appendages
   brachiosaur—dinosaur with forelegs lower than hindlegs
   macrobrachia—excessive development of the arms
   monobrachius—an individual congenitally lacking one arm
   pseudobrachium—appendage for locomotion on a substratum
       formed from elongated ptergials of pectoral fins of
       pediculates

3. CENTE-, "to puncture"
   enterocentesis—surgical puncture of the intestine
   paracentesis—puncture, especially puncture of or tapping of
       the wall of a cavity by means of a hollow needle for
       the purpose of draining off fluid
   pneumonocentesis—surgical puncture of a lung

4. CHIR-, CHEIR-, "hand"
   (gen.) chiropodist, chiropractor, encheiridion
   adenochiri—elaborate accessory copulatory organs which are
       outgrowths of the atrial walls of Turbellaria
   chirography—handwriting
   dyschiria—inability to tell which side of the body has been
       touched
   megalochirous—large-handed
   polycheiria—state of having a supernumerary hand

5. CEL(I)-, COEL-, -COEL, "cavity," "abdominal cavity"
   amphicoelous—concave on both surfaces
   celioparacentesis—tapping of the abdomen
   celiotomy—opening of the abdominal cavity

coelom or *celom*—embryonic body cavity

coeliac—belonging to the cavity of the abdomen

Coelenterata—a phylum of invertebrates lacking a true body cavity, as jellyfish

coelhelminth—coelomate, vermiform invertebrate animals

encephalocoel—cavity within the brain, cerebral ventricle (cf. encephalocele—hernia of the brain)

nephrocoele—the embryonic cavity in a nephrotome (nephrotome—narrow mass of mesoderm from which embryonic kidneys develop)

6. DENDR-, "tree"

dendron—a protoplasmic process of a nerve cell which carries impulses toward the cell body

dendrite or *neurodendron*—fine branch of a dendron

Dendrobium—genus of epiphytic orchids

Dendrochirota—order of holothurians having tube feet and tentacles that branch like trees

zoodendrium—a treelike, branched stalk of certain colonial infusorians

7. HYAL-, "glass," "vitreous body of the eye"

hyalin—a clear, structureless, homogenous, glassy material occurring normally in matrix of cartilage and other bodily colloids and jellies; occurs pathologically in degeneration of connective tissue and epithelial cells

hyalinosis—hyaline degeneration

hyalinuria—hyaline casts in the urine

hyaloid—transparent, glasslike

hyalomere—clear, homogeneous part of the blood

hyaloplasm—ground substance of a cell

8. LARYNG-, "larynx"

laryngopathy—any disease of the larynx

laryngorrhea—excessive secretion of mucus from the larynx

otolaryngology—branch of medicine dealing with the ear, nose and throat

9. LEI-, "smooth"

leiodermia—condition of abnormal smoothness and glossiness of skin

leiodermatous—smooth-skinned

leiotrichous—having smooth or straight hair

10. MALAC-, "soft"

malacology—study of molluscs

malacophilous—adapted to pollination by snails

osteomalacia—failure of calcium to be deposited in a newly formed osteoid

11. MASTIG-, "whip," "flagellum" (MASTIX)

Chilomastix—a genus of flagellated protozoons

heteromastigate—having two different types of flagella

mastigium—defensive posterior lash of certain larvae

mastigobranchia—process of thoracic limbs of crustaceans resembling a brush and used for cleaning gills

Mastigophora—a class of flagellated protozoa

12. MIS-, "hate"

misanthropy—hatred or distrust of mankind

misogamy—morbid aversion to marriage

misoneism—morbid aversion to new things or experiences

13. PTER-, PTERYG(I)-, "wing," "fin"

(gen.) helicopter

anisopterous—unequally winged, applies to seeds

arthropterous—having jointed fin-rays, as fishes

Diptera—an order of flies and mosquitos

hyalopterous—having transparent wings

Hymenoptera—an order of bees, wasps and ants

neuropterous—having wings with a network of nerves; lace-winged

Orthoptera—an order of cockroaches and grasshoppers

pterion—point of junction of parietal, frontal and great wing of the sphenoid; applies to the ossicle, a sutural bone

pteropodium—a winged foot, as of certain bats

14. SCHIZ-, SCHIS(T)-, "to split"

(gen.) schism

anaschistic—applied to a type of tetrads which divides twice longitudinally in meiosis

schist—division along parallel planes

schistocyte—a fragmented part of a red blood cell containing hemoglobin *schistoglossia*—having a cleft tongue

schizogamy—reproduction involving division of the body into a sexual and an asexual individual

schizogenesis—reproduction by fission

schizophyte—a plant which reproduces solely by fission

15. SPLANCHN-, "entrails," "viscera"

macrosplanchnic—large-bodied and short-legged

somaticosplanchnic—relating to the body and viscera

splanchneurysma—distention of the intestine

splanchnodiastasis—displacement or separation of the viscera

16. THI-, "sulfur"

thiobacteria—bacteria which grow where decaying organic matter releases hydrogen sulfide

thiogenic—applies to sulfur-producing bacteria

thioether—an ether containing sulfur instead of oxygen

17. THORAC-, "chest," "thorax"

hemothorax—accumulation of blood in the pleural cavity

thoracomelus—parasitic limb attached to the thorax of a host

thoracocrytosis—excessive curvature of the thorax

18. TOX-, "poison"

cytotoxin—a cell-poisoning substance found in blood serum

toxicodermatitis—skin inflammation due to poison

Toxicodendron—genus of plants including poison ivy and oak

toxicognath—poison fangs of the centipede

toxophore—poison quality of a toxin molecule

19. TRICH- (THRIX-), "hair"

amphitrichous—with flagellum at each pole

melanotrichous—black-haired

schizotrichia—splitting of the hair

trichocryptosis—any disease of hair follicles

tricholith—a calcified hair ball in the stomach or intestine

trichomatosis—matted condition of the hair due to neglect, filth, etc.

Trichopterygidae—beetle's wings fringed with long hairs

20. XER-, "dry"

xeric—characterized by a scanty supply of moisture

xerarch—developing in dry places

xerophobous—having little capacity to resist drought

xerotherm—a plant which survives drought and heat

EXERCISE

List the prefixes, bases and suffixes and give their meanings.

1. *exenterate*—eviscerate

2. *polymerize* or *polymerization*—general terms for a reaction in which a complex molecule of relatively high molecular weight is formed by the union of a number of simpler molecules

3. *hyalinization*—changes characterized by replacement or infiltration of tissues by a firm, hard material

4. *hepatization*—the conversion of tissue into a liverlike substance, as of lungs during pneumonia

5. *brachiate*—to progress by swinging from one hold to another by arms, as gibbons

6. *myelinization*—the process of supplying or accumulating myelin during the development or repair of nerves

7. *autotoxemia*—poisoning by absorption of poisons produced within the body

8. *laryngocele*—a saccular dilatation of the mucosa of the larynx

9. *podagra*—an old term for gout, especially of the great toe

10. *dendrochronology*—dating events by tree-ring analysis

11. *leiomyoma*—a benign tumor consisting largely of smooth muscle cells

12. *cheiragra* or *chiragra*—pain in the hand

13. *encephalomalacia*—a softening of the brain caused by deficient blood supply

14. *pterodactyl*—extinct flying reptile

15. *schizocarp*—a dry seed vessel which splits into two or more one-seeded carpels

16. *cheiropterophilous*—pollinated by bats

17. *thiophilic*—thriving on sulfur; microorganisms that require sulfur for metabolism

18. *misopedia*—morbid dislike of children

19. *xeromorphic*—structurally modified so as to retard transpiration, as a desert plant which exhales vapor through pores

20. *thoracoceloschisis*—congenital fissure of the chest and abdomen

21. *misogynist*—woman-hater

22. *Coniopterygidae*—family of small, humpbacked insects with pollinose wings

23. *polymastigote*—having flagella arranged in a tuft; having several flagella

24. *splanchnocoel* or *splanchnocoele*—that portion of the embryonic body cavity, or coelom, from which are developed the abdominal, pericardial and pleural cavities

25. *thoracocentesis*—operation on the chest cavity for removal of fluid

MORE WORDS TO WORK WITH

abrachiocephalus
achromotrichia
adenomalacia
antitoxin
antixerophthalmic
brachiform
brachioradialis
chirarthritis
chiromancy
chiroplasty
coelozoic
dendrolatry
dendrophagous
endolaryngeal
glossotrichia
gnathoschisis
gonocoel
hyalite
hyalitis
hypertrichosis

ichthyopterygia
ichthyotoxismus
laryngismus
laryngocentesis
laryngoplegia
leiomyosarcoma
lciophyllous
Malacozoa
misanthrope
misology
oligotrichia
onychomalacia
pellagra
pericardiocentesis
peripteral
philodendron
prosopothoracopagus
phytotoxin
pterygiophore
rhinoschisis

schizomycosis
schizonychia
schizophrenia
splanchnectopia
splanchnoptosis
Thiobacillus
thioglycolic acid
thoracodidymus
thoracodynia
toxicology
trichocarpous
Uromastix
xanthopterine
xerodermia
xerography
Xerox
xerophilous
xerophyte
zootoxin

LESSON 13.   Greek Plurals

Although the words we have been studying are English words, some of them still retain enough of their Greek backgrounds that their plurals are those of Greek rather than of English. Thus, the plural of *criterion* is generally *criteria*. Other words sometimes appear in the plural with a Greek ending, sometimes with an English ending, depending upon the habit of the user; for example, the plural of *carcinoma* is either *carcinomata* or *carcinomas*. Still other words, such as *skeleton,* have completely lost their Greek plurals.

Greek plural endings as they appear in English to some extent can be systematized as follows.

1. Words ending in -*ma* in the singular have -*mata* as the Greek plural.

    examples: exanthema—exanthemata

    carcinoma—carcinomata (but also carcinomas)

    trauma—traumata (but traumas is more usual)

2. Words ending in -*sis* in the singular have -*ses* as the Greek plural.

    examples: analysis—analyses

    synthesis—syntheses

    diagnosis—diagnoses

3. Words ending in -*on* in the singular have -*a* as the Greek plural.

    examples: phenomenon—phenomena (occasionally phenomenons)

    criterion—criteria

4. Words ending in -*itis* ("inflammation of") in the singular have -*itides* as the Greek plural. This plural only occurs in highly technical usage.

    examples: meningitis—meningitides

    arthritis—arthritides

5. Words ending in -*nx* in the singular have -*nges* as the Greek plural.

    examples: phalanx—phalanges (but also phalanxes)

    meninx—meninges

6. Words ending in a vowel followed by -*x* in the singular generally have -*ces* as the Greek plural.

> examples: thorax—thoraces (but thoraxes is more usual)
> helix—helices (but also helixes)

As can be seen from the exceptions noted above, except for the plural -*ces*, few of these represent invariable rules. Experience and a dictionary will be your best guides to the formation of plurals. The following are examples from the dictionary.

1. coccyx—coccyges, also coccyxes
2. larynx—larynges, also larynxes
3. octopus—octopuses, octopi, octopodes
4. sarcoma—sarcomas or sarcomata
5. lexicon—lexica or lexicons
6. stigma—stigmata or stigmas
7. metastasis—metastases
8. protozoon—protozoa
9. neuritis—neuritides or neuritises
10. enigma—enigmas, also enigmata

NEW BASES

Learn the following bases and their meanings.

1. ALL-, "other," "different"
   (gen.) allegory, parallel

   allesthesia or *allachesthesia*—a tactile sensation experienced remote from the point of stimulation

   allocheiria—form of allachesthesia; the condition in which if one is pricked on one side, sensation is felt on the other

   allochromatic—accidentally rather than inherently pigmented; mineral without pigmentation when pure

   allogamy—cross-fertilization; opposite of autogamy

   alloplasmatic—applies to the differentiated portion of cell protoplasm *alloplasty*—a plastic operation in which material outside the human body, such as ivory or animal bone, is utilized

allosyndesis—pairing of homologous chromosomes from opposite parents

2. ANKYL-, "bent," "stiff," "adhesion of parts"

ankyloblepharon—adhesion of ciliary edges of the eyelids to each other

ankylocheilia—adhesion of the lips

ankyloglossia—tongue-tied

ankylosis—fixation of a joint due to fusion of bones

3. CYCL-, "circle," "wheel," "ciliary body of the eye"
(gen.) cycle, cyclone, encyclopedia, bicycle

acyclia—state of arrested circulation of body fluids

cyclocoelic—with intestines coiled in one or more distinct spirals

cyclodialysis—detaching of the ciliary body from the sclera to reduce intravascular tension in some glaucomas

cyclotropia—permanent or essential cyclophoria, with eyes rolling outward or inward

excyclophoria—a latent outward tilting of the upper pole of the eye

4. ER-, EROT-, "love"

autoerotism—a combination of sexual emotion and self-admiration; self-gratification of sexual instinct

alloerotism—sexual excitement induced by and directed to another; opposite of autoerotism

erotomania—morbid exaggeration of affections, usually toward opposite sex

zooerastia—sexual relations between a human being and a lower animal

5. GENY-, "jaw," "cheek"; GENI-, "chin"

genioglossus—muscle of the tongue arising from the mandible

genyplasty—surgical reconstruction of the jaw

6. HOL-, "whole," "entire"
(gen.) catholic, holocaust, holographic

holocrine—glands in which secretory cells degenerate and form part of the secretion, as the sebaceous gland *hologastroschisis*—fissure involving the whole length of the abdomen

holognathous—having the jaw in a single piece

hologynic—sex-linked characteristics transmitting directly from female to female

holomastigote—having one type of flagellum scattered evenly over the body

holophytic—animal obtaining the whole of its food after the manner of plants

holotrichous—having a uniform covering of cilia over the whole body

holozoic—having the characteristic animal type of nutrition, requiring the ingestion of organic foods

7.   HOM-, HOME-, "same," "similar"
(gen.) homogeneous, homosexual, homonym, hologous

homacanth—having the spines of the dorsal fin symmetrical

homeozoic—pertaining to a region or series of regions with identical fauna

homochromous—of one color

homodont—having teeth all alike

homoeandrous—having uniform stamens

homogamy—inbreeding due to some type of isolation

homophone—pronounced alike but different in meaning or derivation or spelling

homopterous—having wings alike

8.   HYPN-, "sleep"

hypnagogic—inducing sleep, pertaining to inception of sleep; applies to visions seen just before complete sleep

hypnolepsy or *narcolepsy*—an uncontrollable tendency to attacks of deep sleep of short duration

hypnonarcosis or *narcohypnotism*—sleep induced through hypnosis

hypnophrenosis—a general term for all forms of deep disturbance

hypnotherapy—treatment of disease by hypnosis

9.   IDE-, "idea," "mental image"
(gen.) idea, ideology

ideomotor or *ideomuscular*—movement which is not reflex, but which results from the impingement of ideas on the system

ideophobia—morbid fear of ideas

ideoplasty—process of making subject's mind receptive to suggestions of a hypnotist

monoideism—absorption in a single idea, as in mental depression, hypnosis, trance

10. LEUK- (LEUC-), "white"

leukocyte—one of the colorless cells of the blood

leukocytosis—above-normal increase in leukocytes

leukocytoma—tumorlike mass composed of leukocytes

leukoderma—defective pigmentation of the skin

leukoencephalitis—inflammation of the white substance of the brain

leukomelanoderma—areas of hyperpigmentation and hypopigmentation; vitiligoid

leukotomy—surgical section of brain tissue; lobotomy

leukotrichia—whiteness of the hair

11. ONT-, "being," "individual"
(gen.) ontology

amphiont—zygote or sporont formed by the coming together of two individuals

hyperontomorph—in constitutional medicine, a person of long, thin body type with a short intestine

meront—a uninucleate schizont stage

micront—a small cell formed by schizogony

symbiont—an organism which lives in a state of symbiosis

12. PHYL-, "race," "class"

histophyly—phylogenetic history of a group of cells

homophylic—resembling one another owing to a common ancestor

monophyletic—derived from a single, common parent form

phyloneanic—youthful stage in case history

phylum—a group of animals or plants constructed on a similar general plan, a primary division in taxonomic classification

polyphyletic—having origin from many lines of descent

13. PYEL-, "pelvis, especially of the kidney"

cystopyelitis—inflammation of urinary bladder and pelvis of kidney

pyeloscopy—fluoroscopic examination of the renal pelvis

pyelostomy—incision of the renal pelvis

14. PYG-, "buttocks"

pygidium—the terminal abdominal segment of a beetle

pygopodous—having feet set far back, as some birds

pygostyle—an upturned, compressed bone at the end of the vertebral column of birds

uropygium—hump at the end of a bird's trunk; oil gland

15. STEAR-, STEAT-, "fat," "tallow"

allosteatodes—a perversion or disturbance of sebaceous secretion

asteatosis—absence of sebaceous secretion

cystosteatoma—a sebaceous cyst

steatorrhea or *seborrhea*—an increased flow of the secretion of the sebaceous follicles

steatitis—inflammation of adipose tissue

urostealith—a fatlike substance occurring in some urinary calculi

16. STREPT-, STROPH-, "turned," "twisted"

(gen.) strophe, antistrophe, apostrophe

epistrophe—position assumed by chloroplasts along inner and outer cell walls when exposed to light

phlebostrepsis—the twisting of a vein

strephosymbolia—difficulty in learning to read caused by confusion of "N" and "U" or "P" and "Q," the result of mixed motor dominance of right and left cerebral hemispheres

Streptoneura—a large subclass of gastropods having a loop of nerves twisted in the form of a figure eight

streptolysin—hemolysins from streptococcus (hemolysin—a substance produced in the blood which frees hemoglobin)

strophanthin—a poisonous glycoside cardiac stimulant obtained from plants of the genus Strophanthus, all of which have twisted segments of corolla

17.   THALL-, "young shoot"

heterothallic—requiring branches of two distinct mycelia to form a zygospore

merithallus—a stem unit

thallophyte—plant not differentiated into stem and root, such as algae, fungi and lichens; opposite of cormophyte

18.   THYM-, "mind," "emotions"

euthymia—joyful but tranquil mood

hyperthymia—heightened emotional response

hypothymia—subnormal emotional response and depression

schizothymia—tendency toward schizoid behavior within the limit of normality

19.   TRIB-, TRIP-, "to rub," "to crush"

omphalotripsy—separation of the umbilical cord by a crushing instrument

osteotribe—a bone rasp

splanchnotribe—an instrument for crushing a segment of intestine and so occluding its lumen, previous to resecting it

sternotribe—applies to flowers with fertilizing elements so placed as to be brushed by sternites of visiting insects

triboluminescence—luminescence produced by friction

xerotripsis—dry friction

20.   ZYG-, "yoke"

azygomelous—having unpaired appendages

heterozygosis—descent from two different species, varieties or races

monozygotic—developed from one fertilized ovum

syzygy—a close suture of two adjacent arms; a number of adhering individuals in association of gregarines; reunion of chromosome fragments at meiosis

zygobranchiate—having gills symmetrically placed

zygodont—having molar teeth in which the four tubercles are united in pairs

zygomatic—pertaining to the arch formed by a union of bones

zygoneury—connective between pleural ganglion and ganglion on visceral branch

zygote—cell formed by union of two gametes or reproductive cells; a fertilized ovum

EXERCISE

List the prefixes, bases and suffixes and give their meanings.

1. *ontogeny*—the history of development and growth of an individual organism

2. *schizont*—a stage of parasitic members of class Sporozoa, reproducing in the host by multiple fission

3. *phylogeny*—the racial history of a specified kind of organism; evolution of a race or genetically related group of organisms

4. *allergy*—a hypersensitive state

5. *ideometabolism*—metabolic processes induced by mental and emotional causes

6. *genycheiloplasty*—plastic operation on both cheek and lip

7. *cytosteatonecrosis*—necrosis of fatty tissue

8. *Ancylostomatidae*—a family of nematodes including the hookworms

9. *steatopygia*—excessive accumulation of fat on the buttocks

10. *allosome*—a chromosome other than an ordinary or typical one

11. *ankylodactylia*—deformity resulting from adhesion of fingers or toes to one another

12. *ureteropyeloneostomy*—surgical anastomosis of a ureter with the pelvis of its kidney

13. *metathesis*—transposition; a chemical reaction in which there is an exchange of radicals with no change in valence, e.g., ab + cd = ad + cb

14. *allenthesis*—introduction of foreign substance into the body

15. *heterostrophy*—condition of being coiled in a way other than normal

16. *odontotripsis*—the natural abrasion or wearing away of the teeth

17. *holoacrania*—having no cranial vault

18. *homozygous*—an individual having identical genes for a given character

19. *leukocytopenia*—reduction in number of leukocytes

20. *homothallic*—forming zygoospores from two branches of the same mycelium

21. *homoerotic*—direction of libido toward a member of same sex; a more general term than homosexuality

22. *erogenous*—giving rise to sexual, libidinal or erotic behavior or feeling

23. *phylogerontic*—applies to a decadent stage in race history

24. *pyeloplasty*—plastic repair of the renal pelvis

25. *hypnosia*—uncontrollable drowsiness

26. *streptocarpous*—having fruits spirally marked

MORE WORDS TO WORK WITH

ageniocephalia	homeopathy	pyelonephritis
allomorph	homiothermal	pyeloplication
allotropic	hypnotism	pyeodidymus
ankylotomy	ideogenetic	pygomelus
autohypnotic	ideovascular	pygopagus
cycloplegia	iridocyclitis	steariform
erotic	leukocarpous	stearodermium
erotica	leukemia	Stearodine
erotogenic	lithotripsy	steatocryptosis
genial	microgenia	streptococcus
genioplasty	ontogony	streptokinase
holarthritis	ostealleosis	thallium
holohedral	paleontology	thymocentric
holoptic	phyletic	zygosis
	pyelolithotomy	

LESSON 14.   Bioscientific Terms from Classical Mythology

Innumerable botanical and zoological names, as well as other scientific terms, have been drawn from classical mythology. Some of these names have little or no connection with their source, but others were bestowed because an organism had some characteristic of the fabled person or creature after whom it was named. The Hydra, for instance, in Greek mythology was a poisonous water serpent with nine heads, and whenever one of its heads was cut off, two more grew in its place. It was only the hero Hercules who was

finally able to kill it by having an assistant sear the creature's neck
with a hot iron after he had severed each head. Thus, today, in
nontechnical language, *hydra* means "a persistent evil, one difficult
to eradicate," but in zoology *Hydra* refers to a genus of freshwater
polyps, so called by Linnaeus because cutting apart the bodies of
these animals only serves to increase their numbers.

To cite another example, *atropine*, a highly poisonous alkaloid,
takes its name from Atropos, one of the Three Fates, the grim sis-
ters who, in Greek mythology, were represented as spinning out
the destiny of each man's life as a thread and cutting it at the ap-
pointed time. Another of the Fates, Lachesis, has provided the
name of the bushmaster, *Lachesis mutus,* the most venomous snake
in the Western Hemisphere.

The following are some additional scientific terms derived from
mythology.

	Mythological Association	Scientific Meaning
1. *ammonia*	the temple of Zeus Ammon	alkaline compound of nitrogen and hydrogen
2. *aphrodisiac*	Aphrodite, goddess of love and beauty	substance which excites sexual desire
3. *hermaphrodite*	Hermaphroditus, who became joined in one body with a nymph	having both male and female reproductive organs
4. *narcissism*	Narcissus, who fell in love with his own reflection in a pond	self-love; in psychiatry, fixation of libido on one's own body
5. *Palinuridae*	Palinurus, Aeneas's pilot	family of decapod crustaceans comprising the spiny lobsters
6. *Charon evagatus*	Charon, ferryman who took souls across the river Styx	yellow fever virus

7.	*Eacles penelope*	Penelope, Odysseus's faithful wife, who wove a tapestry	moth that weaves a cocoon
8.	*tendon of Achilles*	Achilles, famous warrior vulnerable only in the heel	strong tendon joining the muscles in the calf of the leg to the bone of the heel

NEW BASES

Learn the following numeral bases and their meanings.

1. HEMI-, "half"
   (gen.) hemisphere

   hemiballismus—a form of hemichorea characterized by sudden violent, spasmodic movements of the extremities of one side of the body

   hemibranch—a gill having filaments on one side only; a half-gill

   hemicephalous—pertaining to absence of cerebrum but with rudimentary cerebellum and basal ganglions

   heminephrectomy—removal of part of a kidney

   hemiopia or *hemianopsia*—blindness in one-half of the visual field

   hemisomus—an individual with one side of the body imperfectly developed

2. MON-, "single," "one"
   (gen.) monocle, monorail, monarch, monopoly, monotheism, monograph, monogamy

   monacanthid—with one row of ambulacral spines, as certain starfish

   monocarpic or *monocarpous*—dying after bearing fruit once; having one ovary developed from gynoecium

   monochronic—occurring or originating only once

   monogeny—production of offspring consisting of one sex

   monomerosomatous—having body segments fused together, as in certain insects

   mononychous—having a single claw

   monoplegia—paralysis of a single limb or muscle

monotrichous—having only one flagellum at one pole

3. PROT-, "first," "original," "primitive"
(gen.) prototype, protagonist, proton

protoplast—the living content of a cell

protocephalon—first of six segments composing an insect's head

protopepsia—solution and alteration of food material accomplished in stomach

protophyte—any plant of the lowest and most primitive type

protoplasm—living cell substance

protopodite—basal segment of an arthropod limb

Protostomia—animals in which a definitive mouth develops directly from the blastopore, as worms and molluscs

protozoan—a unicellular or noncellular animal organism

4. DI-, "twice," "double"
(gen.) dilemma, diploma

diarthrosis—a freely movable articulation

diaster—the stage in mitosis where daughter chromosomes are grouped near spindle poles ready to form a new nucleus

dibranchiate—having two gills

dioecious—having sexes separate; usually refers to plants which have male and female flowers on different individuals

diphyletic—having origin in two lines of descent

diphyllous—having two leaves

5. DICH-, "in two"
(gen.) dichotomy

dichasium—a cymose inflorescence that produces two main axes

dichoptic—having the borders of the compound eyes separate

6. DEUT-, DEUTER-, "second"
(gen.) deuteragonist, deuterogamy

deuterium—hydrogen isotope twice the mass of ordinary hydrogen atom; H^2

deuterogenesis—second phase of embryonic development

deuterostoma—a mouth formed secondarily, as distinct from gastrula mouth

deuterotoxin—the second group in Ehrlich's classification of toxins

Deuterozoic—the newer Paleozoic faunal epoch; as age of fishes

deutomerite—the posterior division of certain gregarines

deutonephros—intermediate part of an excretory organ; mesonephros

7. TRI-, "three"
(gen.) tripod, tricycle, trigonometry, trilogy

trichromatic—able to perceive the three primary colors

tricoccus—a three-carpel fruit

tridactyl—having three digits

trigastric—having three fleshy bellies, as certain muscles

trimorphism—occurrence of three distinct forms or forms of organs in one life cycle or one species

8. TETR(A)-, "four"
(gen.) tetrarch, tetragrammaton

tetracheirus—having four hands

tetracyclic—with four whorls

tetracyte—one of four daughter cells formed from a mother cell by meiosis

tetralogy—a group of four symptoms

tetrapneumonous—having four lung books, as certain spiders

9. PENT(A)-, "five"
(gen.) pentagon, pentangle, Pentateuch, Pentecost

pentactinic—five-rayed

pentadactyl—having all four limbs normally terminating in five digits

Pentastomum—a genus of tongue worms having five stomata

pentosuria or *pentose*—a class of carbohydrates containing five atoms of carbon

10. HEX(A)-, "six"
(gen.) hexagonal, hexameter

hexagynous—having six pistils

hexahedron—a polyhedron having six faces

hexose—any monosaccharide which contains six carbon atoms

11. HEPT(A)-, "seven"

heptagynous—having seven pistils

heptahydrate—a compound with seven molecules of water

heptaphyllite—micas with seven metallic ions per ten oxygen and two hydroxyl ions

12. OCT(A)-, "eight"
    (gen.) octopus, octane, octagonal
    octactine—a sponge spicule with eight rays
    octode—a vacuum tube with eight electrodes
    octodont—having eight teeth
    octophthalmous—having eight eyes

13. ENNE(A)-, "nine"
    ennead—a group of nine
    enneagon—a polyhedron having nine sides
    enneandrous—having nine stamens

14. DEC(A)-, "ten"
    (gen.) decathlon, decaliter, decalogue, *Decameron*
    decahydrate—compound with ten molecules of water
    decahedron—a polyhedron having ten sides
    decapod—having ten legs

15. HECT-, "hundred"
    (gen.) hectograph, hectare
    hectogram—one hundred grams

16. KILO-, "one thousand"
    kilocalorie—a large calorie; the amount of heat required to
        raise one kilogram of water from fifteen to sixteen
        degrees Centigrade
    kilogram—one thousand grams
    kilurane—a unit of radioactivity; one thousand uranium units

EXERCISE

List the prefixes, bases and suffixes and give their meanings.

1. *hemiageusia*—loss or diminution of the sense of taste on one
    side of the tongue

2. *protogynous*—having female elements mature before male

3. *monoecious*—ambisexual, with male and female flowers on
    same plant

4. *andromonoecious*—having male and hermaphrodite flowers on
    same plant

5. *dichogamy*—maturing of sexual elements at different times,
    ensuring cross-fertilization

6. *dimorphism*—state of having two different forms, in sex, color, etc.

7. *octophore*—a modified ascus (spore sac) with eight spores arranged radially

8. *deuteranopia*—inadequate green vision

9. *tetracoccus*—a coccus (bacterium) which divides in two planes and forms a group of four cells

10. *pentapterous*—with five wings, as some fruits

11. *tetrandrous*—having four stamens

12. *hexadactylism*—having six fingers or toes

13. *heptamerous*—having whorls of flowers in sevens

14. *hexacanth*—having six hooks; applies to the embryo of certain flat worms

15. *octopod*—having eight feet or arms

16. *protonephridium*—the primitive excretory tube

17. *decandrous*—having ten stamens

18. *monophagous*—subsisting on one kind of food

19. *monobrachius*—an individual congenitally lacking one arm

20. *hyperhidrosis*—excessive perspiration

21. *dionychous*—having two claws, as torso of certain spiders

22. *hemihypalgesia*—decreased sensitivity to pain on one lateral half of the body

23. *triactinal*—three-rayed

24. *dichromophilism*—capacity for double staining

25. *monophobia*—morbid dread of being alone

26. *pentamerism*—being composed of five parts

MORE WORDS TO WORK WITH

decaliter	heptose	octosporous
deutonymph	hexaphyllous	pentoxide
dicephalism	hexastyle	protein
dioxide	kiloton	tetraethyl
enneapetalous	kilowatt	tetrapod
hemiplegia	monochrome	tetrapterous
	monolithic	

LESSON 15.   Bioscientific Words and the History of Science

The histories of many bioscientific words and expressions give us a fuller realization of the erroneous theories, the false starts, the pursuits up blind alleys which are the frequent and inevitable concomitants of the advancement of learning. Likewise we become aware of the enormous cloud of popular superstition and folklore which long obscured accurate knowledge of the physical universe and which in some measure had to be dispelled before scientific investigation could begin.

Even after such erroneous ideas were discarded, the words they generated remained as tombs to mark the graves of the old concepts. One outmoded concept which has left behind a whole series of such words is known as the humoral theory of physiology. For centuries the prevailing view was that the health of body and mind was determined by the proper mixture of four liquids, or humors, as they were called, for originally *humor* meant "liquid" (compare the modern word *humid*). These four humors were blood, phlegm, yellow bile (or just bile) and black bile. A person's mood or temperament were thought to depend upon the predominance of one or another of these fluids. Thus, a predominance of blood (Lat. *sanguis, sanguinis*) caused a person to be *sanguine,* that is of cheerful, optimistic disposition. An excess of phlegm supposedly made one stolid and unemotional, or *phlegmatic. Chole,* "bile," if present in abundance, made one *choleric,* that is, irascible. The cause of *melancholy* (MELAN-, "black") was laid to a predominance of black bile.

Another field of study, likewise outmoded, which has contributed a number of words to our language is astrology. *Disaster* means literally "ill-starred" (ASTER-, "star"). Not only events, but human nature as well, were once thought to be influenced by the heavenly bodies. A person born under the planet Jupiter, or Jove, was supposedly of a merry disposition, that is, *jovial,* and similarly we gained the words *saturnine,* "gloomy and serious," and *mercurial,* "volatile." *Lunatic* originally meant "moonstruck" (Lat. *luna,* "moon"), while *influenza* in Italian meant simply "influence," from the belief that this disease was caused by an evil influence emanating from certain stars.

The following are some additional examples of words and expressions which have their origin in outmoded scientific ideas: amethyst, atom, planet, rectum, pituitary, malaria, treacle, tarantella, jade, toady, shrew, crocodile tears, lick into shape.

NEW BASES

Learn the following bases and their meanings.

1. BRACHY-, "short"
    brachyodont or *brachydont*—a molar tooth with a low crown
    brachypodous—possessing a short foot or stalk
    Brachyrhinus—large genus of short-snouted weevils
    brachystasis—a process by which a muscle does not relax to
        its former length following a contraction, but main-
        tains its original degree of tension in its new state
    brachysm—dwarfism in plants

2. CAC- (KAK-), "bad"
    (gen.) cacophony
    cacesthesia—any morbid sensation
    cacosmia—imaginary odors, particularly putrefactive odors
    stomatocace—ulcerative stomatitis

3. CAU-, CAUS-, "to burn"
    (gen.) caustic, encaustic, holocaust
    caumesthesia—experience of a sense of heat when temperature
        is not high
    cryocautery—destruction of tissues by application of extreme
        cold
    cauterize—the application of an agent capable of burning or
        destroying tissue

4. CLI-, CLEI-, "to close"; CLEIST-, "closed"
    acleistocardia—condition in which foramen ovule of the heart
        fails to close (foramen ovule—fetal opening between
        two atria)
    cleistogamy—state of having small, inconspicuous, self-fertiliz-
        ing flowers; fertilization without opening of florets
    cleistothecium—an ascocarp which remains closed and pro-
        duces its spores internally
    coreclisis—pathologic closure or obliteration of the pupil
    iridenclaisis—stretching of the iris; iridotasis

5. CLY(S)-, "to wash"
    (gen.) cataclysm
    enteroclysis—injection of a fluid preparation into the rectum
    hypodermoclysis—introduction of large quantities of fluids into
        subcutaneous tissues

venoclysis—injection of food or drugs into a vein

6. CROT-, "pulse beat"

anacrotism—the condition in which two or more notches occur on the ascending limb of the pulse curve

catacrotism—the condition of the arterial pulse, characterized by significant oscillation in its descending limb

tricrotism—the condition of having three waves corresponding to one pulse beat

7. DOLICH-, "long"

dolichoplatycephalus—a person having a long skull which is unusually broad

dolichorrhine—having a long nose

dolichostylous—pertaining to long-styled anthers

8. EDE-, "to swell"

edema—excessive accumulation of fluid in tissue spaces

arthredema—edema affecting the joints

erythredema—pink, itching hands and feet

trophedema—edema due to damaged nourishment or nerve supply

phleboedesis—having circulatory system cavity so distended as to diminish the coelem in molluscs

9. LEPT-, "thin," "delicate"

dolicholeptocephalus—a person whose skull, in addition to being long, is also high and narrow

leptocephaloid—resembling or having the shape of an eel larva

leptocyte—a thin erythrocyte of decreased volume

leptodermatous—thin-skinned

leptomicrognathia—a mild form of micrognathia (micrognathia—abnormal smallness of the jaw)

leptoscope—device for measuring thickness and composition of plasma membrane of a cell

leptosome—tall and slender body type

Leptotrichia—genus of long, filamentous oral bacteria

leptomeninges—pia mater and arachnoid membrane in brain

10. LOG-, "word," "speech," "reason"

(gen.) analogy, homologous, logos

dyslogia—difficulty in expression of ideas by speech

logamnesia—word deafness; word blindness

logoplegia—loss of power of uttering articulate speech

11. MES-, "middle"
(gen.) Mesopotamia
dolichoeuromesocephalus—having a long skull, markedly broad
in the temporal region
mesentery—fold of peritoneum connecting intestine with abdominal wall
mesocarp—middle layer of the pericarp
mesoderm—the third germ layer lying between the ectoderm
and endoderm
mesodont—stag beetles having medium development of mandible projections
mesomorphic—characterized by predominance of structures
from mesodermal layer; muscular, athletic body-
build
mesomyodian—birds with muscles of syrinx attached to middle of bronchial semi-rings
mesophlebitis—middle coat of a vein
mesophyte—thriving in temperate climate with normal amount
of moisture

12. MYX-, "mucus," "slime"
myxasthenia—rare word for overdryness of mucosa or impairment of power to secrete mucus
myxoma—connective tissue tumor composed of cells of stellate
and spindle form with processes separated by mucoid
material
myxopodium—a slimy pseudopodium

13. OXY-, OX-, "sharp," "acid," "oxygen"
(gen.) paroxysm, oxyacetylene, oxygen
oxyaster—stellate sponge spicule with sharp, pointed rays
oxycephalous—having a skull roughly conical in shape
oxyblepsia—acuteness of vision
oxydactyl—having slender, tapering digits
oxyphilous—tolerating only arid soils or substrates
Oxyuris—genus of parasitic nematodes with long, slender tails

14. PETR-, "rock"
(gen.) petrify, petroleum, Peter
osteopetrosis—excessive radiographic density of bone

petrophilous—attached to or living on rocks, especially used of marine life

petrobasilar—pertaining to the petrous part of the temporal bone and the basilar part of the occipital bone

15. PHON-, "sound," "voice"
(gen.) phonetics, telephone, megaphone, euphony, cacophony, antiphonal

baryphonia—a heavy or deep quality of voice

dysphonia—an impairment of voice

heterophonia—abnormal quality or change of voice

hyperphonia—stammering or stuttering resulting from excessive irritability of vocal muscle

rhinophonia—nasal tone in the speaking voice

16. PHOT-, "light"
(gen.) photograph, telephoto

photodromy—movement of particles suspended in a fluid toward light or away from it

photolytic—a substance which is decomposed by action of light

photophore—luminous organ of crustaceans and fishes

photopsia—sparks or flashes of light manifested in certain pathological conditions of the optic nerve or brain

phototrophic—requiring light as a source of energy in nutrition

17. POIE-, "to make"
(gen.) poet, onomatopoeia

angiopoiesis—the process by which certain cells cause the formation of blood vessels in new tissue

hidropoiesis—formation of sweat

nephropoietin—a substance supposed to stimulate growth of renal tissue

18. PRESBY-, "old"
(gen.) Presbyterian

presbyatrics—the branch of medicine dealing with the diseases of old age

presbycusis—progressive hearing loss occurring with age

presbyophrenia—failure of the sense of location and memory in the aged

19. PYR-, PYRET-, "fire," "fever"; PYREX-, "fever"
(gen.) pyre, pyrotechnics, empyrean

pyretogenic—causing fever

pyretolysis—reduction of fever

pyrotoxin—a toxic agent generated in the course of the febrile processes

20. RHIZ-, -RRHIZ-, "root"

mycorrhiza—association of fungal mycelium with roots of a higher plant

polyrrhizal—having many roots

rhizanthous—producing a flower directly from a root

rhizodontropy—pivoting of an artificial crown upon the root of a tooth

rhizome—a thick, horizontal stem running partly along and partly under the ground

rhizoneure—one of the cells that form nerve roots

Rhizopoda—a subclass of protozoons of class Sarcodina with rootlike pseudopods

rhizosphere—soil immediately surrounding the root system of of a plant

EXERCISE

List the prefixes, bases and suffixes and give their meanings.

1. *brachycephalia*—shortness of the head

2. *brachyuric*—short-tailed

3. *arthrocace*—caries of the joints, as in tuberculosis arthritis

4. *cacogeusia*—the sensation of bad taste

5. *causalgia*—the burning pain that is sometimes present in injuries of the nerves

6. *cleistocarpous*—applies to mosses with nonoperculate capsules

7. *otocleisis*—occlusion of the ear

8. *dolichocephalic*—long-headed

9. *phleboclysis*—the injection of a saline solution into a vein

10. *acroedema*—swelling of the extremities

11. *dicrotism*—a condition of the pulse in which with every wave there is the sensation of two beats

12. *leptophyllous*—with slender leaves

13. *neologism*—in psychiatry, meaningless or newly coined words uttered by the insane

14. *mesopodium*—middle part of the molluscan foot

15. *adenomyxoma*—a growth having the character of glandular and mucoid tissue

16. *oxyrrhine*—possessing a sharp, pointed nose; having an acute olfactory sense

17. *hyperoxemia*—excess acidity of the blood

18. *petrophyte*—a rock plant

19. *leukocytopoiesis*—the formation of leukocytes

20. *petromastoid*—pertaining to petrous and mastoid portions of the temporal bone

21. *presbyopia*—condition of vision in the aged whereby the near point of distinct vision is removed farther from the eye

22. *glossopyrosis*—condition characterized by burning sensation of the tongue

23. *photophobic*—not tolerating light; shunning light

24. *phonolite*—a mineral that gives a ringing sound when struck

25. *rhizophorous*—root-bearing

MORE WORDS TO WORK WITH

acrodolichomelia	hyperpyrexia	petrology
acrotism	Kallikak	petrous
anoxemia	leptoclase	phoneme
antipyretic	leptocytosis	photalgia
brachycolic	logorrhea	photogenic
brachydactyly	mesencephalon	photosynthesis
bradycrotic	mesolithic	polylogia
cacogenics	mogiphonia	presbyderma
caustic	myoedema	pyracantha
dolichomorphic	myxadenitis	pyrite
electrocautery	myxobacteria	pyretologist
enterapocleisis	Myxomycetes	pyroclastic
erythropoiesis	myxorrhea	pyromania
glycyrrhizophilia	oxyesthesia	pyropuncture
haemopoietic	petrifaction	tachylogia
homophone	petroglyph	

LESSON 16.   Figurative Usage

Often differences between the meaning of the base of a word derived from Latin or Greek, its etymological meaning and its current meaning are due to the fact that the word has come to be used figuratively, that is, as a figure of speech. The most usual figure of speech used in this regard is the metaphor, a word whose meaning has been transferred from the object or idea which it literally denotes to an object or idea merely suggested by its literal sense. This usage has been particularly prevalent in anatomy, where newly discovered anatomical structures have been named in terms of things already known and familiar. Thus the word *gland* originally meant "acorn," but because the secreting organs often have an acornlike shape, the word came to be used to designate them, losing its original meaning. Likewise, the original meaning of *ventricle* was "little belly" (cf. *ventriloquism*), but, because of the shape of the chambers of the heart, the word came to be used as a name for these, and its previous meaning passed out of use.

The following are some other interesting examples of change of meaning arising from figurative usage.

1. *Delirium* originally referred to getting out of the furrow in plowing (Latin, *de-*, "from," and *lira*, "furrow"). It was probably at first a slang term similar to "off his rocker" or "jumped his trolley," for slang is often nothing more than the use of figures of speech which are more extravagant than necessary.

2. *Muscle* in Latin originally meant "little mouse," and the rippling of muscles under the skin was compared to a mouse running under a rug or blanket.

3. *Cancer* in Latin originally meant "crab," as it still does today in the phrase "Tropic of Cancer" and in the sign of the zodiac. The bioscientific use possibly arose from the resemblance of the swollen veins surrounding some types of malignancies to limbs of a crab.

4. *Acetabulum*, the socket of the hip bone into which the thigh bone fits, in Latin originally meant "vinegar cup" (cf. *acetic* acid, which is found in vinegar) and was used to denote the socket because of the cuplike shape of the depression.

5. *Anthrax*, an infectious disease of cattle, sheep and occasionally man, in Greek originally meant "red-hot coal" (cf. *anthracite*) and was applied to the disease because one of the symptoms is the appearance of fiery red pustules.

6. *Inoculate* was originally a term used in gardening and in Latin meant "to graft," literally, "to take an eye or bud" (*oculus;* cf. "eye" of a potato) from one plant and put it into another." Later, through figurative usage, the word came to mean "to inject serum so as to make immune."

NEW BASES

Learn the following bases and their meanings.

1. GLAUC-, "silvery," "gray-green"

    aglaucopsia—green blindness

    glaucous—pale yellow-green color; a light bluish gray or bluish white color; having a frosted appearance from powder that wears off

    glaucophane—blue, bluish black, grayish silicate of sodium, aluminum, iron and magnesium

    glaucoma—a disease of the eye marked by heightened intra-ocular tension

2. GON(Y)-, GONAT-, "knee"

    gonalgia—pain in the knee joint

    gonarthritis—inflammation of the knee joint

    gonatocele—tumor of the knee

3. (H)APT-, "to touch"; (H)APH-, "sense of touch"

    aphephobia—morbid fear of contact with other persons

    chirapsia—friction with the hand; massage

    haphalgesia—a sensation of pain experienced upon the mere touching of an object

    haptics—the branch of psychology dealing with tactile sense

    haptodysphoria—the disagreeable sensation aroused by the touching of certain objects, as velvet, a peach or a russet apple

    parasynapsis—conjugation or fusion of homologous chromosomes; syndesis

    synapse—the region of connection between neurons

4. KARY-, CARY-, "nucleus," "nut"

    caryoclastic—agent which splits the cell nucleus

    Cryptocarya—genus of tropical trees having a flower with the ripened ovary embedded in a succulent calyx tube

karyochrome—a nerve cell, the nucleus of which stains intensely

karyogamy—the fusion of cell nuclei, as in fertilization

karyotheca—a nuclear membrane

megakaryocyte—a giant cell of bone marrow containing a large, lobulated nucleus

megakaryophthisis—the scarcity of megakaryocytes

synkaryon—a cell nucleus formed by fusion of two existing ones

5. KERAT-, CERAT-, KER-, CER-, "horn," "horny tissue," "cornea"

(gen.) rhinoceros

acanthokeratodermia—thickening of the horny layer of skin on hands and feet

brachycerous—short-horned; with short antennae

ceratotrichia—horny and noncellular actinotrichia (actinotrichia—unjointed, horny rays at edge of fin)

Gyroceras—genus of fossil cephalopods having a shell in form of a spiral

kerotin—a horny type of tissue

keratinization—development of horny quality in a tissue

keratomalacia—softening of the cornea

keratoma—a horny thickening of the skin

keraphyllous—having a layer of hoof between horny and sensitive parts

6. LEPID-, "scale"

homolepidous—with one kind of scales

Lepidosauria—reptiles with scaly skin, including lizards and snakes

lepidosteoid—a ganoid scale lacking cosmine (cosmine—dentinelike material)

Lepidoptera—an order of insects distinguished by featherlike scales

lepidotic acid—an acid found in wings of some insects of the order Lepidoptera

7. NEM-, NEMAT-, "thread"

chromonema—a fine chromatin thread which constitutes the prophase chromosome

micronemous—furnished with short filaments

nemathelminth—a roundworm

nematode—true roundworms

synnema—bundle or column of fused threadlike structures

trophonemata—uterine villi, or hairlike projections, which transfer nourishment to the embryo through the spiracle

8. NOS-, "disease"

paranosic—advantage by illness; applies to primary gain such as freedom from work

epinosic—advantage by illness; applies to secondary gratification received through neurotic illness

nosogeography—the geography of endemic diseases

nosologic—pertaining to the science of classification of diseases

nosophyte—any pathogenic vegetable organism

photonosus—disease from intense or glaring light, such as snow blindness

9. ONC-, -ONCUS, "tumor," "swelling"

adenoncus—an enlargement or tumor of a gland

gonyoncus—a tumor swelling of the knee

mastoncus—tumor of a mammary gland or a nipple

parophthalmoncosis—tumor near the eye

10. PHRA-, "to speak"

(gen.) phrase, paraphrase, periphrasis

aphrasia—loss of power to utter connected phrases

paraphrasia—a form of aphrasia characterized by incoherence of speech

embolophrasia—insertion of meaningless words into speech; embolalia

11. PNEUM-, PNEUMAT-, "air," "gas"

(gen.) pneumatic

pneumatization—progressive development of, or state of having, air-filled cavities in bone

pneumatocele—a sac or tumor containing gas; especially the scrotum filled with gas

pneumatophore—a muscular, gas-containing sac serving as a float for a siphonophore colony

pneumoencephalogram—x-ray of brain after replacement of cerebrospinal fluid with air or gas

12. PHYLAC(T)-, "to guard," "to protect"
    (gen.) phylactery
    cataphylaxis—movement and transportation of phylactic agents (leukocytes, antibodies) to the site of an infection
    exophylaxis—protection afforded against pathogenic organisms by skin secretions
    phylacobiosis—a mixobiosis in which ants live in a termite nest and appear to replace the soldier caste of the termites
    phylactocarp—a modification of the hydrocladium in Hydromedusae for protection of the gonophore

13. PORPHYR-, "purple"
    porphyrin—a heterocyclic ring derived from porphin
    porphyria—an inborn error of metabolism characterized by the presence of pathologic quantities of porphyrins in blood
    porphyrinuria—the excretion of an abnormal amount of porphyrin
    hematoporphyrin—a porphyrin obtained in vitro by treating hemoglobin with sulfuric acid

14. SARC-, "flesh"
    (gen.) sarcophagus
    chondrosarcoma—malignant tumor of cartilage
    ectosarc—external layer of protoplasm in protozoa
    osteosarcoma—osteogenic sarcoma
    sarcobiont—living on flesh
    sarcocarp—the fleshy or pulpy part of a fruit
    sarcocyst—large, intramuscular cyst of sarcocystis
    sarcoma—a malignant tumor composed of cells derived from nonepithelial, mainly connective tissue
    sarcostyle—a fibral or muscle column of muscular tissue

15. SCLER-, "hard"
    otosclerosis—laying down of new bone around the oral window
    rhinoscleroma—a new growth of almost stony hardness, affecting anterior nares and adjacent parts
    sclera—the sclerotic coat of the eyeball; the firm, fibrous outer layer of the eyeball
    scleromeninx—dura mater

16. SEP-, "to rot," "to putrify"

antiseptic—preventing sepsis or poisoning by destruction or exclusion of microorganisms from body tissue

aseptic—pertaining to exclusion of microorganisms causing decay

enteroseptic—intestinal toxemia or sepsis

septic—bacterial poisoning

sepsine—poisonous ptomaine obtained from decomposed yeast and blood

17. SIT-, "food"

apositia—aversion to or loathing of food

autosite—organs are sufficiently developed to carry on a postnatal existence; or a twin which is capable of independent existence and which nourishes the parasite twin

omphalosite—parasitic member of asymmetric, uniovular twins

sitotherapy—the use of food for therapeutic purposes; dietotherapy

sitotropism—tendency to turn in direction of food

18. SPLEN-, "spleen"

splenization—the stage of consolidation in development of pneumonia in which lung tissue grossly comes to resemble the spleen or liver; also called hepatization

gastrosplenic—relating to the stomach and the spleen

splenalgia—pain originating in the spleen

19. STEN-, "narrow"
(gen.) stenographer

dacrystenosis—lacrimal drainage system

stenocardia—obsolete term for angina pectoris

stenocoriasis—narrowing of the pupil

stenostomatous—narrow-mouthed

20. STERE-, "solid," "three-dimensional"
(gen.) stereophonic, stereopticon, stereoscopic, stereotype

stereoarthrolysis—loosening stiff joints by operation or manipulation

stereoblastula—a blastula without a cavity

stereoplasm—more solid part of protoplasm; opposite of hydroplasm

stereoradiography—method of radiography producing a stereoscopic picture which appears three-dimensional

stereotaxy—the mechanical reaction to continuous contact
   with a solid; a taxis in which contact with a solid
   body is the orienting factor

stereotropism—growth or movement toward a solid body

EXERCISE

List the prefixes, bases and suffixes and give their meanings.

1. *gonarthrocuce*—obsolete word for white swelling of the knee
   joint

2. *uroglaucin*—a blue pigment sometimes occurring in urine

3. *haptotropism*—response to contact stimulus, as in tentacles,
   tendrils and stems

4. *gonarthrotomy*—incision into the knee joint

5. *keratoleukoma*—a leukoma or whitish opacity of the cornea

6. *karyokinesis* or *karyomitosis*—mitosis or indirect cell division,
   especially the nuclear transformations as opposed to
   cytokinesis

7. *lepidopterous*—having wings covered with minute, overlapping
   scales; applies to butterflies, moths

8. *nematocyst*—a stinging cell in jellyfish

9. *myoneme*—one of the long, contractile fibrillae of protozoa

10. *tachyphrasia*—morbid rapidity or volubility of speech; occurs
    in the manic phase of manic-depressive psychosis;
    tachylogia

11. *anosognosia*—inability on the part of the patient to recognize
    that he is a hemiplegic

12. *hematoporphyrinuria*—presence of hematoporphyrin in the
    urine

13. *blepharoncus*—a tumor or swelling of the eyelid

14. *septicemia*—a systematic disease produced by microorganisms
    and their poisonous products in the blood stream

15. *anaphylactic*—pertaining to a state of increased susceptibility
    or hypersensitivity following the parenteral injection
    of an antigen in an animal; excessive protein sensiti-

zation caused by prior introduction of the same protein into the body

16. *sitotoxin*—a food poison

17. *pyopneumopericarditis*—pericarditis complicated by the presence of pus and gas in the pericardium

18. *hepatosplenomegaly*—enlargement of the liver and spleen

19. *Sarcophagidae*—family consisting of flesh flies

20. *phlebostenosis*—constriction of a vein

21. *sclerotrichia*—a harsh and dry state of the hair

22. *astereognosis*—inability to recognize objects by sense of touch

23. *metasitism*—a cannibalistic mode of life

24. *anaphia*—defective or absent sense of touch

25. *stenohygric*—adaptable to a narrow variation in atmospheric
humidity

MORE WORDS TO WORK WITH

arteriosclerosis	lepidolite	sarcoderm
ectoparasite	Lepidoptera	sclerodermatous
enterostenosis	lepothrix	sclerophyllous
glaucescent	leprosy	septimetritis
gonatagra	monocerous	splenectomy
gonybatia	nosophobia	stenobaric
haptomonad	oncology	stenophagous
haphephobia	parasite	stenophyllous
hypersplenism	pneumarthrosis	stereobatc
karyolysis	pneumaturia	stereochemistry
karyoplasm	pneumophrasia	stereoscope
keratitis	porphyry	uroneme
keratocentesis	prophylactic	uroporphyrin
keratosis	protonema	

LESSON 17.   Specialization and Generalization of Meaning

Sometimes the difference between the original and the current
meaning of a word may be explained by the process of specializa-

tion, or its opposite, generalization of meaning. Specialization occurs when the meaning of a word shifts from the general to the specific. Thus *disease,* which originally meant "any discomfort," now refers to the particular discomfort caused by illness. *Epilepsy* once referred to any seizure (LEP-, "to take"), but now refers to a specific variety of seizure. *Intoxication,* as its base TOX-, "poison," indicates, in medical terminology is often used to mean poisoning by any of a number of agents, but as generally used, refers only to "poisoning" by alcohol.

The following are some additional examples of specialization of meaning.

1. *physics*—originally "the study of the natural universe"; currently "one branch of the study of the natural universe."

2. *radish*—originally "root" (Latin RADIC-, as in *radical*); currently "a particular type of root in the mustard family."

3. *insanity*—originally "illness" (Latin SAN-, "healthy," as in *sanitary*); currently "a mental illness."

4. *grand mal*—literally French for "great ailment," but currently "the severe type of epilepsy."

Just the opposite process takes place in the case of generalization of meaning, when the meaning of a word broadens and becomes more general. Thus, *vaccine* used to refer to material prepared from cows (Latin VACC-, "cow"), but now the term includes immunizing substances prepared from many other animals, as in the case of the Salk vaccine. *Quarantine* once referred to a period of forty days (Italian *quaranta,* "forty"), but now has come to mean any long period of isolation. *Nausea* once meant "sea-sickness" (cf. *nautical*), but now means "any feeling of being sick to the stomach," whether caused by the motion of the sea or not.

The following are some additional examples of generalization of meaning.

1. *excruciating*—originally "inflicting the pain of literal torture or crucifixion" (Latin CRUC-, "cross"); currently, "causing any great pain."

2. *eradicate*—originally "to pull up by the roots" (Latin RADIC-, "root"); currently, "to get rid of by any means."

3. *spectrum*—originally "the range of colors of the rainbow"; currently, "any wide range," as in the term "broad-spectrum antibiotics."

4. *crescent*—originally "the new moon" (Latin, CRESC-, "to grow"); now, "anything shaped like the new moon."

NEW BASES

Learn the following bases and their meanings.

1. CYN-, "dog"
   (gen.) cynic, cynosure
   cynocephalous—with the head shaped like a dog's
   Cynognathus—genus of extinct carnivorous reptiles resembling mammals
   cynopodous—with nonretractile claws

2. HAPL-, "single"
   haploid—having the number of chromosomes characteristic of mature germ cells for the organism in question
   haplology—contraction of a word by omission of one or more syllables
   haplont—an organism having somatic cells with haploid chromosome number and only the zygote diploid
   haplopia—single vision, as opposed to diplopia
   haplosis—the halving of the somatic chromosome number by meiosis

3. KYM-, CYM-, "wave"
   cardiokymography—a method of recording changes in size of heart by hymographic means
   cymotrichous —having wavy hair
   kymograph—an instrument for recording physiologic cycles or actions in a patient or experimental animal

4. LEMM(A)-, "sheath," "husk"
   lemmocyte—a formative cell for the neurolemma
   myolemma or *sarcolemma*—the sheath of muscle fiber
   neurolemma—delicate elastic membrane outside medullary sheath of nerve fiber
   oolemma—the vitelline membrane of an egg

5. LOPH-, "crest," "ridge," "tuft"; LOPHI-, "small crest," "lophion"
   dilophous—a tetractinal spicule with two rays forked like a crest

ectoloph—the ridge stretching from paracone to metacone in a lophodont molar

lophophytosis—favus of fowls

lophosteon—the heel-bearing part of a bird's sternum

lophiostomate—with crested conceptacle opening (a depression in thallus of certain algae in which gametangia are borne)

lophotrichous—with a tuft of flagellae at one pole

6. LYMPH-, "water," "lymph"

cytolymph—cell sap; the fluid part of protoplasm

endolymphangial—situated in a lymphatic vessel

karyolymph—nuclear sap

lymphadenoma—tumorlike enlargement of a lymph node

lymphocyte—a small mononuclear colorless cell of blood or lymph

lymphoblast—a cell giving rise to lymphocytes

lymphodermia—affection of the lymphatics of the skin

7. MIT-, "thread"

cryptohaplomitosis—type of cell division in some flagellates where chromatin divides into two masses which pass to opposite poles without spireme-formations

karyomitome—the nuclear threadwork

mitosis—indirect or karyokinetic cell division, with chromosome formation, etc.

mitoclastic or *mitoclasic*—interrupting the normal course of mitosis

mitogenesis—formation as a result of mitosis

mitosome—a body arising from spindle-fibers of secondary spermatocytes

8. ORNIS-, ORNITH-, "bird"

Archaeornis—extinct birds

Heliornithidae—a family of tropical aquatic birds comprising the sun grebes

Ornithomimus—a genus of dinosaurs having a birdlike skeleton

ornithophilous—flowers which are pollinated through the agency of birds

9. PALE- (PALAE-), "old," "ancient"

(gen.) paleography

paleoanthropus—a hominid more primitive than *Homosapiens;* an extinct man

paleocranium—type of skull which extends no further back than the vagus nerve

paleencephalon—the phylogenetically old part of the brain

10. PHA-, "to speak"; PHEM-, "voice"

aphemia—an inability to articulate words or sentences due to central lesion

cataphasia—a speech disorder in which patient keeps repeating the same word or series of words

heterophemia—the unconscious saying of one thing while another is meant

paraphemia—aphasia marked by employment of wrong words

schizophasia—word salad; scrambled speech which may occur in schizophrenia

11. PHRAG-, "to block up," "to wall in"
    (gen.) diaphragm

emphractic—any agent that obstructs the function of an organ, especially the excretory function of the skin

endophragm—a septum formed by cephalic and thoracic apodemes in Crustacea

metaphragma—an internal metathoracic septum in insects

phragmoplast—barrel-shaped stage of spindle in mitosis

phragmosis—the spindle during cytokinesis in plant cells possessing rigid cell membranes

phragmosome—a differentiated cytoplasmic diaphragm that develops from the strands of parietal cytoplasm

12. PLAN-, "wandering"
    (gen.) planet

angioplania—irregularity or abnormality in the course of a vessel; angiectopia

aplanogamete—a nonmotile, conjugating germ cell of various plants and animals

diplanetism—condition of having two periods of motility in one life history

planoblast—a free-swimming hydroid individual

planomania—a morbid desire for wandering

13. PLEUR-, "side," "rib," "pleura"

anisopleural—bilaterally asymmetrical

eudipleural—symmetrical about a median plane; bilaterally symmetrical

pleurodont—having teeth fixed by sides to the lateral surface of jaw ridge, as in some lizards

pleurodynia—pain in the abdominal wall

pleuromelus—parasitic accessory limb arising from thorax

pleurapophysis—a lateral vertebral process or true rib

pleurosomatoschisis—lateral abdominal fissure

pleurosteon—lateral process of sternum in young birds

14. -PLO-, "folded," "fold" (as in "threefold")
(gen.) diploma, diplomat

diplocephalus—an organism with two heads

heteroploid—having an extra chromosome; not having a multiple of the basic haploid number of chromosomes

polyploid—with a reduplication of chromosome number, as triploid, etc.

tetraploid—with four times normal haploid number of chromosomes

15. PNE(A)-, PNEUST-, "breathing"

amphipneustic—having both gills and lungs throughout life history

holopneustic—with all spiracles open for respiration

hyperpnea—increase in depth of inspiration

metapneustic—applies to insect larvae with only the terminal pair of spiracles

16. RHAPH-, -RRHAPH-, "to sew," "to suture"

raphe—the seamlike union of the two lateral halves of a part or organ (as of a tongue)

dysrhaphism—defective raphe formation; defective fusion

17. SPA-, "to draw," "to jerk"
(gen.) spasmodic

paraspasm—spasm involving the lower extremities, as in spastic paraplegia

Spasmalgin—trademark for an analgesic and antispasmodic

spasmoneme—contractile filament, as in stalked protozoans

spasmophemia—obsolete term for stuttering

spasmophilia—a morbid tendency to convulsions

18. STAPHYL-, "bunch of grapes," "uvula"

brachystaphyline—having a short alveolar arch

staphylion—the point where the straight line that is drawn tangent to the two curved posterior borders of the horizontal plates of the palatine bones intersects the interpalatine suture

staphylococcus—nonmotile, gram positive, spherical bacteria sometimes occurring in clusters

staphylolysin—hemolysin produced by staphylococci (hemolysin—a substance produced in blood which frees hemoglobin)

19. STETH-, "chest"

mesostethium or *mesoternum*—middle part of the sternum in vertebrates

microstethophone—a stethoscope which amplifies the sounds heard

20. XEN-, "host," "stranger," "foreigner"
(gen.) xenophobia, xenoglossophobia, xenon

antixenic—relating to the reaction which occurs when a foreign substance is introduced into living tissue

monoxenous—confined to a single species of hosts

perixenitis—inflammation around a foreign body embedded in the tissues

xenochroma—the effect of foreign pollen producing a change in color of fruit

xenogamy—cross fertilization

xenogenous—originating outside the organism

xenolith—a fragment of a rock included in another rock

EXERCISE

List the prefixes, bases and suffixes and give their meanings.

1. *mitochondria*—cytoplasmic organelles in the form of granules, short rods or filaments, present in all cells

2. *paleolithic*—pertaining to older, or chipped, Stone Age

3. *ornithosis*—a psittacosislike disease found in birds other than parrots or parakeets

4. *aphasia*—loss or impairment of capacity to use words as symbols or ideas

5. *phlebemphraxis*—plugging of a vein

6. *menoplania*—aberration of the menses

7. *ataxaphasia*—inability to arrange words into sentences

8. *aneuploid*—having an uneven multiple of the basic number of chromosomes

9. *planont*—a swarm spore

10. *stethopolyscope*—a stethoscope having several tubes for the simultaneous use of several listeners

11. *pleurocarpic*—applies to mosses with fructification on lateral branches

12. *staphylorrhaphy*—repair of a cleft palate by plastic operation and suture

13. *orthopnea*—a condition in which there is need to sit up to breathe more easily, associated with cardiac asthma

14. *antispastic* or *antispasmodic* or *spasmolytic*—an agent relieving convulsions or spasmodic pains

15. *xenobiosis*—hospitality in ant colonies

16. *heteroxenous* or *heteroecious*—occurring on or infesting more than one kind of host

17. *myokymia*—constant quivering of a muscle

18. *cyniatrics*—treatment of diseases of dogs

19. *sarcolemma*—the delicate sheath envelope of muscle fiber

20. *diplopia*—seeing two images of a single object

21. *tetralophodont*—applies to molar teeth with four ridges

22. *haplodont*—having molars with simple crowns

23. *thrombolymphangitis*—lymphangitis with thrombosis

24. *thermopolypnea*—rapid respiration due to high temperature

MORE WORDS TO WORK WITH

belpharorrhaphy	cynanthropy	dyspnea
bradyphemia	cynophobia	eupnea
bradypnea	diplacusis	galactoplania
bromopnea	dysphasia	lymphangioma

MORE WORDS TO WORK WITH *(Continued)*

myorrhaphy	phrenemphraxis	spasm
ornithology	phrenospasm	spastic
ornithomancy	plankton	staphyledema
paleobotany	pleurisy	staphylitis
paleontology	proctorrhaphy	staphyloplasty

LESSON 18.   Changes of Meaning in Technical Usage

Often a scientific term, when used in a specifically technical sense, will have quite a different meaning from that which it has when used in popular speech. Its scientific meaning is usually closer to the actual meaning of the Latin or Greek. Thus *photogenic,* which most people think of as meaning "photographing well," technically means "producing light," as in the phrase, "photogenic organs of fireflies." *Cryptic,* which in ordinary language means "having a hidden meaning," in biology means "hiding," as "cryptic in habit, seeking protection under stones." And *topical,* which commonly means "relevant," in medicine refers to an agent applied to the surface of an area of the body (TOP-, "place").

The following are some additional examples of words which have different meanings when used as technical terms, together with phrases illustrating their use.

1. *abduction*—the drawing away of a part from the axis of the body (Latin, *ducere,* "to lead"); "abduction of a limb"

2. *acumen*—a point (Latin, *acuere,* "to sharpen"); "leaves gradually narrowed to a long acumen"

3. *cancellation*—a latticelike pattern (Latin, *cancelli,* "lattice," "grating"); "wall ornamented by a rather coarse cancellation"

4. *coronation*—a crownlike structure (Latin, *corona,* "crown"); "the forward margin forming a narrow coronation"

5. *excursion*—outward movement (Latin, *currere,* "to run," "to go"); "excursion of the lung"

6. *incarnate*—flesh-colored (Latin, *carnem,* "flesh"); "pilei usually pale incarnate or a deeper reddish color"

7. *intramural*—within the material of the wall of an organ (Latin, *murus,* "wall"); "an intramural abscess"

8. *radical*—pertaining to the root (Latin, *radicem*, "root"); "leaves mostly radical and often spreading on the ground"

NEW BASES

Learn the following bases and their meanings.

1. BALAN-, "acorn," "the glans penis"
   Balanidae—sessile barnacles comprising acorn barnacles
   balanoid—acorn-shaped, pertaining to barnacles
   balanitis—inflammation of the glans penis

2. BRY-, "moss"
   Bryanthus—genus of mat-forming, evergreen heaths
   bryophyte—any of the mosses or liverworts
   bryozoan—a polyzoan named from its mosslike appearance; a colony of many zooids

3. CAMP(T)-, CAMPYL-, "bent"
   acampsia—inflexibility or rigidity of a joint or limb; anbylosis
   camptosaur—a duck-billed dinosaur
   camptotrichia—jointed dermal fin-rays in certain primitive fishes
   campylotropous—pertaining to ovules in which nucellus and embryo sac are bent so that the micropyle points almost back to the placenta
   gonycampsis—deformity of the knee due to abnormal bending or curving

4. CARP-, "wrist"
   carpitis—arthritis of the carpal joint in domestic animals
   carpocerite—fifth antennal joint in certain Crustacea
   carpometacarpal—pertaining to carpal and metacarpal bones, joints and ligaments
   metacarpal—part of hand between carpus and phalanges

5. CERC-, "tail"
   cercus—jointed appendage at end of abdomen occurring in many arthropods
   cysticercus—larvae form or bladderworm stage of certain tapeworms
   heterocercal—having a vertebral column terminating in upper lobe of caudal fin, which is usually larger than lower

leptocercal—with long, slender, tapering tail, as some fishes

lophocercal—having a rayless caudal fin like a ridge

6. CLEID-, "clavicle"

hypocleidium—the interclavicle

7. DOCH-, "to take or receive"

elaeodochon—the preen gland or oil gland of birds

hematodocha—the fibro-elastic bag at the base of the palpal organ in Araneae

sialodochoplasty—plastic surgery of a salivary gland duct

8. ECH-, "echo," "repetition"

echoacusia—the subjective sensation of hearing echoes following sounds heard normally

echopathy—in psychiatry, a morbid condition marked by automatic and purposeless repetition of a word or sound heard or an act seen

echolalia—the meaningless repetition of words spoken by others

9. GANGLI-, "mass of nerve tissue," "small cyst or swelling"

diplogangliate—with ganglia in pairs

gangliocyte—a ganglion cell outside the central nervous system

ganglioblast—mother cell of a gangliocyte

paraganglia—scattered cell clusters along the aorta and in other parts of body considered to secrete adrenaline

paraganglioneuroma—tumor of the paraganglious cells of the sympathetic and parasympathetic nervous systems

10. GLI-, "glue"

glioma—a tumor composed of cells and fibers representative of special supporting tissue of the central nervous system

angiogliomatosis—a glioma rich in blood vessels

ectoglia—an outer layer in the central nervous system

Gliocladium—genus of molds in which conidium on the sporehead becomes surrounded by a slimy deposit

neuroglia—fibrous or protoplasmic cells supporting nerve cells and nerve fibers

gliosis—excessive development of neuroglia

oligodendroglia—small supporting cells of the nervous system

oogloea—egg cement

11. IN-, "fiber," "muscle"

inochondritis—inflammation of fibrocartilage

inocyte—old term for a fibrocyte

inogen—obsolete term for a hypothetical, complex substance of high energy in muscle whose breakdown was thought to supply energy for muscular contraction

inosemia—excess of fibrin in blood

inotropic—pertaining to influences that modify muscle contractibility

perinium—an outer microspore coating or outer layer of a spore wall

12. RHACH(I)-, RACH(I)-, -RRHACH-, "the spine"

hematorhachis—hemorrhage into spinal meninges

meningorhachidian—pertaining to spinal cord and its membrane

rachiocampsis—curvature of the spine

rachiodont—having gular teeth consisting of modified ventral vertebral spines, as a snake

rachitic—pertaining to rickets

rachitomous—vertebrae in which parts remain separate

13. -RRHAG-, "excessive discharge, usually of blood"

antimenorrhagic—a controller of profuse, prolonged menstrual flow

enterorrhagia—intestinal hemorrhage

leukorrhagia—excessive leucorrheal flow

otorrhagia—discharge of blood from the ear

14. SPHYGM-, "pulse"

sphygmograph—instrument for graphically recording pulse and variations in blood pressure

sphygmogram—the tracing made by the sphygmograph

sphygmoid—pertaining to continuous pulsation

sphygmomanometer—instrument for measuring the tension of blood current or arterial pressure

15. SPONDYL-, "vertebra"

astereospondylous—having centrum with radiating, calcified cartilage

Palaeospondylus—genus of extinct vertebrates with segmented vertebral column *phyllospondylous*—vertebrae consisting of hypocentrum and neural arch contributing to transverse process

polyspondyly—condition of having multiple vertebral parts

spondylolysis—dissolution or destruction of a vertebra

spondylopyosis—suppurative inflammation of a vertebra

16. STERN-, "chest," "breastbone"

chondrosternal—pertaining to rib cartilage and sternum

episternum—a dermal bone or pair of bones ventral to the sternum of certain fishes and reptiles

eusternum—a sternal sclerite of insects

sternopleurite—thoracic sclerite formed by union of episternum and sternum in insects

sternotribe—flowers with fertilizing elements so placed as to be brushed by sternites of visiting insects

17. THEL-, "nipple"

endothelium—tissue lining blood and lymph vessels

epithelium—tissue forming epidermis and lining hollow organs

mesothelium—tissue lining body cavities

endotheliolysin—a cytotoxin endowed with the capacity of dissolving endothelial cells

myoepithelial—referring to contractile cells of ectodermal origin

thelion—central point of a nipple

18. TOC-, TOK-, "childbirth"

amphitoky—parthenogenetic reproduction of both males and females

deuterotoky—reproduction of both sexes from parthenogenetic eggs

oligotocous—bearing few young

ootocous—egg-laying

tokocyte—reproductive cells of spores

tocostome—a genital pore

19. TRE(T)-, "to bore," "to perforate"

atretostomia—inperforation of the mouth

dacryagogatresia—obstruction of a tear duct

helicotrema—small opening near the summit of the cochlea

trema—a foramen

20.   ZYM-, "ferment," "enzyme"
zymosis—fermentation
enzyme—catalytic substance promoting chemical change
erythrozyme—enzyme capable of decomposing ruberythric acid
microzyme—microorganism of fermenting liquids
zymogenic—causing fermentation; pertaining to or producing
        a zymogen
zymophore—active part of an enzyme; that which bears the
        ferment
zymoplastic—enzyme producing

EXERCISE

List the prefixes, bases and suffixes and give their meanings.

1.   *balanorrhagia*—hemorrhage from the glans penis
2.   *bryology*—the science dealing with mosses and liverworts
3.   *camptodactyly*—a condition in which one or more fingers are
        constantly flexed
4.   *camptodrome*—pertaining to leaf venation in which secondary
        veins bend forward and unite before reaching the
        margin
5.   *anisocercal*—with lobes of tail fin unequal
6.   *carpectomy*—excision of a carpel bone or bones
7.   *adiadochokinesis*—inability to perform rapidly alternating
        movements, such as pronation and supination, as in
        cerebellar disease; incessant movement
8.   *craniocleidodysostosis*—congenital defect of the clavicle asso-
        ciated with imperfect ossification of bones of the
        cranium
9.   *autoecholalia*—stereotypy in which the patient continually
        repeats some word or phrase of his own
10.   *choledocholithotomy*—surgical removal of a calculus by incision
        of the common bile duct
11.   *echokinesis* or *echopraxia*—automatic imitation of another
        person's movements or mannerisms, seen in catatonic
        form of schizophrenia

12. *ganglioglioma* or *neuroastrocytoma*—tumor in the brain

13. *gliococcus*—a micrococcus having a gelatinous envelope

14. *mastorrhagia*—hemorrhage from the breast

15. *hyperinosis*—an exaggerated tendency to form fibrin in the blood

16. *rachiodynia*—spasmodic pain in the spinal column

17. *sphygmochronography*—the registration of the extent and oscillations of the pulse wave

18. *hyperglycorrhachia*—excess of sugar in the cerebrospinal fluid

19. *angioendothelioma*—a tumor composed of endothelial cells and blood or lymph vessels

20. *stereospondylous*—having each vertebra fused into one piece

21. *polythelia*—the presence of supernumerary nipples

22. *schistosternia*—sternal fissure

23. *zymolysis*—fermentation; action of enzymes

24. *oxytocin*—a hormone which increases contraction of uterine muscles in late pregnancy or during parturition

25. *proctatresia*—an imperforate condition of the anus or rectum

26. *ditrematous*—with separate genital openings

MORE WORDS TO WORK WITH

acephalorrhachus	dystocia	prosoposternodidymus
astroglia	echographia	rachianesthesia
atretorrhinia	echophony	rachicentesis
balanoplasty	eutocia	rachiometer
bradytocia	ganglioid	sphygmosystole
Bryopia	hemorrhage	spondyloarthritis
campylognathia	inophragma	sporodochium
carpopodite	monocercous	sternodynia
choledochoenterostomy	monotocous	sternotomy
choledochorrhaphy	odontorrhagia	Thelodontidae
cleidagra	oogloea	thelorrhagia
cleidotomy	perispondylitis	tocophobia
colpatresia	peritreme	zymosthenic
cryptomerorachischisis	pneumatorhachis	

LESSON 19.   Diseases Named from Symptoms

Sometimes the etymological meaning of a term for a disease will have little to do with the actual nature of the illness but instead describe a symptom which was first noticed or seemed most prominent. Thus an analysis of the term *hydrophobia* indicates that its original meaning was "fear of water," from the aversion to water and inability to swallow which characterizes the disease in human beings. *Diabetes* (Greek, *dia-*, "through," and *bainein* [BA-] "to go") refers to the excessive discharge of urine which often accompanies the disease. *Diptheria* (Greek, *dipthera*, "skin," "leather") was coined with reference to the membrane which forms in the air passages of a person suffering from this illness.

The following are some further examples of the tendency to name diseases from prominent symptoms.

1. *cirrhosis* (Greek, "tawny")—a degenerative disease of an organ, especially the liver, named from the orange-yellow appearance of a liver affected by this condition

2. *myxedema* (Greek, MYX-, "mucus," and EDEMA-, "swelling")—a disease caused by the decrease or absence of the thyroid hormone, the name coming from the accompanying puffy appearance of the face and hands (which is *not* caused by an accumulation of mucus)

3. *hemorrhoid* (Greek, HEM-, "blood," and *rhoos*, "flowing" [cf. *-rrhea*, "discharging blood"])—a varicose condition of the veins of the anus, sometimes accompanied by bleeding

4. *shingles* (Latin, *cingulum*, "girdle")—an inflammatory disease of the skin along the course of a nerve, often partially encircling the waist

5. *leprosy* (Greek, *lepros*, "rough," "scaly")—an infectious disease of the skin, one of the symptoms of which is the appearance of white, scaly scabs

NEW BASES

Learn the following bases and their meanings.

1. ADELPH-, "brother"
   (gen.) Philadelphia
   adelphogamy—brother and sister mating, as in certain ants

adelphotaxis—the tendency of motile cells to arrange themselves into definite positions

adelphous—joined together in bundles, as filaments of stamens

endadelphus—encloses a more or less complete individual within its own body

ilioadelphus—conjoined twins united in the iliac region; iliopagus

isadelphia—conjoined twins united by unimportant tissues; each body is normal in the development of all essential organs

pentadelphous—having five clusters of more or less united filaments

2. ANCON-, "elbow"

anconoid—obsolete term for that which resembles the elbow

anconeus—a small muscle at the back of the elbow joint

anconitis—inflammation of the elbow joint

3. CALYPT(R)- "hidden"

calyptobranchiate—with gills not visible from exterior

calyptopsis—a larva with short-stalked eyes, as larvae of some arthropods

calyptra—tissue enclosing developing sporogonium in liverworts; remains of archegonium which surrounds apex of capsule in mosses; root cap

4. CHORD-, "cord"

notochord—the dorsal supporting axis of lowest vertebrates

Chordaceae—a family of brown algae having slender, cordlike fronds

chordate—having a notochord at some stage of development

chorditis—inflammation of the spermatic cord

chordoma—a tumor derived from persistent remnants of the notochord

parachordal—on either side of the notochord

urochord—the notochord when confined to the caudal region, as in tunicates

5. CHOR(I)-, "fetal membrane" (chorion), "tunic of the eyeball" (choroid)

chorioblastosis—abnormal proliferation of cells of the chorion

choriocarcinoma—a highly malignant tumor composed of cyto-
trophoblast and syncytial trophoblast

choriocele—hernial protrusion of choroid coat of the eye

choroiditis—inflammation of choroid coat of the eye

monochorionic—having a single chorion, applies to uniovular
twins

6. CLON(US)-, "muscle spasm"

cataclonus—rhythmic, convulsive movements which are of
functional or hysterical nature

clonograph—apparatus for recording spasmodic movements
of head, lower jaws, trunk, etc.

clonospasm—a clonic spasm

synclonus—tremor or clonic spasm of several muscles at the
same time

logoclonia—explosive or spasmodic enunciation of words;
logospasm

7. COLL(A)-, "glue"
(gen.) protocol

collagen—the albuminoid substance of the white fiber of connective tissue, cartilage and bone

collencyte—a clear cell with threadlike pseudopodia, found in
sponges

colloid—a gelatinous substance which does not readily diffuse
through animal or vegetable membrane

collodion—solution of nitrate cellulose in alcohol and ether,
used as a protective coating for wounds

phycocolloid—a class name for polysaccharides derived from
brown or red seaweeds which form colloidal disper-
sions with water

8. EC-, OEC-, OEK-, OIK-, OIC-, "house"
(gen.) economy, ecumenical, diocese

cladautoicous—with antheridia on a special stalk, as in mosses

ecology—that part of biology which deals with the relationship
between organisms and their surroundings

ecotopic—tending to or involving adjustment to specific local
habitat conditions

gynoecium—pistils, carpels and female organs of a flower

metoecious—with two hosts

oikophobia—morbid fear of home or of a house

zooecium—a chamber or sac enclosing a polyzoan nutritive zooid

9. NOT-, "the back"

notanencephalia—congenital absence of the cerebellum

notencephalocoel—an occipital hydroencephalocele

stenonotal—with a very small thorax, as a worker insect

10. OM-, "shoulder"

acromion—the flat, long process formed by the lateral extension of the scapular spine situated just above the glenoid cavity

metacromion—posterior branch process of the acromion process

omitis—obsolete word for the inflammation of the shoulder

11. OPISTH-, "behind"

dolichoeuro or *opisthocephalus*—having a long skull, very broad in the occipital region

opisthion—median point of posterior margin of foramen magnum (foramen magnum—opening in skull for spinal cord)

opisthodetic—lying posterior to the beak

opisthodont—having back teeth only

opisthognathous—having retreating jaws

opisthosoma—posterior body region

opisthure—projecting tip of the vertebral column

12. PHY-, "to grow"

(gen.) physics, physiology, physical, metaphysics

apophysis—a process, outgrowth or projection of some part or organ, as of a bone

dactylosymphysis—syndactyly

epiphysis—any part or process of bone formed from a separate center of ossification which later fuses with bone; the pineal body; the stout bar firmly fixed to the alveolus of each jaw of sea urchins

hypophysin—pituitary extract

neurapophysis—two apophysis on each vertebra which blend and form the neural arch *symphysis*—coalescence of parts

synarthrophysis—progressive ankylosis of joints

xenophya—foreign bodies deposited in interspaces of certain Sarcodena, or used in formation of shells in certain protozoa

13. POR-, "passage," "pore"
(gen.) porous

blastopore—channel leading into archenteron of gastrula

digonoporous—with two distinct genital apertures, male and female

opisthoporeia—involuntary walking backward in an attempt to go forward; occurs in parkinsonism

polyporin—antibiotic derived from polypore fungus

porencephalitis—encephalitis with a tendency to form cavities

porocyte—a perforated cell of Porifera

porogamy—entrance of a pollen tube into an ovule by micropyle to secure fertilization

14. PTY-, "to spit"; PTYAL-, "saliva"

ptyalin—diastatic enzyme found in saliva

ptyalocele—a cyst containing saliva; usually due to obstruction of a duct of a salivary gland

pyoptysis—expectoration of pus

15. RHABD-, "rod"

rhabdite—one of short rodlike bodies in epidermal cells in Polycladida

rhabdomyoma—tumor of striated muscle

Rhabdonema—a genus of parasitic round worms

rhabdophobia—morbid fear of being beaten; unreasoning fear at the sight of a stick

rhabdopod—an element of the clasper in some male insects

statorhabd—a short tentacular- or process-carrying statolith in Trachomedusae

16. SPOR-, "seed," "spore"
(gen.) sporadic, diaspora

acrospore—spore on end of sporophore

angiosporous—having spores contained in a theca or spore capsule *aplanospore*—a nonmotile resting spore of algae

Cercospora—fungus having long, slender multiseptate spores

hypnospore—a resting spore

sporogony—spore formation; sporogenesis

sporokinete—a motile spore from the oocyst of certain Haemosporidia

sporont—gametocyte stage in the life history of Sporozoa; a cell which forms spores by encystment and subsequent division

stylosporous—pertaining to a stalked spore

trichosporosis—fungous infection of a hair shaft

17. STIG-, "pricking," "mark," "point"

astigmatism—the faulty vision which results from irregularity in the curvature of one or more refractive surfaces of the eye

metastigmate—having posterior tracheal openings or stigmata, as mites

osteostixis—surgical puncturing of a bone

protostigma—one of two primary gill slits in an embryo

stigmata—that portion of a pistil which receives pollen; eyespots of some protozoa; apertures connected with the trachea of some insects

stigmonose—a disease characterized by transparent spots in leaves and spotting, dwarfing, etc.

18. TEL(E)-, "completion," "end," "purpose"
(gen.) teleology

atelosis—dwarfism

atelognathia—imperfect development of a jaw

atelomitic—nonterminal, applied to spindle fiber attachment of chromosomes

atelopodia—defective development of the foot

hypertely—excessive imitation in colors or patterns, being of problematical utility; overdevelopment

telangioma—tumor composed of dilated capillaries

teleodont—applied to forms of stag beetles with largest mandible development

telokinesis—last stage of mitosis

telomere—end of each chromosome arm distal to the centromere

telosyndesis—end-to-end union of chromosome halves in meiosis

19. TROCH-, "wheel," "disk"

cephalotrocha—a turbellarian larva with eight processes around the mouth

mesotrochal—applies to annulate larva with circlet of cilia around middle of body

telotroch—pre-anal tuft of cilia of trochosphere

troche or *trochiscus*—lozenge

trochocephalia—an abnormal roundness of the skull caused by premature union of frontal and parietal bones

20. XYL-, "wood"

(gen.) xylophone

melanoxylon—black wood

xylem—the lignified portion of the vascular bundle; the woody tissue of plants

metaxylem—secondary xylem with many thick-walled cells

xylochrome—wood dye or pigment of tannin, produced before death of wood cells

xyloma—a tree tumor

xylophyte—a woody plant

xylotomous—able to bore or cut wood

EXERCISE

List the prefixes, bases and suffixes and give their meanings.

1. *diadelphous*—having stamens in two bundles owing to fusion of filaments

2. *anconagra*—gout of the elbow

3. *idiocalyptrosome*—outer zone derived from idiosphaerosomes in sperm cells (idiosphaerosome–acrosome; body at apex of spermatozoan)

4. *calyptoblastic*—pertaining to hydroids in which gonophore is enclosed in a gonotheca

5. *polymyoclonus*—a rare degenerative disease occurring in adult life manifested by irregular rapid muscular twitch-

ing; a rod-shaped elastic structure of cells forming primitive supporting axis of the body in lower vertebrates

6. *cephalochord*—cephalic portion of the notochord

7. *chordamesoblast*—the middle germ layer before segregation into notochord and mesoblast

8. *colleterial*—a mucus-secreting gland in the female reproductive system of insects

9. *synoekete*—a tolerated guest in a colony

10. *syndesmochorial*—pertaining to maternal connective tissue and chorionic ectoderm

11. *notopodium*—dorsal lobe of polychaetan parapodium (parapodium—a paired lateral locomotory structure on body segments of polychaetes)

12. *iridochoroiditis*—inflammation of both the iris and choroid of the eye

13. *opisthorchiasis*—infestation of the liver with a fluke

14. *ecomania*—a psychosis marked by a domineering and haughty attitude toward members of the family but an attitude of humility toward those in authority

15. *polyphyodont*—having many successive sets of teeth

16. *omarthralgia*—pain in the shoulder joint

17. *hemoptysis*—the spitting of blood from larynx, trachea, bronchi and lungs

18. *myelopore*—an opening in the spinal cord

19. *rhabdolith*—a calcareous rod found in some protozoa, strengthening the walls

20. *androsporangium*—a sporangium containing androspores (androspore—a male spore)

21. *anastigmatic*—free from astigmatism

22. *atelomyelia*—congenital defect of the spinal chord

23. *xylophagous*—wood-eating

24. *polytrochal*—having several circlets of cilia between mouth and posterior end, as in certain annulates

25. *trochocardia*—displacement of the heart by rotations on its long axis

MORE WORDS TO WORK WITH

adelphosite	colloblast	osteoporosis
anconad	colloidopexy	phyma
anconal	ecotype	phymatosis
atelomyelia	eucalyptus	polyadelphous
blepharoclonus	glycoptyalism	porophyllous
calyptrogyne	hemichordate	ptyalagogue
chordamesoderm	hypoptyalism	ptyalolithiasis
Chordata	ichthyocolla	rhabdomancy
chordencephalon	monophyodont	rhabdomere
chordotomy	monostigmatous	rhabdosphere
chorioretinal	notalgia	sporobola
choroideremia	nototribe	sporodochium
choroidocyclitis	omodynia	telencephalon
clonic	Opisthobranchia	trochocardia
clonism	opisthocoelous	xylocarp

LESSON 20.   Changes in the Forms of Greek and Latin Words

Up to now, we have discussed words borrowed directly from Greek and Latin by scholars or systematically coined by scientists familiar with Greek and Latin bases, and the form of these words seems fairly constant and regular. It is necessary to point out, however, that some Greek bases have come into our language by less direct routes or have been borrowed by nonscholars. In such cases, bases often exhibit radically altered forms that are scarcely recognizable on the basis of what you have already learned. Thus the bases GLYC-, "sweet," + -RRHIZ-, "root," appear in English as *licorice;* HEMI-, "half," and CRANI-, "cranium," appear as *migraine. Paralysis* first entered English as *palsy.*

The following are some additional examples of such changes in the form of Greek and Latin words.

1.   *date*—from Greek DACTYL-, "finger," hence the term "finger dates"

2.   *dropsy*—from Greek *hydrops* (HYDR-), "abnormal accumulation of serous fluid ('water')," "edema"

3.   *sciatica*—from Greek *ischiadikos* (ISCHI-, "hip")

4. *elixir*—apparently from Greek XER-, "dry," the *el* coming from the Arabic definite article *al*, added when the word, along with much else of Greek science, passed to the Arabs

5. *frenzy*—from the Greek *phrenitis* (PHREN-, "mind,"), "inflammation of the brain"

6. *almond*—from Greek AMYGDAL-, "almond"

7. *ague*—from Latin *febris acuta*, "violent, acute fever"

8. *grotto*—from Greek CRYPT-, "hidden"

9. *gillyflower*—from Greek *karyophyllon*, literally, "nut-leaf"

NEW BASES

Learn the following bases and their meanings.

1. ALEX-, "to ward off"
   (gen.) Alexander

   alexin—a complement; a complex substance resembling a ferment formed in the blood, plasma or serum of animals; it has the capacity, in cooperation with antibody and cellular elements, to destroy a variety of pathogenic organisms and other foreign substances

2. ANTR-, "cavity," "sinus"

   antritis—maxillary sinusitis

   antrocele—an accumulation of fluid in the maxillary sinus

   antrostomy—opening of the antrium for drainage

3. BRONCH(I)-, "air tube"

   bronchadenitis—inflammation of bronchial lymph nodes

   bronchitis—inflammation of mucous membrane of bronchial tubes

   bronchocele—a dilatation of a bronchus

   bronchophony—an abnormal increase in the intensity of voice sounds; heard by auscultation over the chest wall when density of the lung tissue has been increased by disease

   ectobronchus—lateral branch of the main bronchus in birds

4. CHLAMYD-, "cloak," "envelope"

   Chlamydosaurus—a genus of reptiles including frilled lizard of Australia *haplochlamydeous*—having rudimentary leaves in connection with sporophylls

heterochlamydeous—having a calyx differing from corolla in color

5. CHY-, "to pour"; CHYM-, CHYL-, "juice"

chyle—a milk-white emulsion of fat globules in lymph formed in the small intestine during digestion

chyme—the viscid fluid contents of the stomach, consisting of food which has undergone gastric digestion

actinenchyma—cellular tissue having a stellate appearance

aerenchyma—cortex of submerged roots in certain swamp plants; aerating tissue in the floating portions of some aquatic plants

blastochyle—the fluid in a blastocoel or segmentation cavity

chylophyllous—with fleshy leaves; applies to certain desert plants

cytochylema—the interreticular portion of protoplasm; cell juice

enchylema—old term for hyaloplasm (hyaloplasm—the fluid portion of protoplasm)

parenchyma—the essential or specialized part of an organ as distinguished from supporting connective tissue

6. CONDYL-, "knob," "knuckle"

condyle—any rounded eminence such as occurs in the joints of many bones

occipital *condyle*—rounded eminence on joint of occipital bone

amphicondylous—having two occipital condyles

condyloma—a wartlike growth or tumor

epicondyle—a medial and a lateral protuberance at distal end of humerus and femur

7. CORM-, "trunk of a tree or body"

atretocormus—having one or more of the body openings imperforate

camptocormia—a special form of hysteria seen most often in soldiers; characterized by extreme forward flexion of the spine

rhizocorm—an underground stem like a single-jointed rhizome; popularly, a bulb

schistocormus—having a cleft thorax

8. GON(I)-, "angle"

(gen.) trigonometry, pentagon

goniometer—an instrument for measuring angles

microgonioscope—an apparatus for measuring extremely small angles, as in ophthalmology

trigonid—triangle of cusps of the lower molar teeth

trigonocephalus—an individual having a triangular or egg-shaped head due to early synostosis of the metopic suture

9. HAL-, "salt"

halite—rock salt

halobios—sum total of organisms living in the sea

halogen—any one of the nonmetallic elements: iodine, chlorine, bromine, fluorine

halophyte—a shore plant; a plant capable of living on salt

Halosauridae—extinct deep-sea fishes with cycloid scales

10. PALI(N)-, "again," "back"

(gen.) palindrome, palinode, palimpsest

palindromia—recurrence or intensification of a disease; relapse

palingenesis—rebirth of ancestral characters; recapitulation

palintrope—recurved posterior section of either valve of some brachiopod shells

paliopsia—recurrence of a visual impression after stimulus has ceased

palirrhea—recurrence of mucus discharge; regurgitation

11. POIKIL-, "varied," "irregular," "mottled"

osteopoikilosis—a bone affection of unknown cause, which gives rise to no symptoms and is discovered by chance in x-rays when ellipsoidal dense foci are seen in all bones

poikilocyte—a large red blood cell of irregular shape

poikilothermal—a cold-blooded animal, whose temperature varies with its surroundings

12. PYCN-, PYKN-, "thick," "frequent"

pycnometer—instrument for determining specific gravity of fluids

pycnomorphous—applies to nerve cells in which chromophil substance of cytoplasm is compactly arranged *pycnopodia*—a genus of starfishes including the twenty-rayed stars

pycnosis—thickening; degenerative change in cells whereby the nuclei are condensed and shrink to dense, structureless masses of chromatin

pycnoxylic—having hard, dense wood because of a high proportion of secondary xylem

pyknic—referring to constitutional body type marked by roundness of contour, amplitude of body cavities and considerable subcutaneous fat

13. PYL(E)-, "gate," "entrance"

apopyle—exhalant pore of a sponge

micropyle—aperture for admission of pollen tube at ovule apex

pylethrombophlebitis—inflammation and thrombosis of the portal vein

pylome—in certain Sarcodina, an aperture for emission of pseudopodia and reception of food

14. SPERM(A)-, SPERMAT-, "seed," "semen"

coelosperm—a carpel hollow on its inner surface

gymonspermous—having seeds not enclosed in a true ovary, as conifers

melanospermous—applies to seaweed with dark-colored spores

spermatozoon—a male reproductive cell

necrospermia—impotence due to loss of motility of spermatozoa

spermateleosis—development of spermatozoon from spermatid in spermatogenesis

spermatheca—a sac in female or hermaphroditic invertebrates for storing spermatozoa

spermatocyst—a seminal sac

15. SPHEN-, "wedge"

diplosphene—wedge-shaped process on the ventral arch of certain fossil reptiles

sphenoid—a basal compound skull bone of some vertebrates

episphenoid—parasite fetus or fetal parts attached to sphenoid region

sphenotresia—a variety of craniotomy in which the sphenoid bone is perforated

sphenotribe—instrument for crushing the basal portion of the fetal skull

16. SPIR-, "coil"
    (gen.) spiral
    acrospire—the first shoot or sprout, being spiral, at the end of
        a germinating seed
    Leptospira—a genus of spirochetes able to survive in water,
        characterized by sharply twisted filaments
    spiraster—a spiral and ragged sponge spiracle
    spireme—threadlike appearance of nuclear chromatin during
        prophase of mitosis
    spirochete—a spiral macroorganism

17. SYRING-, "pipe," "tube" (SYRINX)
    dacryosyrinx—a lacrimal fistula; a syringe for use in lacrimal
        ducts
    sialosyrinx—a salivary fistula; a syringe for use in salivary
        ducts
    syringadenoma—a sweat-gland tumor
    syringium—a muscular, tubular organ connected to the mouth
        in certain insects and used to eject poisonous saliva
    syringograde—jet-propelled; moved by alternate suction and
        ejection of water through siphons
    syringomyelocele—a spinal bifida with protrusion of meningeal
        sac containing part of the spinal cord
    Syringophilus—genus of parasitic mites that live in the gullets
        of birds

18. TA-, "to stretch"
    bronchiectasis—dilatation of bronchi
    entasia—spasmodic muscular action
    iridotasis—stretching the iris, as in treatment of glaucoma
    myotasis—muscular tension or toxicity
    phlebectasia—dilatation of a vein, varicosity
    ptyalectasia—dilatation of the duct of a salivary gland
    syntasis—a stretching or tension

19. TON-, "stretching," "tension"
    (gen.) tone, tonic
    angiohypertonia—a condition in which walls of blood vessels
        are constricted
    tonus—the state of partial contraction characteristic of normal
        muscle

atonia—absence of tonus

isotonic—of equal tension; of equal osmotic pressure

metratonia—atony of the uterus

opisthotonus—the condition in which, from a tetanic spasm of the muscles of the back, the head and lower limbs are bent backward and the trunk is arched forward

ophthalmotonometer—an instrument for measuring inter-ocular tension

psychentonia—mental strain or overwork

20. TRACHEL-, "neck"

laparotrachelotomy—low caesarean section in which the peritoneal cavity is not opened, the approach being through cervix of uterus

schistotrachelus—cervical fissure

trachelagra—rheumatic or gouty pain in the neck

trachelopexia—surgical fixation of the neck of the uterus

trachelosyringorrhaphy—operation for vaginal fistula with stitching of the cervix uteri

EXERCISE

List the prefixes, bases and suffixes and give their meanings.

1. *ecchymosis*—extravasation of blood into subcutaneous tissues

2. *rhinantralgia*—pain in, or referred to, the walls of the cavities of the nose

3. *hydrospermatocele* or *spermatocele*—cystic dilatation of a duct in the head of the epididymis or in the rete testes; rupture into the tunica vaginalis which produces spermatic hydrocele

4. *bronchorrhaphy*—the suturing of a bronchus

5. *condylotomy*—osteotomy; division through the condyles of a bone

6. *spiranthy*—displacement of flower parts through twisting

7. *acanthosphenote*—echinoid spine made of solid wedges separated by porous tissue

8. *syringomyelia*—a chronic disease characterized pathologically by the presence of long cavities surrounded by gliosis, which are situated in relation to the central canal of the spinal cord and frequently extend up into the medulla

9. *sphenoiditis*—inflammation of the sphenoid air sinus

10. *amyotonia*—lack of muscular tone

11. *spironeme*—coiling thread in an infusorian stalk

12. *hysterotrachelorrhaphy*—amputation of the cervix of the uterus

13. *catatonic*—pertaining to a phase or type of schizophrenic reaction in which the patient seems to lack the will to talk or move and stands or sits in one position, assumes fixed postures, etc.

14. *gonicheiloschisis*—transverse facial cleft; intermaxillary fissure

15. *chlamydospore*—a thick-walled resting spore of certain fungi and protozoa

16. *achlamydeous*—having neither calyx nor corolla

17. *eurypylous*—wide at the opening; applies to the canal system in sponges

18. *cormophyte*—a plant which possesses stem and root; opposite of thallophyte

19. *ectocondyle*—the outer condyle of a bone

20. *pycnophrasia*—thickness of speech

21. *poikiloderma*—a skin syndrome characterized by pigmentation

22. *poikilodermatomyositis*—poikiloderma in association with muscular sclerosis

23. *euryhaline*—applies to marine organisms adaptable to a wide range of salinity

24. *pyknolepsy*—a very mild form of epileptic variant resembling petit mal

25. *palikinesia*—constant and involuntary repetition of movements

26. *antialexin*—an anticomplement agent which destroys alexin

27. *aerenterectasia*—excessive amount of air or gas in the intestines

MORE WORDS TO WORK WITH

angiospermous
antrectomy
antroatticotomy
antronasal
bronchomycosis
bronchoscope
Chlamydobacteriaceae
chylocyst
chylopoiesis
chyluria
condyloid
cormidium
haloplankton
octagonal
paliphrasia

peritonitis
pneumatopyle
poikilitic
poikilothrombocyte
poikilozoospermia
polygonal
procondylism
propalinal
pycnidia
pycnidiophore
pylemphraxis
pylorus
sclerenchyma
somatotonia
spermatocide
spermatogenesis

spermatogonium
spermatoid
spermatolysis
sphenosis
sphenotripsy
Spirochetaceae
spirochetemia
stenohaline
syringe
syringobulbia
syringomylia
syringotomy
telangiectasis
trachelodynia
zygosphere

PART II
BIOSCIENTIFIC WORDS
DERIVED FROM LATIN

LESSON 21. Introduction to Latin Bases and Prefixes

As with words derived from Greek, words derived from Latin are frequently compounds made up of prefixes, bases and suffixes. The bases were originally Latin words from which the characteristic Latin endings, such as *-us, -a, -um* and *-are,* have been removed. Thus, from the Latin word *similis,* "like," comes the English base SIMIL- (as in *similar* and *assimilate*); from the Latin *magnus,* "great," comes the base MAGN- (as in *magnify* and *magnate*). As in the case of Greek bases, Latin bases will be written in capital letters followed by a dash.

Most dictionaries, in describing the origin of an English term from Latin, will give the actual Latin word from which it has been derived (e.g., *similis* and *magnus*) rather than the base. In many instances such original Latin words have not been anglicized and appear in English with their original endings retained, as, for instance, *terminus, via* and *finis.* Also, many unchanged Latin phrases are used in scientific writing; e.g., *corpus luteum, caput medusae* and *arrectores pilorum.* There will consequently be one very significant difference between Part I and Part II of this book. In the lists of Latin bases and their meanings, in the case of nouns and adjectives, the actual Latin words will be listed along with the bases, thusly: COST-, "rib" *(costa).*

With that brief introduction, let us turn to learning Latin bases. Sometimes a base appears in English by itself, without the addition of prefixes or suffixes. Occasionally a final silent *e* is added. The following are examples of this simple type of borrowing.

Latin Base	English Derivative
FORT-, "strong"	fort
VERB-, "word"	verb
GRAV-, "heavy"	grave
FIN-, "end"	fine

Usually, however, two or more bases are combined, or prefixes and suffixes are added, as in the following.

> *in-,* "on" + GRAV-, "heavy" + *-esc(e),* "to become" + *-ent,* "-ing"
> ingravescent ("becoming worse")
>
> FIN-, "end" + *-al,* "pertaining to" + *-ity,* "state of"   finality

When two or more Latin bases are combined, generally an *i* ap-

165

pears between them as a connective, although frequently *o* and other vowels are used.

SACR-, "sacred" + (i) + FIC-, "to make"	sacrifice
EQU-, "equal" + (i) + VAL-, "to be worth" + *-ent*	equivalent
SACR-, "sacred" + (o) + SANCT-, "sacred"	sacrosanct

Sometimes Greek and Latin bases may be combined in the same word. Although this practice in coining words is frowned upon by purists, it has frequently occurred, and such words are called *hybrids*.

(Gr.) AUT(o)-, "self" + (Lat.) MOB-, "to move" + *-ile*	automobile
(Gr.) NE(o)-, "new" + (Lat.) NAT-, "born" + *-al*	neonatal

Similarly, Greek prefixes and suffixes may be used with Latin bases and vice versa.

(Gr.) *dys* + (Lat.) FUNCT-, "to perform" + *-ion*	dysfunction
(Gr.) *hyper*- + (Lat.) TENS-, "to stretch" + *-ion*	hypertension
(Lat.) *ex*- + (Gr.) ENTER-, "intestine" + *-ate*	exenterate
(Lat.) *de*- + (Gr.) HYDR-, "water" + *-ate*	dehydrate

Latin prefixes frequently are attached to bases. These prefixes were originally Latin prepositions or adverbs but now seldom occur by themselves but are placed in front of a base to modify the meaning of the base. A base may be preceded by more than one Latin prefix.

con-, "with" + *re*-, "again" + LAT-, "to bear"	correlate
in-, "not" + *ex*-, "out" + PLIC-, "fold" + *-able*	inexplicable

There are two problems connected with Latin prefixes which do not arise in the case of prefixes derived from Greek.

1. Often, when a prefix is used before certain consonants in a base, it undergoes phonetic change. The most usual type of change is that by which the last consonant of a prefix becomes the same as the first consonant of a base. This process is called assimilation.

ad-, "to" + GRESS-, "to go" + *-ion*	aggression
ad- + TRACT-, "to drag"	attract
con-, "together" + LID(e)-, "to strike"	collide
dis-, "apart" + FER-, "to bear"	differ

ex-, "from"	+ FECT-, "to make"		effect
in-, "not"	+ LEG-, "to read"	+ *-ible*	illegible
ob-, "against"	+ FEND-, "to hit"		offend
sub-, "under"	+ FER-, "to bear"		suffer

Similarly, a final *n* in a prefix becomes *m* before *p* or *b* in a base.

in-, "not"	+ POSS, "to be able"	+ *-ible*	impossible
con-, "with"	+ PLET(e)-, "to fill"		complete

2. Occasionally the base itself may exhibit a slight change in form when a prefix is added.

Latin Base	English Derivative
FACT-, "to make"	factory, manufacture, but also efFECT, deFECT
SED-, "to sit"	sedentary, but also reSIDe
SPEC-, "to look"	specimen, but also conSPICuous

Actually there are relatively few bases which are subject to this type of change. These will be listed with their variant forms in the following manner: FACT- (-FECT-), SED- (-SID-), SPEC- (-SPIC-).

Learn the following prefixes and their meanings.

1. *ab-, a-, abs-,* "away from," "from"

    This prefix is never assimilated.

    > examples: abduction, abnormal
    > aversion, avocation
    > abstract, abstain

2. *ad-, ac-, ag-,* etc.,* "to," "toward," "near"

    Sometimes this prefix appears as *a-*, usually before *-sc-, -sp-* or *-st-*, as in *aspire* and *ascribe*. This occurs so infrequently, however, that it is generally safe to assume that the prefix *a-*, is a form of *ab-*, "away." Although a prefix, sometimes *ad-* is used at the end of a word.

---

*The process of assimilation causes the last consonant of the prefix to become the same as the first consonant of the base.

examples: adrenal, adverb
access, aggression, alleviate
cephalad, orad, proximad

3. *ambi-, ambo-,* "both," "around"

examples: ambidextrous, ambition, ambisexual
amboceptor, ambosexual

4. *ante-,* "before," "in front of"

This suffix should not be confused with the Greek prefix *anti-,* "against."

examples: anteroom, antecedent

5. *circum-, circu-,* "around"

examples: circumference, circumstance
circuitous

6. *con-, com-, co-,* etc.,* "with," "together," "very"

examples: conduct, confine
compose, compress
correspondent, correspond
cooperate, collect

7. *contra-, contro-,* "opposite," "against" (through French, *counter-*)

examples: contradict, contraceptive
controversy, controvert
counteract, counterindicate

8. *de-,* "down," "away," "off," "thoroughly"

examples: describe, descend, depression

9. *dis-, di-, dif-,* "apart," "in different directions," "thoroughly"

examples: dissect, dispersion
divorce, digress, divert
differ, diffusion

NEW BASES

Learn the following bases and their meanings.

1. CAUD-, "tail" (cauda)

---

*The process of assimilation causes the last consonant of the prefix to become the same as the first consonant of the base.

caudostyle—a terminal structure in certain parasitic amebas

ecaudate—without a tail

nudicaudate—having a tail not covered with hair or fur

caudocephalad—in the direction from the tail toward the head

sacrocaudal—pertaining to the sacrum and tail region

Caudata—an order of Class Amphibia (salamanders, newts, etc.) having long bodies, with long tails retained through life

2. CEREBR-, "brain" (cerebrum)

cerebellum—fourth division of the brain

deutocerebron—that portion of the insect brain derived from fused ganglia of the antennary segment of head

syncerebrum—a secondary brain formed by union of one or more of ventral cord ganglia with the brain, as in some arthropods

cerebrotonia—a pattern of temperament typical of the ectomorphic individual marked by predominance of intellectual over social or physical and by exhibition of sensitivity, introversion and shyness

cerebrin—a nitrogenous glycoside obtained from brain and similar tissue

3. CID-, CIS-, "to cut," "to kill"

(gen.) matricide, regicide, genocide, decision, precise, concise

succise—abrupt; appearing as if a part were cut off

incisura—a notch, depression or indentation, as in bone, stomach, liver, etc.

schizonticide—substance destructive to schizonts (schizont—a stage in asexual life cycle of plasmodium, covering the period from beginning of division of nuclear material until the mature merozoites are formed)

4. DORS-, "back" *(dorsum)*

antedorsal—situated in front of the dorsal fin in fish

dorsiferous—with sori on back of a leaf; carrying young on the back

dorsifixed—having the filament attached to the back of the anther

dorsigrade—having back of a digit on the ground when walking

dorsalgia—pain in the back

dorsocephalad—toward the dorsal aspect of the head

dorsocaudad—to or toward the dorsal surface and caudal end of the body

5. DUC-, DUCT-, "to lead," "to draw"
    (gen.) conduct, reduce, induce, deduction

    nephrogonoduct—combined excretory and genital duct

    spermiducal—applies to glands into or near which sperm ducts open in many vertebrates

    abduction—withdrawal of a part from the axis of the body or of an extremity

    abducent—abducting, drawing away from a median line

    levoduction—movement to the left, especially of the eye

6. ERR-, "to wander," "to deviate"
    (gen.) err, errata

    errant—with a tendency toward moving; straying or deviating

    Errantia—a division of class Polychaeta comprising free-swimming worms

    erratic—having no fixed course; characterized by a lack of regularity

7. FLEX-, FLECT-, "to bend"
    (gen.) flex, reflection, inflexible

    reflex—an involuntary, invariable, adaptive response to a stimulus

    biflex—twice-curved

    inflected—curved or abruptly bent inward or toward the axis

    dorsiflexion—bending the foot toward the dorsum or upper surface of the root

    retroflexion—the state of being bent backward

    circumflex—winding around; designating a number of arteries

    deflexed—bent or turned abruptly downward

    reflection—a bending or turning back

8. FUND-, FUS-, "to pour," "to melt" (through French, FOUND-)
    (gen.) refund, foundry, confusion, refuse, fusion

    diffuse—to spread out

    infundibular—funnel-shaped

    infusion—the process of extracting the active principles of a substance by means of water, but without boiling; the slow injection of fluid into a vein

perfusion—the introduction of fluids into tissues by their injection into arteries; the passage of fluids through spaces

suffusion—the spread or flow of any liquid of the body into surrounding tissue

Infusoria—a group of minute organisms typically found in infusions of decaying organic matter

9. GREG-, "flock" *(grex)*
    (gen.) congregate, segregate, egregious

    gregaloid—pertaining to colony of protozoa of indefinite shape

    gregarious—tending to herd together; colonial; growing in clusters

    gregaria—an irregularly recurrent phase in the life cycle of migratory or plague grasshoppers induced by crowded breeding conditions and marked by development of strongly gregarious behavior

10. LACT-, "milk" *(lac)*

     lactation—suckling; the period during which the child is nourished from the breast; the formation or secretion of milk

     lactase—an enzyme that hydrolyzes lactose to dextrose

     lactiferous—forming or carrying milk

     lactochrome or *lactoflavin*—a nitrogenous coloring matter in milk

     lactosuria—presence of lactose (milk sugar) in urine

     lacteal—chyliferous or lymphatic vessels of the small intestine; ducts which carry lactase

     prolactin—a hormone which stimulates lactation in the mammalian breast

     Lactarius—family of mushrooms that exude a white or colored milky substance when cut

11. LATER-, "side" *(latus)*

     laterigrade—walking sideways, as a crab

     ambilateral—relating to or affecting both sides

     dorsolateral—relating to the back and the side

     heterolateral—pertaining to or situated on the opposite side

lateropulsion—a tendency to move to one side in forward locomotion

12.   MEDI-, "middle" *(medius)*
(gen.) mediate, immediate, intermediate

mediodorsal—both median and dorsal; on the median line of
the back

mediad—toward the median plane or line

mediastinum—a partition separating adjacent parts; the space
in the middle of the chest between the two pleura

hematomediastinum—an effusion of blood into the mediastinal
space

13.   OV-, "egg" *(ovum)*

binovular—pertaining to two ova; dizygotic; applies to twin-
ning

mesovarium—the mesentery of the ovary

synovial—pertaining to the clear fluid normally present in
joint cavities

ovicide—an insecticide effective against an egg stage

14.   PON-, POSIT-, -POSE, "to place," "to put" (through French,
POUND-)

(gen.) exponent, expository, expose, expound, impound, im-
position

anteposition—the placing of one word or group of words before
another, especially in cases where usual order is the
inverse; superposition of whorls in a flower typically
alternating

apposition—the state of being in juxtaposition or proximity

decompound—more than one compound

transposition—a change of position

suppository—a medicated solid body intended for introduction
into the various orifices of the body

15.   RUG-, "wrinkle" *(ruga)*

ruga—a fold or wrinkle, as of the mucous membrane of certain
organs

rugosity—a condition exhibiting many folds in a tissue or
integument

erugatory—tending to remove wrinkles

16.   SANGUI(N)-, "blood" *(sanguis)*

(gen.) sanguine, sanguinary, sangfroid

sanguification—conversion into blood

sanguimotor—of or relating to the circulation of the blood

Sanguisorba—a genus of herbs of styptic quality

17. SICC-, "dry" *(siccus)*

exsicatta—dried specimens

exsiccant—drying or absorbing moisture

siccant—drying; tending to make dry

18. VAL-, "to be strong," "to be well"

(gen) valid, valedictory, evaluate, equivalent, valor

bivalent—applies to paired homologous chromosomes

valence—capacity of atoms to combine with other atoms in different proportions

pentavalent—having a valence of five

19. VARIC-, "twisted and swollen (vein)" *(varix)*

varicose—descriptive of blood vessels that are dilated, knotted and tortuous

neurovaricosis—a varicosity on a nerve fiber

varicomphalus—a varicosity at the navel

varicellate—applies to shells with small or indistinct ridges

varix—prominent ridges across the whorls of univalve shells

20. VERT-, VERS-, "to turn"

(gen.) aversion, extrovert, perversion, advertise, convert

diverticulum—a pouch or sac springing from a hollow organ

versatile—hung or attached near the middle and moving freely, as an anther

versicolor—variously colored

verticellate—cyclical

dextroversion—a turning to the right side

eversion—a turning outward, as of an eyelid

EXERCISE

List the prefixes and bases and give their meanings.

1. *abscise*—to become separated; to fall off, as leaves, fruit, etc.

2. *aberrant*—deviating from the usual or normal

3. *caudad*—toward a cauda

4. *dorsad*—toward the back

5. *ablactation*—the weaning of an infant; the end of mammary secretion

6. *affusion*—the pouring of water upon a part or upon the body to reduce the temperature and calm the nervous system, as in fever

7. *ambivalence*—tendency to be pulled in psychologically opposite directions, as between love and hate; coexistence within a person, to a similar degree, of opposed traits, attitudes or sentiments

8. *ambiversion*—tendency to have a balance between introversion and extroversion

9. *circumcision*—removal of the foreskin

10. *anteversion*—a tipping, tilting or displacement forward of an organ or part, especially of the uterus

11. *circumduction*—the movement of a limb in such a manner that its distal part describes a circle, the proximal end being fixed

12. *admedial*—located near or approaching the median plane or central axis

13. *corrugated*—formed into folds or furrows

14. *consanguineous*—related by birth or blood

15. *ovipositor*—a specialized structure in insects for placing eggs in a suitable place

16. *decomposition*—disintegration

17. *collateral*—accessory or secondary; not direct or immediate

18. *contralateral*—opposite; acting in unison with a similar part on the opposite side of the body

19. *decerebrate*—having the brain removed

20. *desiccate*—to dry up or cause to dry up

21. *divaricate*—widely divergent

22. *aggregate*—the whole sum

23. *disgregation*—dispersion; separation, as of molecules or cells

24. *adduction*—any movement whereby one part is brought toward another or toward the median line of the body

25. *anteflexion*—a bending forward

MORE WORDS TO WORK WITH

amebicide
autotransfusion
bicaudate
bilateral
cerebral
cerebration
composite
convalescent
dorsal
ductile
ductule
effusion
equilateral

error
excision
exsanguination
flexor
germicidal
hyperlactation
incisor
introvert
latericumbent
median
obverse
ovary
oviduct
oviparous

ovulation
rugulose
sanguicolous
sanguivorous
segregation
siccolabile
superimposed
transfusion
transverse
valerian
valetudinarian
version
vertigo

LESSON 22.   Latin Prefixes I

Learn the following prefixes and their meanings.

1.   *ex-, e-, ef-,* "out," "from," "removal," "completely"

        examples: exclude, expel, exclamation
                  emit, elect, elongate
                  effective, effeminate

    After *ex-*, an initial *s* in a base sometimes disappears.

        ex- + SPIR(e)-, "to breathe"   expire
        ex- + SPECT-, "to look"   expect

2.   *extra-, extro-,* "outside of," "beyond"

        examples: extraordinary, extrasensory
                  extrovert

3.   *in-, im-,* etc.,* "into," "on" (through French, *en-*)

        examples: incision, induce
                  illuminate, imprint, irrigation
                  enclose

---

*The process of assimilation causes the last consonant of the prefix to become the same as the first consonant of the base.

4. *intra-, intro-,* "within"

> examples: intramural
> introduce, introvert

5. *in-, im-,* etc.,* "not"

> examples: infirm, inefficient
> impossible, illegible, irresponsible

6. *infra-,* "below"

> examples: infrared, infrahuman, infraspecific

7. *inter-,* "between," "among"

> examples: interrupt, intercept, interact

8. *juxta-,* "by the side of," "close to"

> examples: juxtaposition, juxtaspinal

9. *ob-,* etc.,* "against," "toward," "completely"

In many words it is difficult to see the force of this prefix.

> examples: obstruct, obstacle, obvious
> oppose, offer, occur

10. *per-,* "through," "wrongly," "completely"

> examples: perfect, permeate, pervade, perjury

NEW BASES

Learn the following bases and their meanings.

1. ARTICUL-, "joint" *(articulus)*
   (gen.) article, articulate
   interarticular—between articulating parts of bones; applies to
           certain ligaments and fibrocartilages
   biarticulate—two-jointed
   coarticulation—a synarthrosis
   polyarticular—affecting many joints

2. BUCC-, "cheek," "mouth" *(bucca)*
   buccal—pertaining to the cheek; toward the cheek
   buccolingual—pertaining to the cheeks and tongue

---

*The process of assimilation causes the last consonant of the prefix to become the same as the first consonant of the base.

buccomesial—pertaining to the buccal and mesial walls of a dental cavity

buccoversion—condition of a tooth being out of the line of the normal occlusion in the buccal direction

3. CLUD-, CLUS-, CLOS-, "to close," "to shut"
    (gen.) conclude, inclusive, preclude, disclose

eclosion—the act of emerging from the pupal case; the act of hatching from the egg

buccoclusal—pertaining to the buccal and occlusal walls of a dental cavity; pertaining to the grinding or biting surface of a tooth

disto-occlusal—relating to the distal and occlusal surfaces of premolar and molar teeth

perclusion—the inability to execute any movement

exclusion—the process of extruding or shutting out in a surgical operation by which part of an organ is disconnected from the rest but not excised

4. CORD-, "heart" *(cor)*
    (gen.) accord, concord, cordial, record

cordate—heart-shaped

subcordate—tending to be heart-shaped

postcordial—situated behind the heart

precordium—the area of the chest overlying the heart

5. COST-, "rib" *(costa)*

bicostate—having two longitudinal ridges or ribs, as a leaf

costate—with one or more longitudinal ribs or ridges

intercostobrachial—the lateral branch of the second intercostal nerve which supplies the upper arm

costalia—the supporting plates in the theca of Cladoidea

subcostalgia—pain beneath the ribs or over a subcostal nerve

ecostate—without ribs

6. CRUR-, "leg" *(crus)*

crus—term applied to certain parts of the body from their resemblance to legs

crura (plural of *crus*)—the shanks; leglike or columnar structures; lumbar parts of the diaphragm of muscle fibers

subcrureal—applies to subcrureus or articularis genus muscle, extending from lower femur to knee

genitocrural—pertaining to genitalia and leg

7. CUR(R)-, CURS-, "to run," "to go"
    (gen.) current, occur, cursive, incursion, concur
    decurrent—having leaf base prolonged down extensions or rib
    excurrent—pertaining to ducts, channels or canals where there
        is an outgoing flow; with undivided main stem; hav-
        ing midrib projecting beyond the apex
    intercurrent—occurring or taking place between, as a disease
        arising or progressing during the existence of another
        disease in the same person
    succursal—subsidiary

8. DENT-, "tooth" *(dens)*
    (gen.) indent, trident
    dentition—the process of teething; the arrangement of the
        teeth
    bidenticulate—with two small teeth or toothlike processes, as
        some scales
    dentin—a hard, elastic substance, chemically resembling bone,
        composing the greater part of teeth
    osteodentin—a variety of dentin which closely approaches bone
        in structure
    denticle—a small, toothlike process
    dentary—the membrane bone of the lower jaw of many ver-
        tebrates
    dentate—having teeth or teethlike projections; having a toothy
        or serrated edge; having a scalloped edge, as a den-
        tate ligament
    dedentition—loss of teeth

9. FEBR-, "fever" *(febris)*
    febrile—pertaining to or characterized by a fever
    Antifebrin—a proprietary name for acetanilid
    febricula—a slight and transient fever

10. FER-, "to bear," "to carry," "to produce"
    (gen.) suffer, differ, refer, transfer
    afferent—bringing toward; applies to nerves carrying impulses
        to nervous centers
    dorsiferous—with sori on back of leaf; carrying the young on
        the back

lactiferous—forming or carrying milk

oviferous—serving to carry eggs

proliferate—to multiply

toxiferous—producing or conveying poison

biferous—producing two crops of fruit in a season

11. FOLI-, "leaf" *(folium)*
    (gen.) folio, foliage

    foliaceous—having the form or texture of a foliage leaf; thin and leaflike

    foliolate—like leaflets

    prefoliation—the form and arrangement of foliage leaves in a bud

    effoliation—shedding of leaves

12. HER-, HES-, "to stick"
    (gen.) inherent, hesitate, adhesive

    adherent—attached to a substratum

    cohesion—the attractive force between the same kind of molecules

    adhesiotomy—the surgical cutting or division of adhesions

13. JECT-, "to throw"; JACUL-, "dart" *(jaculum)*
    (gen.) eject, reject, project, conjecture

    projectile vomiting—a form of vomiting observed in some diseases of the brain stem; the vomitus is suddenly projected out of the mouth to some distance, usually without nausea

    ovijector or *ovejector*—a highly muscular part of the oviduct in many nematode worms that forces the eggs through the genital pore

    jaculatory—darting out; capable of being emitted

    retrojection—the washing of a cavity from within outward

    jactitation—a tossing about; great restlessness

14. MUR-, "wall" *(murus)*
    (gen.) immure

    intermural—situated between the walls of an organ

    extramural—outside the wall of an organ

    mural—pertaining to a wall, as a mural pregnancy

15. NOMIN-, NOM-, "name" *(nomen)*

(gen.) nominal, nominalism, nominate, denomination

paranomia—nominal aphasia, characterized by an inability to name objects

binomial—consisting of two names

16. RADI-, "spoke of a wheel," "ray" *(radius)*
(gen.) radiator, radio

radioreceptor—a terminal organ for receiving light or temperature stimuli

radiole—a spine of a sea urchin

radiatiform—with radiating marginal florets

equibiradiate—with two equal rays

radiotherapy—treatment of disease by x-rays, radium and other radioactive substances

radiate—radially symmetrical; radiating

17. SEMIN-, "seed" *(semen)*
(gen.) dissemination, seminary, seminar

semination—dispersal of seeds; discharge of spermatozoa

seminoma—a testicular tumor of low malignancy made up of large, uniform cells with clear cytoplasm which resembles spermatogonia; also called dysgerminoma, spermatocytoma

seminuria—the discharge of semen in the urine

18. TEG-, TECT-, "to cover"
(gen.) protect, detect

subtegminal—under the tegmen or inner coat of a seed

tectorial—covering; applies to the membrane covering the spiral organ of the corti

tectospondylic—having vertebrae with several concentric rings of calcification

tectrices—small feathers covering the base of remiges (remiges —large feathers of wings)

tegmen—the integument; the inner seed coat; the thin plate of bone over the tympanic atrium

19. TUSS-, "cough" *(tussis)*

tussive—pertaining to or caused by a cough

Tussilago—genus of plants used as remedy for cough

Tussol—a trademark for antipyrine mandelate, used as a remedy for whooping cough

20. VEN-, "vein" *(vena)*

rectivenous—with straight veins

venation—the system or disposition of veins or nervures; nervation

venule—small vein of a leaf or insect wing, small vessel conducting venous blood from capillaries to vein

venose—with many and prominent veins

supervenosity—condition in which blood has become venous to a high degree

venomotor—causing veins to contract or dilate

EXERCISE

List the prefixes and bases and give their meanings.

1. *edentate*—without teeth or teethlike projections

2. *extrabuccal*—outside of the mouth; extraoral

3. *exfoliation*—the shedding of leaves or scales from a bud

4. *irradiation*—exposure to radiation of varying wave lengths

5. *efferent*—carrying away, as efferent nerves; conveying impulses away from the central nervous system

6. *intravenous*—within or into the veins

7. *integument*—a covering, investing or coating structure or layer; the coat of an ovule

8. *infracostal*—old name for the subcostal muscle

9. *intramural*—within the substance of the walls of an organ, as the intramural fibroid of the uterus

10. *intercrural*—situated between the crura

11. *introjection*—absorption of the external world into oneself; hence, reacting to external events as if they were merely subjective; projecting one's own qualities into inanimate objects, or acting as if they were animate

12. *seminiferous*—secreting or conveying seed or seminal fluid; bearing seed

13. *innominate*—unnamed, unnamable, as innominate artery; an irregular bone forming one side and anterior wall of the pelvic cavity

14. *juxta-articular*—near a joint

15. *obcordate*—inversely heart shaped; applies to leaves which have stalk attached to apex of the heart

16. *pertussal* or *pertussoid*—like whooping cough

17. *occlusion*—a closing or shutting up; absorption by a metal or gas in large quantities; the full contact in a position of rest of the masticating surfaces of the upper and lower teeth

18. *percurrent*—extending from the base to the apex; used of the midrib of a leaf

19. *intrafebrile*—during the course of a fever

20. *insemination*—the planting of seed; the introduction of semen into the vagina; impregnation

21. *incoherent*—disconnected, illogical and inconsistent

22. *excursion*—a wandering from the usual course; the extent of movement, as of the eyes from a central position, or, of the chest during respiration

23. *disarticulation*—separation at a joint; amputation at a joint

24. *perfoliate*—having the stem apparently passing through the leaf; said of opposite leaves joined at their base

25. *jaculiferous*—bearing dartlike spines

MORE WORDS TO WORK WITH

abarticular	dentil	radiologist
adhesion	ejaculate	radium
brevifoliate	febrifacient	recurrent
buccogingival	febrifuge	retrobuccal
bucconasal	febriphobia	seminal
chrondocostal	infradentary	tegular
coherent	malocclusion	trajectory
conifer	muriform	trinomial
cordiform	nomenclature	tussal
crursus	perfoliate	venoclysis
defoliate	procursive	venovenostomy
	quadrifoliate	

LESSON 23.   Latin Prefixes II

Learn the following prefixes and their meanings.

1. *post-,* "behind," "after"

> examples: postpone, postscript, postgraduate

2. *pre- (prae-),* "before," "in front of"

> examples: prevent, prepare, precaution
> praenomen, praetorian

3. *pro-,* "forward," "in front of"

> examples: progress, project, prolong

4. *re-, red-,* "back," "again," "against"

> examples: reduce, reject, recede
> redundant, redemption

5. *retro-,* "backward," "behind"

> examples: retroactive, retrospect, retrograde

6. *se-,* "aside," "away"

> examples: secede, select, secrete

7. *sub-, sus-, suc-,* etc.,* "under," "up from under," "somewhat"

> examples: submarine, subscribe, submerge
> suspend, suffer, support

8. *super-, supra-,* "above"

> examples: supernatural, superstructure, supersonic
> supranational, suprarenal

9. *trans-, tran-, tra-,* "across," "through"

> examples: transmit, transfer, transfusion
> transcribe, transcend
> trajectory, travesty, tradition

10. *ultra-,* "beyond"

> examples: ultraviolet, ultramodern, ultrasonic

---

*The process of assimilation causes the last consonant of the prefix to become the same as the first consonant of the base.

NEW BASES

Learn the following bases and their meanings.

1. ARBOR-, "tree" *(arbor)*

    arboreous—treelike or pertaining to trees

    arborization—a conformation or arrangement resembling the branching of a tree

    arboretum—a place where trees, shrubs and herbaceous plants are cultivated for scientific purposes

    arborvitae—a type of tree

    arbor vitae—arborescent appearance of the white substance in a median section of the cerebellum; series of ridges and folds within the mucosa of the uterine cervix

2. CAL-, "to be warm"

    calefacient—an externally applied medicine that causes a sensation of warmth

    calorescence—the conversion of invisible heat rays into luminous heat rays

    calorie—a heat unit; amount of heat required to raise 1 kg of H_2O from 0° to 1° C

    calenture—a fever formerly thought to affect sailors in the tropics, causing them to imagine the sea a green field and leap into it; any fever supposedly caused by heat

    calentura—term used in the Philippines for an epidemic disease of horses

    decalescence—the decrease in temperature when rate of heat absorption exceeds rate of heat input

3. CARIN-, "keel" *(carina)*

    (gen.) careen

    carina—any keellike structure

    paracarinal—beside a carina, especially urethral carina

    carina nasi—a narrow, cleftlike space between the agger nasi and the inner surface of the dorsum nasi

4. CERN-, CRET-, CRE-, "to separate," "to distinguish," "to secrete"

    (gen.) secret, discernment, indiscretion

    secernment—secretion, applied to the function of a gland

    incretion—internal secretion

    secretagogue—a substance promoting or causing secretion

5. CILI-, "eyelid," "eyelash" *(cilium)*
   (gen.) supercilious
   cilia—hairlike, vibratile outgrowths of the ectoderm
   ciliospore—a ciliated protozoan swarm spore
   Ciliata—a class of phylum Protozoa characterized by the presence of cilia

6. CORN(U)-, "horn" *(cornu)*
   (gen.) cornet, corn (on toe), cornucopia, unicorn, Capricorn
   bicornute—with two hornlike processes
   cavicorn—hollow-horned; applies to certain ruminants
   corniculate—having small horns
   subcorneous—under a horny layer; slightly horny
   interramicorn—a piece of a bird's bill beyond the mandibular rami forming the gonys
   cornification—degenerative process by which cells of epithelium are converted into dead, horny tissue

7. CUB-, CUMB-, CUBIT-, "to lie"
   (gen.) succumb, incumbent, recumbent, incubus
   decubitus—recumbent or horizontal posture; ulcer, bedsore
   succubous—with each leaf covering part of leaf beneath it
   accumbent—applies to embryo having cotyledons with edges turned toward radicle

8. DORM-, DORMIT-, "to sleep"
   (gen.) dormitory
   obdormition—numbness of a part due to interference with nervous function; sensation of a part "being asleep"
   dormidera—California poppy, known for narcotic effect of its seeds
   dormitive—inducing sleep

9. FET- (FOET-), "offspring," "fetus" *(fetus)*
   fetation—the formation of a fetus; pregnancy
   exfetation—extopic or extrauterine fetation
   multifetation or *superfetation*—the production of a second fetus after one is already present in the uterus

10. FRANG- (-FRING-), FRAG-, FRACT-, "to break," "to bend"
    (gen.) frangible, infringe, fraction, fragile, fragment
    refract—to cause the deviation of a ray of light from a straight

line in passing obliquely from one transparent medium to another of different density

refractory—resisting treatment; slow to melt; resisting stimulation, as muscle or nerve

diffraction—the separation of light into component parts by
means of prisms

frangulin—a glycoside obtained from frangula (Alder Buck-
thorn), so called for the frangibility of its bark

11. GRAD-, GRESS-, "to step," "to go"
(gen.) grade, graduate, aggressive, progress, congress

digitigrade—walking with only digits touching the ground

dorsigrade—having back of digit on ground when walking

orthograde—walking or standing in the upright position

subplantigrade—incompletely plantigrade; walking with the
heel slightly elevated

antiaggressin—an antibody which neutralizes an agressin or
spreading agent produced by microorganisms

12. LINGU-, "tongue," "language" *(lingua)*
(gen.) linguistics, bilingual, lingo

fissilingual—having a bifid tongue

vermilingual—having a worm-shaped tongue

Linguatula—a genus of tongue worms

linguoversion—displacement of a tooth on the lingual side of
its proper occlusal position

13. MENT-, "chin" *(mentum)*

mentigerous—supporting or bearing the mentum; a projection
between the head and foot of some gastropods

mental—pertaining to the chin

mentalis—a muscle of the lower lip

14. PLIC-, PLICIT-, "to fold"
(gen.) complicate, complicity, implicit, inexplicable, duplicate

plica—a fold of skin or membrane

complicate—folded; applies to leaves folded longitudinally so
that right and left halves are in contact; applies also
to insect wings

conduplicate—applies to cotyledons folded to embrace the
radicle; applies to vernation when one half of leaf is
folded on the other

induplicative—applies to vernation or estivation with induplicate foliage or floral leaves respectively

plication—the act or process of folding

15.   POT-, "to be powerful"
(gen.) potential, potentate, plenipotentiary, omnipotent

totipotent or *equipotent*—applies to blastomeres which can develop into complete embryos when separated from the aggregate of the blastomere

unipotent—giving rise to only one cell or tissue type; said of an embryonic or multiplying cell

potentiation—effect of a substance, which, when added to another, makes the latter more potent as a drug

16.   PUR-, "pus" *(pus)*
purulent—containing, consisting of or forming pus

purohepatitis—suppurative inflammation of the liver

puruloid—puriform

17.   REN-, "kidney" *(ren)*
adrenal—adjacent to the kidneys; relating to or derived from adrenal glands or their secretion

adrenergic—liberating adrenaline

subreniform—slightly kidney shaped

renotrophic—pertaining to the ability of certain compounds, such as testosterone, to produce hypertrophy of the kidney

renotropic—specifically attracted to kidney tissue

18.   SON-, "sound" *(sonus)*
(gen.) dissonant, consonant, sonorous, sonata

assonance—a morbid tendency to employ alliteration

asonia—tone deafness

sonification—the act or process of producing sound, as stridulation of insects

19.   SUD-, "to sweat"
exudation—process of oozing out slowly

sudoriferous or *sudomotor*—conveying, producing or secreting sweat

sudatorium—a hot air bath or a room for such a bath

sudoresis—excessive sweating

sudorific—inducing sweating

sudamen—eruption of translucent, whitish vesicles due to noninflammatory disturbance of the sweat glands

20. TRUD-, TRUS-, "to push," "to thrust"
(gen.) intrude, inobtrusive, abstruse

detrusor—an ejection or expulsion; a thrusting down or out

contrusion—obsolete term for the act of crowding together, as teeth

extrusion—a forcing out; in dentistry, extension of a tooth beyond the occlusal plain

EXERCISE

List the prefixes and bases and give their meanings.

1. *predormition*—applied to the stage of unconsciousness immediately preceding actual sleep

2. *postcornual*—applies to glands situated behind horns, as in chamois

3. *replicatile*—applies to wings folded back on themselves when at rest

4. *prepotent*—transmitting the majority of characteristics; applies to a flower exhibiting a preference for cross-pollination

5. *retrofract*—bent backward at an angle

6. *retrolingual*—behind the tongue; applies to a gland

7. *suppurate*—to form pus

8. *prosecretin*—the precursor of secretin, i.e., a hormone produced in the epithelial cells of the duodenum, which excites the pancreas to activity

9. *subcarinate*—somewhat keel shaped

10. *submental*—beneath the chin

11. *feticide*—the killing of the fetus in the uterus

12. *superciliary*—pertaining to the eyebrow

13. *subarborescent*—somewhat like a tree

14. *suprarenal*—situated above a kidney

15. *laterigrade*—walking like a crab

16. *ciliograde*—progressing by movement of cilia

17. *transudation*—the passing of fluid through a membrane, especially of blood serum through vessel walls

18. *procumbent*—prone; lying face down; in dentistry, said of a tooth whose long axis approaches the horizontal

19. *ultrasonic*—pertaining to sounds with a frequency above that of audible sound

20. *transcalent*—permeable to radiant heat rays

21. *prolactin*—a hormone which stimulates lactation

22. *transonance*—transmitted resonance; the transmission of sounds through an organ, as of the cardiac sound through the lungs and chest wall

23. *recrement*—a substance secreted from a part of the body, as from a gland, and again absorbed by the body

24. *retrogression*—in biology, the passing from a higher to a lower type of structure in the development of an animal; in medicine, a going backward, degeneration, involution or atrophy, as of tissue

25. *retrusion*—in dentistry, the process of pressing teeth backward

MORE WORDS TO WORK WITH

adrenal gland	duplicity	longicorn
adrenaline	ecarinate	mucopurulent
arborescent	effete	multiciliate
arboriculture	elinguation	pronograde
bicarinate	excrement	protrusive
biplicate	excretion	puriform
buccolingual	extrude	refringent
calorimeter	hypersonic	renal
carinulate	incubation	renette
centigrade	incubatorium	resonate
ciliolate	impotence	sonic
cornea	interrenal	sudation
discrete	labiomental	supersonic
dormant	latericumbent	ventricumbent
	linguodental	

LESSON 24.   Latin Suffixes I

As in the case of words derived from Greek, suffixes from Latin are often attached to bases, and more than one suffix may be found in a single word:

VAL-, "to be strong" + -*id*, "tending to" + -*ity*, "state of"
    validity

SON-, "sound" + -*or*, "state of" + -*ous*, "full of"   sonorous

Note that when a suffix which ends in *e* is followed by an additional suffix the *e* generally disappears:

ANIM-, "spirit" + -*ose*, "full of" + -*ity*, "state of"   animosity

URB-, "city" + -*ane*, "pertaining to" + -*ity*, "state of"
    urbanity

Learn the following suffixes. All four groups carry the same meanings. The Latin form of each suffix is given in parentheses.

1. -*al* (-*ial*, -*eal*), "pertaining to," "like," "belonging to," "having the character of" (-*alis*)

ABDOMIN-, "abdomen"	+ -*al*	abdominal
LEG-, "law"	+ -*al*	legal
OR-, "mouth"	+ -*al*	oral
CORPOR-, "body"	+ -*al*	corporal

2. -*ile*, -*il*, same meanings as number 1 (-*ilis*)

HOST-, "enemy"	+ -*ile*	hostile
JUVEN-, "youth"	+ -*ile*	juvenile
VIR-, "man"	+ -*ile*	virile
CIV-, "citizen"	+ -*il*	civil

3. -*ar*, same meanings as number 1 (-*aris*)

LUN-, "moon"	+ -*ar*	lunar
SOL-, "sun"	+ -*ar*	solar
POPUL-, "people"	+ -*ar*	popular

4. -*ine*, same meanings as number 1 (-*inus*)

BOV-, "cow"	+ -*ine*	bovine
MAR-, "sea"	+ -*ine*	marine
FEMIN-, "woman"	+ -*ine*	feminine

NEW BASES

Learn the following bases and their meanings.

1. ACIN-, "grapes in a cluster" *(acinus)*

   acinar—pertaining to an acinus, a small seed or kernel, as of a grape; a small sac

   interacinar—among alveoli of a racemose gland

   aciniform—grape- or berry-shaped; applies to a type of silk gland in a spider

2. AL-, "wing" *(ala)*

   ala—any winglike projection or structure

   exalate—not having winglike appendages; apterous

   alisphenoid—winglike portion of sphenoid forming part of cranium

   aliferous—having wings

   alinotum—the dorsal plate of an insect to which wings are attached

3. ANNUL-, "ring" *(annulus)*

   annulus—any ringlike structure

   exannulate—having a sporangium not furnished with an annulus; applies to certain ferns

   Annelida—a phylum of segmented worms including earthworms

   annulose—possessing rings

4. APIC-, "tip," "summit," "apex" *(apex)*

   apiculate—forming abruptly to a small tip, as a leaf

   subapical—nearly at the apex

   periapical—around an apex

   apicitis—inflammation of any apex, as a tooth root or a lung

5. ARGENT-, "silver" *(argentum)*

   argenteal—applies to layer of eye containing calcic crystals

   argenteous—like silver

   argentaffin or *argentophile*—the capacity of certain tissue elements to reduce silver in staining solution

   argentiferous—producing or containing silver

   Argentinidae—family of small, silvery marine fishes

6. CAN-, "dog" *(canis)*

(gen.) canary

canicola fever—an acute febrile disease in man and dogs caused by *Leptospira canicola*

Canidae—family which includes dogs, wolves and jackals

caniniform—having the form of a typical canine tooth

7. CAPIT- (-CIPIT-), "head" *(caput)*
    (gen.) capital, capitulate, precipitate, decapitate, cattle
    bicipital—pertaining to biceps
    capitulum or *capitellum*—knoblike swelling on end of bone
    bicapitate—having two heads; dicephalous
    Capitellidae—family of worms with small heads

8. DUR-, "hard," "dura mater" *(durus)*
    (gen.) endure, dour, duration, obdurate
    duramen—hard, darker central region of a tree stem; heartwood
    epidural—space between the dura mater and the wall of the vertebral canal; situated upon or over the dura
    duroarachnitis—inflammation of the dura mater and arachnoid membrane
    induration—the hardening of a tissue or part; a hardened area of tissue
    thermoduric—able to survive high temperatures, specifically pasteurization
    aciduric—refers to bacteria which can grow in an acid medium, but which grow better in alkaline medium

9. EQU-, "horse" *(equus)*
    (gen.) equestrian, equitation
    equitant—overlapping saddlewise, as leaves in a leaf-bud
    equiline—an estrogenic hormone occurring in urine of pregnant mare
    Equidae—family of mammals having a single extant genus, Equus, which includes the horse, ass and zebra

10. LACRIM- (LACHRYM-), "tear" *(lacrima)*
    (gen.) lachrymose
    lacrimal—pertaining to tears or to tear-secreting organs; the lacrimal bone
    adlacrimal—lacrimal bone of reptiles
    nasolacrimal—pertaining to the nose and lacrimal apparatus

11. LACUN-, "small pit," "gap" *(lacuna)*

   lacuna—a space between cells; a sinus; a cavity in bone; a small cavity or depression on the surface of lichens; a leaf gap

   lacunose—having many cavities; pitted

   lacunome—a system of lacunar spaces sometimes demonstrated in animal cells

   lacunosorugose—having deep furrows or pits, as some seeds and fruits

   Lacunidae—family of marine gastropods with slit in shell comprising the chinks, or keyhole limpets

12. LIMIN-, "threshold" *(limen)*
   (gen.) eliminate

   limen—threshold; minimum stimulus or quantitative difference in stimulation that is perceptible; boundary

   limen nasi—boundary between the osseous and cartilaginous portions of the nasal cavity

   liminal—pertaining to a threshold; applies to stimulus, sensations

   supraliminal—lying above a threshold

13. MAL-, "cheek," "cheekbone" *(mala)*

   malar—pertaining to the cheek or to the zygoma

   deutomalae—the broad plate in Chaetognatha, formed by fusion of second pair of mouth appendages

14. OCUL-, "eye" *(oculus)*; OCELL-, "little eye" *(ocellus)*
   (gen.) monocle

   ocellate—like an eye or eyes; applies to markings in many animals

   oculomotor—causing movements of the eyeball

   inocular—applies to antennae inserted close to eye

   monocule—a one-eyed animal, as certain insects

   oculist—ophthalmologist

   oculogyric—referring to movements of the eye

   transocular—extending across the eye

15. PALAT-, "palate," "roof of the mouth" *(palatum)*

   palatine—pertaining to or in the region of the palate; applies to artery, bone, foramen

salpingopalatine—pertaining to the eustachian tubes and palate

transpalatine—a cranial bone of crocodiles connecting pterygoid with jugal and maxilla bones

palatitis—inflammation of the palate

palatiform—resembling the palate

16. PARIET-, "wall" *(paries)*

paries—wall of a hollow structure

parietal—pertaining to or forming part of the wall of a structure; applies to cells, membrane, placentation, etc.; the parietal bone in the roof of the skull

gastroparietal—pertaining to the stomach and body wall

parietomastoid—connecting mastoid with parietal, as a suture

uteroparietal—pertaining to the uterus and abdominal wall

17. PLANT-, "sole of the foot," "sprout" *(planta)*
(gen.) transplant, implant, plantation

planta—the sole of the foot; the first tarsal joint of insects

autotransplantation—transplantation of a tissue or organ to another part of same organism

explantation—tissue culture removed from the organism of its origin

latiplanter—having the hinder tarsal surface rounded

plantula—a pulvilluslike adhesive pad on the tarsal joints of some insects

replantation—the replacement of teeth which have been extracted or otherwise removed from sockets, usually after appropriate treatment, such as filling root canals and scraping the roots

18. PONT-, "bridge" *(pons)*
(gen.) pontoon

pons—a process or bridge of tissue connecting two parts of an organ; a convex white eminence situated at the base of the brain

pontic—portion of a prosthetic bridge which is between the abutments and serves as the artificial substitute for a lost tooth

cerebropontine—relating to cerebrum and pons

pontobulbar—pertaining to the pons and the medulla oblongata

19. PULVIN-, "cushion" *(pulvinus);* PULVILL-, "little cushion"
     (pulvillus)

     pulvinus—a cellular swelling at the junction of axis and leaf
     stalk

     pulvilliform—like a small cushion

     pulvination—a convex curve or swelling, as on a frieze

     Pulvinaria—genus of scales named from the appearance of
     their cottony egg cases

     pulvillus or *pulvinulus*—pad, process or membrane on the foot
     or between the claws; the lobe between each claw

20. SEN-, "old" *(senex)*

     (gen.) senior, senate, señor, monsignor

     presenility—premature old age

     senopia—the change of vision in the aged in which persons
     formerly myopic acquire what seems to be normal
     vision because of preslyopia

     senium—old age

EXERCISE

List the prefixes, bases and suffixes and give their meanings.

1. *abapical*—away from or opposite the apex

2. *periacinar*—located about, or surrounding an acinus (acinus—
     a saccular terminal division of a compound gland)

3. *subliminal*—below the threshold of consciousness or of sensa-
     tion

4. *lacrimotome*—a cutting instrument used in operating on the
     nasolacrimal duct or lacrimal sac

5. *subdural*—beneath the dura mater

6. *canine*—resembling dogs; pertaining to the sharp cutting teeth
     of mammals

7. *senilicide*—killing of the aged

8. *plantar*—pertaining to the sole of the foot

9. *interparietal*—between walls; between parietal bones

10. *pontine*—pertaining to a process or bridge of tissue connecting
     two parts of an organ

11. *occipital*—pertaining to the occiput, the back of the head

12. *protomala*—a mandible of myriopods

13. *pulvillar*—pertaining to a pulvillus

14. *glossopalatine*—connecting the tongue and soft palate

15. *argentine*—silver; small, silvery marine fishes; a pearly variety of calcite

16. *lacunar*—having or resembling small spaces, or lacunae

17. *precipitin*—an antibody to a soluble antigen

18. *alar*—winglike

19. *subfebrile*—constituting a body temperature slightly above normal but not febrile

20. *equine*—pertaining to or derived from a horse; horselike

21. *plantigrade*—walking on full sole of the foot

22. *annular*—pertaining to a ring of tissue about an opening

23. *aliped*—wing-footed, as a bat

24. *intraocular*—within the eye

25. *ambiocular*—pertaining to both eyes

MORE WORDS TO WORK WITH

acinotubular	biparietal	lacunule
alation	dextrocular	laminiplanter
alula	duralumin	maloplasty
annulation	duritis	palatorrhaphy
annulospiral	equisetosis	plantad
apicad	Equisetum	ponticulus
apical	inoculate	pulvinulus
apicifixed	intradural	recapitulation
argentaffinoma	lacrimation	senescence
argentite	lacrimatory	senile
binocular	lacunula	succiput

LESSON 25.   Latin Suffixes II

Learn the following suffixes and their meanings.

1. *-ic, -tic,* "pertaining to," "like" *(-icus, -ticus)*

PELV-, "pelvis"	+ -ic	pelvic
CIV-, "citizen"	+ -ic	civic
LUN(A)-, "moon"	+ -tic	lunatic

2. *-ary,* "pertaining to," "connected with," "having the character of" *(-arius)*

MILIT-, "soldier"	+ -ary	military
LITER-, "literature"	+ -ary	literary
SANGUIN-, "blood"	+ -ary	sanguinary

3. *-an, -ane,* "pertaining to," "like," "belonging to," "having the character of" *(-anus)*

URB-, "city"	+ -an, -ane	urban, urbane
VETER-, "old"	+ -an	veteran
AMERIC-	+ -an	American

4. *-form,* "like," "having the shape of" *(-formis)*

REN-, "kidney"	+ -(i)*form*	reniform
MUR-, "wall"	+ -(i)*form*	muriform
OV-, "egg"	+ -(i)*form*	oviform

NEW BASES

Learn the following bases and their meanings.

1. AQU(A)-, "water" *(aqua)*
   (gen.) aqueduct, aquamarine

   aqua regia—a mixture of nitric and hydrochloric acids which dissolves gold

   subaqueous—occurring beneath the water

   deaquation—the act or process of removing water from a substance; dehydration

   aquifer—a water-bearing bed or stratum of permeable rock, sand or gravel

2. BREV-, "short" *(brevis)*
   (gen.) brevity, abbreviate, breviary

   breviped—having short legs

   brevifoliate—having short leaves

   brevilingual—with a short tongue

3. CAPILL-, "hair" *(capillus)*

capillitium—protoplasmic threads forming a network in the spore capsule

capillarectasia—dilatation of the capillaries

capillovenous—pertaining to a junctional vessel between a capillary and a venule

capillariasis—infestation with a disease caused by a nematode worm of the genus Capillaria

capillaceous—having hairlike filaments

capilliculture—treatment to cure or prevent baldness

4. COLL-, "neck" *(collum)*
(gen.) collar, decolletage
decollation—decapitation
collar bone—the clavicle

5. CORON-, "crown" *(corona);* COROLL-, "little crown" *(corolla)*
(gen.) coronation, coroner, coronet
corolla—the petals of a flower
corolliferous—having a corolla
corollaceous—pertaining to a corolla
Coronilla—genus of herbs named for crown-shaped flower clusters
coronula—peripheral ring of spines on shell of certain echinoids
Coronula—a group of cells forming a crown on the oosphere

6. CORTIC-, CORT-, "bark," "outer layer" *(cortex)*
cortex—outer or more superficial part of an organ; the cerebral cortex
corticiferous—forming or having a barklike cortex
cortisone—constituent of adrenal cortical extract
infracortical—beneath the cortex
decorticate—to remove bark or cortex
corticipetal—conducting toward the cortex
isocortex—those parts of the cerebral cortex exhibiting the six characteristic layers or strata, each layer having certain predominant cells and histologic features common to all isocortical areas
neocortex—that part of the cerebral cortex which is phylogenetically the most recent in development

7. CRUC-, "cross" *(crux)*
    (gen.) crucify, excruciating

    crucifer—a plant with four petals and tetradynamous stamens;
        a member of the family Cruciferae

    cruciate—cross-shaped

8. CUNE-, "wedge" *(cuneus)*

    cuneate—wedge-shaped

    praecuneus—the medial surface of the parietal or the quadrate
        lobe of the cerebrum

    entocuneiform—the most internal of distal tarsal bones

9. ENS-, "sword" *(ensis)*

    ensiform—sword-shaped

    ensomphalus—conjoined twins united by a band in the epi-
        gastric and lower sternal regions; xiphopagus

10. FALC-, "sickle" *(falx)*
    (gen.) defalcate

    falx—sickle-shaped fold of dura mater; inguinal aponeurosis

    falcate—sickle-shaped; hooked

    falculate—curved and sharp at the point

11. FUG-, "to flee," "to put to flight"
    (gen.) refuge, fugitive

    fugue—a state of amnesia of considerable duration, sometimes
        involving a flight from familiar surroundings

    nidifugous—leaving the nest soon after hatching

    cerebrifugal—applies to nerve fibers which pass from the brain
        to the spinal cord

    basifuge—a plant unable to tolerate basic soils

    fugacious—evanescent; falling off early

    lactifuge—a drug or agent that lessens secretion of milk

    nucleofugal—moving away from a nucleus

12. LINE-, "line" *(linea)*
    (gen.) lineage, delineate, linear, lineal, lineament

    linella—a system of filaments in certain Sarcodina holding
        together the xenophya

    lineolate—marked by fine lines or striae

    lineation—an arrangement of lines

13. LUC-, "light," "to shine" *(lux)*

(gen.) lucid, elucidate

noctilucent—phosphorescent, luminescent

radiolucent—partly or wholly transparent to roentgen rays or other forms of radiation

translucid—semitransparent

14. MATR-, MATERN-, "mother" *(mater, maternus)*
(gen.) matricide, matron, matrimony, maternal

dura mater—the fibrous membrane forming the outermost covering of the brain and spinal cord

matrilocal—located or centered around the residence of the wife's family or people

matroclinous—derived from or inherited from the maternal line

matripotestal—pertaining to the power exercised by a matriarch and her family

matrix—something within which something else originates or takes form or develops

15. MONT-, "mountain" *(mons)*
(gen.) promontory, Montana, Vermont

monticolous—inhabiting mountainous regions

monticulus—largest part of the superior vermis of the cerebellum

verumontanum—a ridge on floor of the urethra

monticules—small eminences or prominences

16. MULT-, "many" *(multus)*
(gen.) multiply, multitude, multiversity, multifarious

multicarinate—having many carinae, or ridges

multicostate—with many ribs or veins; with many ridges

multiocular—many-eyed

multiciliate—with some or many cilia

17. RET-, "net," "network" *(rete)*

rete—a network or net

retial—pertaining to a rete

reticle or *reticulum*—a delicate network of cell protoplasm; in veterinary medicine, the honeycomb bag or second stomach

reticulocyte—an immature erythrocyte, of reticular appearance when stained

retina—the light-receptive layer and terminal expansion of the optic nerve in the eye

retinula—group of elongated pigment cells; the innermost element of an ommatidium

18. ROSTR-, "beak" *(rostrum)*

rostrum—beak or beaklike process

rostrulum—a small rostrum

rostrulate—with or like a rostrulum

adrostral—near to or closely connected with beak or rostrum

erostrate—having no beak; applies to antlers

longirostral—with a long beak

rostelliform—shaped like a small beak

19. TORQU-, TORT-, TORS-, "to twist"

(gen.) tort, retort, contortion, extortion, torture, distortion

torsion—the act of twisting

contortuplicate—applies to a bud with contorted and plicate leaves

detorsion—the correction of a torsion, as the twisting of a spermatic cord or ureter

torticone—a turreted, spirally twisted shell

adtorsion—a convergent squint

extorsion—outward rotation of a part

laterotorsion—a twisting to one side

20. VERM-, "worm" *(vermis)*

(gen.) vermillion, vermicelli, vermin

vermiculation—wormlike or peristaltic movement; fine, wavy markings

vermiculose—vermiform

vermilingual—having a worm-shaped tongue

vermiparous—producing wormlike young, as do blowflies

EXERCISE

List the prefixes, bases and suffixes and give their meanings.

1. *montane*—pertaining to the mountains, as a plant which grows on them

2. *capillary*—hairlike; relating to a hair, to a hairlike filament, to a tube with a minute bore or to a minute blood ves-

sel; also applies to moisture held between and around particles of soil

3. *coronary*—a term applied to vessels, nerves or attachments that encircle a part or an organ

4. *vermiform*—worm-shaped, as a vermiform process

5. *cuneiform*—wedge-shaped; cuneate

6. *cruciform*—crucial; shaped like a cross

7. *retrocollic*—pertaining to the muscles at back of the neck

8. *ensiform*—shaped like a sword, as the ensiform cartilage

9. *vermifuge*—any agent that kills or expells intestinal worms

10. *falciform*—having the shape of a sickle

11. *corticifugal*—conducting away from the cortex

12. *retiform*—net-shaped; reticular

13. *cortilactin*—an extract of adrenal cortex alleged to increase lactation

14. *aquatic*—living in or frequenting water

15. *adrenocorticotropic*—exhibiting a hormonal influence on the adrenal cortex; formerly spelled "adrenocortico-trophic"

16. *brevicollic*—pertaining to a congenital short neck

17. *brevirostrine*—pertaining to extinct mastodons with much shortened jaws

18. *torticollar*—affected with wry-neck or torticollis

19. *collinear*—in optics, lying in the same straight line

20. *matrilineal*—relating to tracing, or based on descent, through the maternal line

21. *lucifugal*—fleeing from or avoiding light

22. *Brevicipitidae*—family of tropical frogs or toads lacking maxillary teeth and having small mouths

23. *luciferin*—an organic substrate found in luminescent organisms which, when oxidized in the presence of the enzyme luciferose, emits light, as in fireflies and glow worms

24. *brevilineal*—pertaining to a body type which is shorter and broader than normal; brachymorphic

25. *multicipital*—with many heads or branches arising from one point

MORE WORDS TO WORK WITH

aquarium
aqueous
aquiclude
brevicaudate
centrifugal
collic
corona
coroniform
crucial
cuneifoliate
dextrotorsion

ensate
falcial
febrifuge
hypocorticism
intercapillary
matrilateral
monticulate
multiplicate
patrilineal
pellucid
pericoronal

psychocortical
rectilinear
recurvirostrate
reticulation
retinoscopy
rostel
rostrocarinate
torque
tortuous
translucent
vermicide

LESSON 26.   Latin Suffixes III

Learn the following suffixes and their meanings.

1. *-ate* (occasionally *-ite*), "having," "having the shape of," "characterized by having" *(-atus)*

ef- + FEMIN-, "woman"	+ *-ate*	effeminate
ad- + CUR-, "care"	+ *-ate*	accurate
DENT-, "tooth"	+ *-ate*	dentate
FAVOR-, "favor"	+ *-ite*	favorite

2. *-(u)lent, -(o)lent*, "full of," "disposed to" *(-lentus)*

FRAUD-, "deceit"	+ *-(u)lent*	fraudulent
PUR-, "pus"	+ *-(u)lent*	purulent
SANGUIN-, "blood"	+ *-(o)lent*	sanguinolent
VIR-, "poison"	+ *-(u)lent*	virulent

3. *-ose*, "full of" *(-osus)*

VERB-, "word"	+ *-ose*	verbose
RUG-, "wrinkle"	+ *-ose*	rugose
COMAT-, "lethargy"	+ *-ose*	comatose

4. *-ous (-ious, -eous)*, "full of," "having the character of" *(-osus, -us)*

VARI-, "varied"	+ *-ous*	various
POPUL-, "people"	+ *-ous*	populous
NERV-, "nerve"	+ *-ous*	nervous

5. *-aceous*, "belonging to," "resembling" *(-aceus)*

HERB-, "plant"	+ *-aceous*	herbaceous
CRET-, "chalk"	+ *-aceous*	cretaceous
CHART-, "paper"	+ *-aceous*	chartaceous

NEW BASES

Learn the following bases and their meanings.

1. BULL-, "bubble," "blister" *(bulla);* BULLI-, "to boil" (gen.) (papal) bull, bulletin, ebullient, bouillon, bullion

    bulla—a large bleb or blister forming either within or beneath the epidermis and filled with lymph

    bulliform—applied to large, thick-walled epidermal cells of most Gramineae and Cyperaceae

    vesioluobullous—characterized by both vesicles and bullae at the same time

2. COL-, "to inhabit"

    fungicolous—living in or on fungi

    latebricolous—inhabiting holes

    deserticolous—desert-inhabiting

    arboricolous—inhabiting trees, as certain molluscs

    radicicolous—with the flower seated immediately upon the crown of a root; dwelling in the root, as a parasite

3. CORI-, "skin" *(corium)*

    corium—the deep layer of the skin

    Coriaria—a genus of poisonous shrubs used in dyeing and tanning

4. CRIST-, "crest" *(crista)*

    crista—a crest

    crista terminalis—crest on wall of right atrium

    intercristal—between the surmounting ridges of a bone, organ or process; used particularly in intercristal diameter of pelvis, distance between two clear crests

Cristispira—genus of large, flexious, coarsely spiral bacteria

5. FEC-, "excrement," "sediment" *(feces)*

fecalith—concretion or calcified mass of fecal material; coprolith

fecaloid—resembling feces

fecula—the starchy part of a seed; sediment subsiding from an infusion; the fecal pellet of an insect

6. FLA-, FLAT-, "to blow"

exsufflation—forced discharge of the breath

souffle—a blowing sound; an auscultatory murmur

fetal *souffle*—inconstant murmur heard over the uterus during pregnancy

7. FLOR-, "flower" *(flos)*
(gen.) florist, florid, Florida

efflorescence—spontaneous conversion of a crystalline substance into powder by loss of water of crystallization; eruption of exanthematous disease

extrafloral—situated outside the flower

liguliflorous—having ligulate flowers

prefloration—the form and arrangement of foliage leaves in the bud

8. FORNIC-, "arch" *(fornix)*

fornix—an arched body or surface

fornical—like or pertaining to a fornix

9. GER-, GEST-, "to carry," "to bear"
(gen.) suggest, exaggerate, gesticulate, gesture

digest—to convert food into assimilable form

ingest—to take substances into the body

oviger—egg-carrying leg of Pycnogonida

lactigerous—lactiferous

Progestin—trademark for *progesterone,* a hormone connected with pregnancy

10. GUTT-, "drop" *(gutta)*
(gen.) gutter

guttate—having droplike markings

guttation—formation of drops of water on plants

guttiform—drop-shaped

guttulate—in the form of a small drop, as markings

Guttiferae—family of tropical trees with resinous sap

11. NEV-, "birthmark," "mole" *(nevus)*

nevus—birthmark

nevoxanthoendothelioma—a group or groups of yellowish brown nodules sometimes found on extremities in early childhood

neval—of or related to a nevus

12. NID-, "nest" *(nidus)*

nidamental—applies to glands which secrete material for an egg-covering

innidiation—development of cells in a new part to which they have been carried; colonization

nidation—the renewal of uterine lining between menstrual periods

pilonidal—pertaining to or containing an accumulation of hairs in a cyst

denidation—disintegration and ejection of superficial part of uterine mucus

prenidatory—before nidation

13. PULVER-, PULV-, "dust" *(pulvus)*

pulviplume—a powder-down feather

Pulvule—trademark for a capsule containing a powdered drug

pulveraceous—covered with a layer of powdery granules

14. RADIC-, "root" *(radix)*

(gen.) radical, eradicate, radish

radiculose—having many rootlets

radicicolous—inhabiting roots

radicle—a small root; a primary root

monoradicular—having only one root; said of teeth

myeloradiculitis—inflammation of spinal cord and roots of spinal nerves

15. RAM-, "branch" *(ramus)*

(gen.) ramification

biramose—divided into two branches

ramate—branched

ramiflorous—having flowers on branches

ramigerous—bearing branches

interramicorn—a piece of a bird's bill beyond the mandibular rame forming the gonys

ramuliferous—with small branches

16. SAX-, "rock" *(saxum)*

saxicavous—applies to rock-borers, as some molluscs; lithophagous

saxifrage—plant of the family Saxifraga, perennial herbs frequently found growing in rock crevices

saxigenous or *saxicolous*—inhabiting or growing around rocks

17. SCUT-, "shield" *(scutum)*
(gen.) escutcheon

scutum—the broad apex of a style; a bony, horny or chitinous shield

scute—an external scale, as of reptiles, fish or scaly insects

scutellum—a small, shield-shaped plant structure; a hard plate or scale, as on birds and insects

exscutellate—having no scutellum; applies to insects

scutate—protected by large scales or horny plates

scutellation—arrangement of scales, as on the tarsus of a bird

scutelliplantar—having tarsus covered with small plates, or scutella

18. SERR-, "saw," "saw-tooth" *(serra)*
(gen.) sierra

biserrate—having marginal teeth that are themselves notched

serratiform—like a saw

serratodenticulate—with many-toothed serrations

subserrate—somewhat notched or saw-toothed

Serricornia—a genus of beetles with saw-toothed antennae

19. STERCOR-, STERC-, "excrement" *(stercus)*

stercome—fecal matter of Sarcodina, in masses of brown granules

stercoral—a dorsal pocket or sac of proctodaeum in spiders

stercobilin—the brown pigment of feces

stercomarium—the system of stercome-containing tubes of certain Sarcodina

stercoma—a fecalith; a hard fecal mass, usually in the rectum

Sterculia—a type of plant with a fetid odor

20. SULC-, "furrow," "groove" *(sulcus)*
    sulcate—furrowed; grooved
    bisulcate—having two grooves
    sulcomarginal—situated at the margin of the spinal cord adjacent to the ventral median fissure

EXERCISE

List the prefixes, bases and suffixes and give their meanings.

1. *feculent*—abounding in sediment or noxious matter; fecal
2. *fugaceous*—in biology, falling off, as the falling off or fading of petals after the full bloom of a flower
3. *argenteoguttate*—with silver spots
4. *nevose*—spotted; having nevi
5. *capillaceous*—having filaments; like a hair
6. *nidifugous*—leaving the nest soon after hatching
7. *nidicolous*—living in the nest for a time after hatching
8. *monticolous*—inhabiting mountainous regions
9. *coriaceous*—leathery; applies to leaves
10. *bullate*—blistered; puckered; vesiculate
11. *saxicoline*—living or growing on rocks; saxacolous
12. *cristate*—crested; shaped like a crest
13. *flatulent*—having gas in the stomach and intestinal tract
14. *nidulent*—partially encased or lying free in a cavity; embedded in a pulp, as the seeds in a berry
15. *radiciflorous*—with flowers arising at the extreme base of the stem; rhizanthous
16. *pulverulent*—powdered, as if dusted over
17. *subramose*—slightly branching
18. *scutigerous*—bearing a shieldlike structure
19. *serratirostral*—with serrate bill; applies to birds
20. *stercoricolous*—living in dung
21. *retroserrate*—toothed, with teeth directed backward
22. *multisulcate*—much-furrowed

23. *stercoraceous*—fecal; having the nature of or containing feces, as stercoraceous vomiting

24. *mentigerous*—supporting or bearing the mentum

25. *fornicate*—having an arched form

MORE WORDS TO WORK WITH

biflorate	floscule	nidulation
bullation	fornication	nudiflorous
congestion	gestation	pulverize
cristulate	gout	radicivorous
defecate	guttiferous	sanguicolous
deflate	inflate	Saxicola
defloration	insufflator	serrulate
egesta	metascutum	stangicolous
excoriate	multiflorous	stercolith
feces	multiramose	sulculus
flora	nevoid	

LESSON 27.   Latin Suffixes IV

Learn the following suffixes and their meanings.

1. *-ent (-ient), -ant (iant),* equivalent to the English present participial ending, *-ing (-ens, -ans)*

   This suffix often forms words which are used as nouns, and in such cases it comes to mean "person who," "that which."

e-	+ LOQU-, "to speak"	+ *-ent*	eloquent
in-	+ NOC-, "to harm"	+ *-ent*	innocent
	DORM-, "to sleep"	+ *-ant*	dormant
	VIGIL-, "to watch"	+ *-ant*	vigilant
	AG-, "to do"	+ *-ent*	agent
	CURR-, "to run"	+ *-ent*	current
in-	+ HABIT-, "to live"	+ *-ant*	inhabitant

2. *-ile,* "able to be," "able to," "tending to" *(-ilis)*

   The fact that this suffix is attached to verbal bases, whereas *-ile,* "pertaining to," etc. (Lesson 24), is generally attached to noun and adjective bases, will enable you to distinguish the two.

FRAG-, "to break"	+ -*ile*	fragile
DUCT-, "to lead," "to draw"	+ -*ile*	ductile
AG-, "to do"	+ -*ile*	agile

3. -*able*, -*ible*, "able to be," "able to," "tending to" (-*abilis*, -*ibilis*)

If this suffix is followed by an additional suffix, it appears as -*abil*-, -*ibil*-.

DUR-, "hard," "to last"	+ -*able*	durable
ad- + APT-, "to fit"	+ -*able*	adaptable
in- + CRED-, "to believe"	+ -*ible*	incredible
FLEX-, "to bend"	+ -*ible*	flexible
ad- + APT-, "to fit"	+ -*abil*- + -*ity*	adaptability
FLEX-, "to bend"	+ -*ibil*- + -*ity*	flexibility

4. -*id*, "tending to," "inclined to" (-*idus*)

FERV-, "to boil"	+ -*id*	fervid
FRIG-, "to be cold"	+ -*id*	frigid
VIV-, "to live"	+ -*id*	vivid

5. -*uous*, "tending to," "inclined to" (-*uus*, -*uosus*)

con- + TIN-, "to hold"	+ -*uous*	continuous
ad- + SID-, "to sit"	+ -*uous*	assiduous
im- + PET-, "to seek"	+ -*uous*	impetuous

NEW BASES

Learn the following bases and their meanings.

1. AUD-, AUDIT-, "to hear"
   (gen.) audit, auditor, inaudible, auditorium, audition
   audiometer—an instrument for measuring the acuity and range of hearing
   anaudia—loss of speech; aphonia
   autoaudible—audible to the patient; applied to heart sounds
   auditive—auditory
   psychauditory—pertaining to the conscious or intellectual interpretation of sounds
   subaudition—act of comprehending what is not expressed

2. CAMER-, "chamber" *(camera)*
    (gen.) camera

    cameration—division into a large number of separate chambers

    camerostome—hollowed-out place under the surface of the "hood" of certain Trogulidae

    unicameral—having only one cavity or chamber

3. CAD- (-CID-), CAS-, "to fall," "befall"
    (gen.) cadence, decadent, accident, casual, occidental

    incidence—the act or manner of falling upon; the way in which one body strikes another, as angle of incidence; the angle at which a ray of light strikes a reflecting or refracting surface

    adeciduate—not falling or coming away; applies to evergreens; also applies to Adeciduata, a division of mammals including those not having a deciduate placenta

    caducous—in botany, dropping off very early, as compared with other parts

    indeciduate or *noncaducous*—with maternal part of placenta not coming away at birth

    decidua—the mucous membrane lining the pregnant uterus, cast off after parturition

    deciduoma—decidual tissue produced in uterus by mechanical methods in absence of embryo; an intrauterine tumor containing decidual relics and believed to arise from some hyperplasia of a retained portion of the decidua

4. CAP- (-CIP-), CAPT- (-CEPT-), "to take," "to seize"
    (gen.) captive, recipient, reception, inception, accept

    amboceptor—a specific antibody or immune body necessary for fermentationlike action of a complement on a toxin or a red corpuscle; contains two specialized elements

    exteroceptor—a receptor which receives stimuli from outside the body

    conception—the fecundation of the ovum by the spermatozoon

    proprioceptor—a receptor located in a muscle, tendon, joint, etc., whose reflex function is locomotor or postural

    beneceptor—a receptor for stimuli that tend to promote the well-being of the body

    intussusception—receiving of one part within another, especially invagination; slipping a passage of one part of intestine into another

5. CREPIT-, "to creak," "to crackle"
    (gen.) decrepit

    crepitation or *crepitus* or *crepitatio*—the grating of fractured
            bones; crackling of the joints; noise produced upon
            tissues containing an abnormal amount of air or gas;
            in insects, the discharge of fluid with an explosive
            sound

    decrepitation—the breaking up or crackling of certain crystals
            on heating

6. GRAV-, "heavy" *(gravis)*

    ingravescence—increasing in weight or severity

    multigravida—a pregnant woman who has had two or more
            previous pregnancies

    primigravida—a woman who is pregnant for the first time

    gravimetric—measurement of weight or density

    gravigrade—any of several large, heavy-footed mammals, as
            elephants

    Gravigrada—a division of Edentata comprising ground sloths

7. JAC-, "to lie"

    adjacent—lying nearby; having a common border

8. LAB-, LAPS-, "to slip," "to fall," "to glide"
    (gen.) collapse, lapse

    labile—unstable; readily changing; moving from place to place

    lability—in psychiatry, very rapid fluctuations in intensity
            and modality of emotions, usually without external
            cause

    tremolabile—easily inactivated or destroyed by agitation

9. MOLL-, "soft" *(mollis)*
    (gen.) molligy

    mollities—softness

    mollisol—surface layer of permanently frozen ground in which
            ice melts during the summer (SOL-, ground)

    molluscum—a chronic skin disease with pulpy nodules

10. MORB-, "disease" *(morbus)*

    morbific—old term for producing disease, pathogenic

    morbilli—old term for measles

    morbose—diseased, morbid

    morbus anglicus—rickets

morbus divinus or *morbus caducus*—epilepsy

morbus hungaricus—typhus

11. MOV-, MOT-, "to move"
     (gen.) promote, demotion, remote, mobile, remove

oculomotor—causing movements of eyeball; applies to third cranial nerve

vasomotor—applies to nerves supplying muscles in wall of blood vessels and regulating caliber of blood vessels

motorium—motor area; part of the nervous system where the motorial sense is located

venomotor—causing veins to contract or dilate

12. NASC-, NAT-, "to be born"
     (gen.) native, nature, renascence, Renaissance, nation

adnate—congenitally attached or united

innate—inherited; basifixed; applies to anther with filament attached only at base

antenatal—occurring or existing before birth; prenatal

denature—to change, to render different from normal

13. PATI-, PASS-, "to suffer," "to endure"
     (gen.) impatient, dispassionate, compassionate

compatibility—congruity; the power of a medicine or a substance in a medicine to mix with another without deliterious chemical change or loss of therapeutic power; refers to blood types

passion—an intense emotion

inpatient—a person in a hospital or infirmary who receives lodging and food as well as treatment

14. PLAN-, "flat" *(planus)*
     (gen.) plan, plane, aquaplane

deplanate—leveled, flattened

planiform—with nearly flat surfaces

planation—a process of erosion that produces flat surfaces

planarian—a turbellarian worm

planoconcave—flat on one side and concave on the other

planula—very young, flat-bodied larva of free-swimming coelenterates

15. PRUR-, PRURIT-, "to itch"

antipruritic—relieving or preventing itching

prurigo—a chronic inflammatory disease of the skin characterized by itching

pruritus—itching

16. REG- (-RIG-), RECT-, "to make straight," "to rule"; RECT-,
"straight," "rectum" *(rectus)*
(gen.) regent, dirigible, direct, erect, rectitude, corrigenda,
correct

arrector—a muscle which erects

pararectal—beside or near the rectum

regimen—a systematic plan or course including food, sanitary
arrangements and medication to maintain or improve
health

17. RUMP-, RUPT-, "to break," "to burst"
(gen.) abrupt, corrupt, disrupt, interrupt

abruption—a tearing away

rupture—a forcible tearing of a part; a hernia

ruptio—rupture of a vessel or organ

18. SCIND-, SCISS-, "to cut," "to split"
(gen.) rescind

scissile—separating; easily split

abcission—the separation of parts

discission—state of being torn apart; in eye surgery, an operation for a soft cataract in which the capsule is lacer-
ated a number of times to allow the lens substance to
be absorbed

electroscission—the cutting of tissues by an electrocautery
knife

abscind—to cut off

19. TANG- (-TING-), TIG-, TACT-, "to touch"
(gen.) tact, contact, intact, contingent

tactile—pertaining to the sense of touch

atactilia—loss of the tactile sense

myotactic—relating to the muscular sense

20. VESIC-, "bladder," "blister" *(vesica)*

vesicle—a small bladder, especially a small sac containing fluid;
a small bulla

perivesiculitis—inflammation around a seminal vesicle

vesiculation—the formation of vesicles

vesication—the formation of a blister; a blister

bronchovesicular—pertaining to an intermediate stage in the transition from normal vesicular to completely bronchial breath sounds

EXERCISE

List the prefixes, bases and suffixes and give their meanings.

1. *audile*—applies to a person who tends to understand better by hearing than by seeing; ear-minded

2. *transaudient*—allowing the transmission of sound

3. *multicamerate*—with many chambers

4. *contiguous*—in contact, or adjacent

5. *susceptible*—state of being readily affected

6. *gravid*—pregnant

7. *subcrepitant*—almost crepitant; rattling, crackling, as a subcrepitant rale

8. *subjacent*—lying beneath

9. *applanate*—flattened

10. *prolapse*—the falling or sinking down of a part

11. *neonatal*—applies to the first four weeks after birth

12. *morbid*—pertaining to disease or diseased parts

13. *siccolabile*—altered or destroyed by drying

14. *motile*—able to move; capable of spontaneous motion

15. *emollient*—a substance used externally to soften the skin

16. *nascent*—pertaining to gaseous substances at the moment of their liberation from chemical combination

17. *incompatible*—incapable of being used or put together because of resulting chemical change or of antagonistic qualities, as two drugs or two types of blood

18. *vesicant*—a blistering agent

19. *incorrigible*—incapable of being corrected

20. *prurient*—causing an itching sensation

21. *erumpent*—breaking through suddenly, as fungal hyphae

22. *connate*—firmly joined together from birth

23. *circumscissile*—splitting along a circular line; applies to dehiscence

24. *ruptile*—bursting in an irregular manner

25. *deciduous*—falling off at the end of growth period or at maturity

MORE WORDS TO WORK WITH

abcise
aggravate
auditory
clairaudience
contraception
crepitant
erectile
eruption
frigolabile
gravity
hydroplane

hypermotility
incipient
locomotion
mollusc
morbilliform
morbus gallicus
natimortality
octigravida
passive
patient
prenatal
procidentia

pruriginous
rectalgia
recidivism
rectilinear
relapse
superjacent
tactual
tangent
thermolabile
tricamerous
Vesicaria

LESSON 28.   Latin Suffixes V

Learn the following suffixes and their meanings.

1. *-ulous*, "tending to," "inclined to" *(-ulus)*

in-	+ CRED-, "to believe"	+ *-ulous*	incredulous
	TREM-, "to tremble"	+ *-ulous*	tremulous
	GARR-, "to chatter"	+ *-ulous*	garrulous

2. *-ive*, "tending to," "inclined to" *(-ivus)*

	ACT-, "to do"	+ *-ive*	active
ad-	+ GRESS-, "to go"	+ *-ive*	aggressive
ad-	+ HES-, "to stick"	+ *-ive*	adhesive

3. *-ory*, "tending to," "serving for" *(-orious)*

pre-	+ PAR-, "to prepare"	+ *-ate*	+ *-ory*	preparatory
intro-	+ DUCT-, "to lead"	+ *-ory*		introductory
ex-	+ CRET-, "to separate"	+ *-ory*		excretory

4. *-itious,* "tending to," "characterized by" *(-icius)*

FICT-, "to invent"	+ *-itious*	fictitious
ex- + CRE-, "to separate"	+ *-ment* + *-itious*	excrementitious

5. *-acious,* "tending to," "inclined to" *(-ax)*

VIV-, "to live"	+ *-acious*	vivacious
AUD-, "to dare"	+ *-acious*	audacious
LOQU-, "to speak"	+ *-acious*	loquacious

NEW BASES

Learn the following bases and their meanings.

1. AMBUL-, "to walk"
   (gen.) amble, preamble, perambulate, ambulatory

   ambulant or *ambulatory*—walking or able to walk; designating a patient not confined to bed but requiring medical care

   ambulacrum—locomotor tube foot of echinoderms

   somnambulism—sleepwalking; hypnotic sleep in which the subject appears to be awake, but his consciousness is under the control of the hypnotizer

2. CED-, CESS-, "to go," "to yield"
   (gen.) concede, excess, recede, procession, intercession, succession

   introcession—a depression, as of a surface

   process—a prominence or outgrowth

   succedaneous—relating to or acting as a substitute; pertaining to that which follows after, as a permanent tooth that replaces a deciduous tooth

3. DEXTR-, "righthand" *(dexter)*
   dextral—dexiotropic, turning from left to right, as whorls

   dextroduction—movement of the visual axis toward the right

   dextrogyrate or *dextrorotatory*—rotating the plane of polarized light to the right

4. FAC- (-FIC-), FACT- (-FECT-), "to do," "to make"
   (gen.) factory, efficient, deficient, faculty, effective, confection

   artifact—in microscopy and histology, a structure that has been produced by mechanical, chemical or artificial means

facultative—voluntary; optional; having the power to do or not to do a thing

5. FID-, FISS-, "to split"
(gen.) fissure, fission
fissile—fissionable
fissirostral—with deeply cleft beak
pentafid—divided in five divisions or lobes
palmatifid—applies to leaves divided into lobes to about the middle at acute angles to each other

6. GUST-, "to taste"
(gen.) disgust
gustation—the sense of taste; the act of tasting
degustation—the act of tasting
gustometer—an apparatus used to determine taste thresholds

7. INSUL-, "island" *(insula)*
(gen.) insulate, peninsula
insuloma—a tumor arising from the cells of the islets of pancreas
insula—that portion of the cortex overlying the corpus striatum
insulin—the antidiabetic hormone arising from the islets of Langerhans of the pancreas

8. JUNCT-, "to join"; JUG-, "yoke" *(jugum)*
(gen.) junction, conjunction, injunction, subjunctive
conjugation—the temporary union or complete fusion of two gametes or unicellular organisms; the pairing of chromosomes
bijugate—with two pairs of leaflets
disjunction—divergence of paired chromosomes at anaphase
subjugal—below jugal of the cheekbone (malar bone)
exconjugant—a protozoan immediately after the separation following conjugation

9. LEV-, "lefthand" *(laevus)*
levoduction—movement to left, said especially of the eye
levogyrate or *levorotatory*—rotating the plane of polarized light to the left
levophoria—a tending of the visual lines to the left

10. MACUL-, "spot" *(macula)*

macula—a spot or patch of color; small pit or depression

macula lutea—the yellow spot of the retina; point of clearest vision

maculation—the arrangement of spots on a plant or animal

emaculation—removal of freckles or skin lesions, especially skin tumors

maculopapular—having characteristics of a macule (spot) and a papule

11. NOCT-, "night" *(nox)*

noctiphobia—morbid fear of night

pernoctation—obsolete word for wakefulness, insomnia

Noctuidae—family of night-flying moths, including owlet moths

noctivagant—going about in the night; night-wandering

12. PAR-, PART-, "to give birth to," "to produce"

multiparous—bearing several or more than one offspring at a birth

biparous—having two young at a time

ramiparous—producing branches

primipara—a woman bearing or giving birth to her first child

octipara—a woman who has been in labor eight times

13. PEND-, PENS-, "to hang," "to weigh," "to pay"
(gen.) depend, impend, expensive, recompense

compensation—a psychic phenomenon in which strong feelings of guilt or inferiority prompt excessive defensive reactions

14. PRED-, "prey" *(praeda)*
(gen.) depredation

predatism—the habit or practice of living by predation

predacious—preying on other animals

predacity—quality or state of being predacious

15. ROT-, "wheel" *(rota)*
(gen.) rotation, rotund

rotate—shaped like a wheel; rotiform

rotula—one of five radially directed bars bounding the circular aperture of the esophagous of a sea urchin *rotuliform*—shaped like a small wheel

mutarotation—a change in optical rotation of solutions of certain sugars

16. SALI- (-SILI-), SALT- (-SULT-), "to leap," "to jump"
(gen.) exult, result

insult—trauma or other stress to tissues or organs

dissilient—springing open; applies to capsules of various plants which dehisce explosively

saltigrade—moving by leaps, as some insects

saltation—the act of leaping or jumping

resilium—the horny, flexible hinge of a bivalve

resilifer—projection of a valve carrying the resilium

17. SORB-, SORPT-, "to suck in"

absorbtion—in physiology, the taking up of fluids or gases through osmosis and capillarity; infiltration into the skin; incorporation into the body through blood and lymph

adsorption—the power of taking up fluids possessed by certain substances

absorbefacient—an agent which promotes absorption

18. STRING-, STRICT-, "to draw tight"
(gen.) stringent, restrict, district

strict—stiffly upright, rigid, erect

astringent—an agent that produces contraction of organic tissues or arrests hemorrhage, diarrhea, etc.

abstriction—the process of detaching spores by rounding off of the tips of sporophores, as in mildew

electrostriction—the contraction of a solvent resulting from the development of an electrostatic field by a dissolved electrolyte

restringent—an astringent or styptic

stricture—the narrowing of the lumen of a canal or hollow organ, as of the esophagus

19. TEN- (-TIN-), TENT-, "to hold"
(gen.) tenant, tenure, continuous, abstention, detention, abstinence

tenaculum—a holdfast of algae; an ectodermal area modified for adhesion of sand grains in certain sea anemones

retinaculum—a small, glandular mass to which an orchid pollinium adheres at dehiscence

sustentacular—supporting; applies to connective tissue acting as a supporting framework for an organ

20. VIV-, "living" *(vivus)*
(gen.) survive, vivid, vivacious

vivification—the act of making alive

vividiffusion—passage of diffusible substances from the blood of a living animal flowing through collodion tubes into surrounding isotonic saline solution

viviparous—bringing forth the young alive

EXERCISE

List the prefixes, bases and suffixes and give their meanings.

1. *efficacious*—having the power to bring about a desired effect

2. *pendulous*—bending downward from the point of origin; overhanging

3. *procursive*—running forward, as procursive epilepsy, a form in which the patient runs during an epileptic attack

4. *tenacious*—adhesive; cohesive; persistent

5. *factitious*—pertaining to a state or substance which is brought about or produced by means other than natural

6. *capacious*—able to contain a great deal; not narrow or constricted

7. *conjunctivitis*—inflammation of the conjunctiva (conjunctiva —the mucous membrane covering the anterior portion of the globe of the eye)

8. *predation pressure*—effects of predation on a natural community

9. *ambidextrous*—able to use both hands equally well

10. *ambulatory*—walking

11. *resilient*—rebounding; elastic

12. *resorptive*—pertaining to the removal by absorption

13. *suspensory*—serving for suspension or support, as a suspensory ligament or suspensory bandage

14. *constrictive*—contracting or tightening

15. *incontinent*—not having the ability to control the natural evacuations, as the feces or the urine

16. *recessive*—in biology, a characteristic of one of the parents of a hybrid which is found in the minority of offsprings

17. *fissiparous*—propagating by fission

18. *accessory*—auxiliary, assisting

19. *ovoviviparous*—reproducing by means of eggs hatched within the body

20. *saltatory*—dancing or leaping

21. *ambilevous*—clumsy in the use of both hands; ambisinister

22. *circuminsular*—surrounding the insula of the cerebral cortex

23. *immaculate*—without spots or marks

24. *gustatory*—pertaining to the sense of taste

25. *noctambulation*—sleepwalking

MORE WORDS TO WORK WITH

abortifacient
abscess
ambulacriform
ambulance
antivivisection
appendix
bifid
bimaculate
decedent
dextrad
dextrocardia
dextrose
dextrosuria
dispensary
distention
equinox

fissilingual
fissiped
gustatism
hypoinsulinism
infection
insulinemia
levophobia
levorotatory
levulose
lyosorption
muciparous
noctalbuminuria
noctilucent
nocturnal
orifice
parent
parturition

perpendicular
petrifaction
postpartem
predator
predatory
putrefaction
quadrimaculate
retention
revive
salient
sejunction
subsultory
suspensorium
tenacious
tentacle
vasoconstrictor

LESSON 29.   Latin Suffixes VI—Diminutives

Diminutive suffixes are attached to bases in order to denote smallness. Occasionally their addition results in a change in the form of the base.

CASTR-, "camp"	+ -le	castle
CEREBR-, "brain"	+ -ellum	cerebellum
OCUL-, "eye"	+ -ellus	ocellus
LAMIN-, "thin plate"	+ -ella	lamella

Since the Latin forms of these suffixes frequently appear in English words, in the presentation below the Latin forms generally will be given along with the anglicized diminutives. Learn the following suffixes and their meanings.

1. A.   *-ule, -ole, -le,* "little"

GLOB-, "ball"	+ -ule		globule
GRAN-, "grain"	+ -ule	+ -ar	granular
ARTERI-, "artery"	+ -ole		arteriole
CIRC-, "ring"	+ -le		circle
SCRUP-, "small stone"	+ -le		scruple

　　 B.   *-ulus, -ula, -ulum,* etc., "little"

GLADI-, "sword"	+ -olus	gladiolus
FORM-, "form"	+ -ula	formula
CUP-, "tub"	+ -ola	cupola
CAPIT-, "head"	+ -ulum	capitulum

2. A.   *-el,* "little"

TUN(N)-, "tub"	+ -el	tunnel
SCALPR-, "knife"	+ -el	scalpel
MORS-, "bite"	+ -el	morsel

　　 B.   *-ellus, -ella, -ellum,* "little"

LAMIN-, "thin plate"	+ -ella	lamella
FLAGR-, "whip"	+ -ellum	flagellum
CAPIT-, "head"	+ -ellum	capitellum
CEREBR-, "brain"	+ -ellum	cerebellum

3. 　　 *-cule, -cle,* "little" (*-culum,* etc.)

MOLE-, "mass"	+ -cule	molecule
MUS-, "mouse"	+ -cle	muscle
PART-, "part"	+ -(i)cle	particle

4. A. *-il*, "little"

COCIC-, "book," "document"	+ *-il*	codicil
PUP-, "boy," "girl"	+ *-il*	pupil
FIBR-, "fiber"	+ *-il*	fibril

    B. *-illus, -illa, -illum*, "little"

FIBR-, "fiber"	+ *-illa*	fibrilla
PRISC-, "Priscus" (Roman name)	+ *-illa*	Priscilla
ARMAD-, "armored"	+ *-illo*	armadillo

5. A. *-uncle*, "little"

CARB-, "live coal"	+ *-uncle*		carbuncle
AV-, "grandfather"	+ *-uncle*	+ *-ar*	avuncular
FUR-, "thief"	+ *-uncle*		furuncle

    B. *-unculus*, "little"

PED-, "foot"	+ *-unculus*	pedunculus
RAN-, "frog"	+ *-unculus*	ranunculus

6. *-ette, -et*, "little" (of French origin)

STATUE	+ *-ette*	statuette
SYRING-	+ *-ette*	Syrette
CORN-, "horn"	+ *-et*	cornet
LANCE-, "lance"	+ *-et*	lancet

NEW BASES

Learn the following bases and their meanings.

1. AC(U)-, "sharp," "sour," "needle" *(acus)*
    (gen.) acumen

    acupuncture—puncture of the tissues with long, fine needles; used for centuries for relief of neuralgic pain or release of fluid

    acusector—an electric needle, operating on a high-frequency current, which cuts tissues like a scalpel

    acuticostal—having projecting ribs

    aculeolate—beset with small prickles

2. ARE-, "space" *(area)*

    areola—any minute interstice or space in a tissue; a colored or pigmented ring surrounding some central point or space, as a nipple or a pustule; the part of the iris enclosing the pupil *areolet*—a small areola

areolate—marked with areoles; divided into distinct spaces; reticulate

3. AUR-, "ear" *(auris)*

aurist—a specialist in diseases of the ear

aurophore—an organ projecting from the base of the pneumatophore of certain Siphonophora

auricle—any earlike, lobed appendage; the external ear; the atrium, or anterior chamber, of the heart

endaural—pertaining to the inner surface or part of the external auditory canal

4. CALC-, "limestone," "pebble," "calcium" *(calx)*

calcicole—a plant which thrives in soils rich in calcium salts

calcification—the deposition of lime salts in tissue

calcareous or *calcarious*—pertaining to or having the nature of limestone; having a chalky appearance or consistency

calcipenia—calcium deficiency

nephrocalcinosis—renal calcinosis, marked by the precipitation of deposits of calcium phosphate in kidney tubules

5. CAPS-, "box" *(capsa)*

encapsulation—the process of surrounding a part with a capsule

decapsulation—removal of a capsule or enveloping membrane

capsulitis—inflammation of a capsule, as that of the lens, liver (perihepatitis) or the labyrinth (otosclerosis)

Capsella—a genus of weeds with notched, markedly flattened pods, such as shepherd's purse

6. CAR(N)-, "flesh" *(caro)*

(gen.) carnal, incarnation, reincarnation, carnation, carnival

carnification—alteration of tissue so that it resembles skeletal muscle in color and consistency; this sometimes affects the lungs

incarnative—an agent which produces flesh or promotes granulation

carnassial—pertaining to cutting teeth of animals of the order Carnivora; the fourth premolar above and first molar below

carneous—flesh-colored

caruncle—an excrescence or appendage at or above the hilum of a seed

carunculate—having a caruncle

carnose—like or relating to flesh; of fleshy consistency, like the succulent parts of plants

7. CUT-, "skin" *(cutis)*

intracutaneous—within the skin substance; applied to injection of substances into the skin

cutireaction—a local skin reaction following the inoculation with or the application of extracts of pathogenic organisms

cutin—a substance allied to cellulose found in external layers of thickened epidermal cells

cutinization—the deposition of cutin in cell wall, thereby forming a cuticle

cutisector—an instrument for taking small sections of skin from the living subject

8. FIBR-, "fiber" *(fibra)*

fibril—a component filament of a fiber, as of a muscle or a nerve

fibrillose—furnished with fibrils; applies to the mycelia of certain fungi

fibrin—the fibrous, insoluble protein in the network involved in blood clotting

fibrinogen—a soluble protein of blood which by activity of thrombin yields fibrin and produces coagulation

neurofibril—exceedingly fine fiber composing a medullated nerve fiber

leiomyofibroma—a benign tumor composed of cells of smooth muscle and fibrous connective tissue

adenofibroma—a leiomyofibroma containing glandular tissue

9. FOLL-, "bag" *(follis)*

follicle—a capsular fruit which opens on one side only; a cavity or sheath; an ovarian follicle; a hair follicle; a small secretory cavity or sac as an acinus or alveolus

perifollicular—surrounding a follicle

folliclis—a tuberculid involving the extremities and sometimes the face

10.   FUN-, "rope," "cord" *(funis)*

funiculus—a bodily structure suggesting a cord; one of the three main divisions of white matter in the brain; old term for fasciculus; old term for umbilical or spermatic cord; a bundle of nerve fibers; the stalk of a plant ovule

funicular—having the form of or associated with a cord; a funiculus

funiculitis—inflammation of a funiculus, specifically, of the spermatic cord

funic—relating to or originating in the umbilical cord

funipendulous—suspended by a rope or cord

11.   LOC-, "place" *(locus)*
(gen.) local, location, allocate, locomotion, collocation

bilocular—containing two cavities or chambers

locellus—a small compartment of an ovary

loculicidal—dehiscent dorsally down the middle of carpels

translocation—removal to a different place or habitat; diffusion, as of food material; change in position of a chromosome segment to another part of the same chromosome or to a different chromosome

apicolocator—an instrument for locating the apex of a tooth

12.   LUN(A)-, "moon" *(luna)*

lunate—somewhat crescent shaped; semilunar

lunette—the transparent lower eyelid of snakes; an opening in a vault, especially for a window

semilunar—half-moon-shaped

13.   OSTI-, "door," "opening" *(ostium)*

ostium—any mouthlike opening; the openings of the fallopian tubes

ostiate—furnished with ostia

ostiole—the opening of a conceptacle, perithecium, stoma or another sac; the inhalant aperture of a sponge

14.   PART-, "part," "to divide" *(pars)*
(gen.) participate, particular, impartial, partition

digitipartite—having leaves divided in a handlike pattern

pedatipartite—a palmate leaf with cymose branching of the third order

bipartite—having two parts

15. PED-, "foot" *(pes)*
(gen.) pedal, pedestrian, expedient, impede, velocipede
pedicel—any slender stalk; especially one that supports a fruiting or spore-bearing organ
pedicellate—supported by a pedicel or petiole
scutiped—having the foot or part of the foot covered by scutella
pediculation—the process of developing a pedicel
pedicure—the care of the feet
suppedaneous—pertaining to the soles of the feet
pedatifid—divided in a pedate manner nearly to the base;
palmately divided with lateral divisions cleft

16. PELL-, "skin" *(pellis)*
pellicle—a thin skin or film; a film on the surface of a liquid
pelliculate—having a pellicle on an external surface
pellagra—a syndrome resulting from nicotinic acid deficiency,
characterized by dermatitis in sun-exposed areas

17. PLUM-, "feather" *(pluma)*
filoplume—a delicate, hairlike feather with a long axis and a
few free barbs at the apex
plumate—plumelike
plumigerous—feathered
pulviplume—a powder-down feather

18. RACEM-, "cluster of grapes or berries" *(racemus)*
racemation—a cluster, as of grapes
racemiferous—bearing racemes
racemose—bearing flowers in clusters
racemic acid—an optically inactive mixture of dextrorotatory
and levorotatory forms of optical isomers, etc.,
named from its being found in the juice of grapes
racemization—conversion of the optically active form of a
compound to its racemic form, commonly by heating

19. RIM-, "crack," "chink" *(rima)*
rimate—having fissures
rimiform—in the shape of a narrow fissure
birimose—having two clefts or slits

20. VOR-, "to eat"
    (gen.) voracious
    herbivorous—living on vegetable food
    fungivorous—fungus-eating animals and plants
    insectivorous—living on insects

EXERCISE

List the prefixes, bases and suffixes and give their meanings.

1. *caruncle*—a small, fleshy, red mass or nodule
2. *racemulose*—in small clusters
3. *subareolar*—situated or occurring beneath the mammary areola
4. *ostiolar*—pertaining to an ostiole
5. *locelli*—small compartments of an ovary
6. *interauricular*—located between the auricles of the heart
7. *lunula*—the white, semilunar area of the nail near the root; the thin, crescentic area of a semilunar valve of the heart
8. *calculus*—a solid concretion composed chiefly of mineral substances and salts found principally in ducts, passages, etc.
9. *capsuliferous*—with, or forming, a capsule
10. *fibrillate*—to form fibers; in the case of muscular fibers, to quiver
11. *cuticle*—a horny or chitinous, sometimes calcified, layer formed by and covering an epithelium; a popular term for epidermis
12. *peduncle*—a narrow part acting as a support
13. *particulate*—composed of particles
14. *acidulous*—slightly sour
15. *plumule*—a primary bud on epicotyl; a plumula, or adult down feather
16. *multilocular*—having many cells or chambers
17. *rimulose*—having many small clefts
18. *calcivorous*—applies to plants which live on limestone

19. *funicle*—a slender cord

20. *acicular*—needlelike; shaped like a needle

21. *dextraural*—right-eared; pertaining to the right ear

22. *carnivorous*—meat-eating

23. *folliculose*—having follicles, or small sacs

24. *aculeate*—in botany, armed with prickles, as the rose or other brier; in zoology, having a sting

MORE WORDS TO WORK WITH

acid	cutization	multicapsular
acuity	destropedal	omnivorous
acute	dislocate	ostial
areolar	fibroid	pedometer
aural	fissiped	Pellicularia
bicapsular	folliculitis	piscivorous
binaural	funambulist	plumiped
biped	hypocalcemia	quadruped
calcifuge	incarnate	raceme
calculate	lactivorous	sanguivorous
capsular	locellate	subcutaneous
centipede	lunar	tripartite
cutidure	lunatic	tririmose
	monaural	

LESSON 30.   Latin Suffixes VII

Learn the following suffixes and their meanings.

1. A. *-ory,* "place for," "apparatus"

    DORMIT-, "to sleep"   + *-ory*   dormitory
    LAVAT-, "to wash"   + *-ory*   lavatory

   B. *-orium,* "place for," "apparatus"

    AUDIT-, "to hear"   + *-orium*   auditorium
    SANAT-, "to heal"   + *-orium*   sanatorium

2. A. *-ary,* "place for," "apparatus"

    MORTU-, "dead person"   + *-ary*   mortuary

LIBR-, "book"	+ -ary	library
in- + FIRM-, "strong"	+ -ary	infirmary

B. -arium, "place for," "apparatus"

AQU-, "water"	+ -arium	aquarium
SAN-, "healthy" + -ity	+ -arium	sanitarium
HERB-, "plant"	+ -arium	herbarium

3. A. -y, "quality of," "state of," "act of"

MISER-, "wretched"	+ -y	misery
MODEST-, "modest"	+ -y	modesty
per- + JUR-, "to swear"	+ -y	perjury

B. -ia, "quality of," "state of," "act of"

NEUR-, "nerve" + ALG-, "pain" + -ia	neuralgia
in- + SOMN-, "sleep" + -ia	insomnia
a- + SON-, "sound" + -ia	asonia

NEW BASES

Learn the following bases and their meanings.

1. ANS-, "jug handle," "loop" *(ansa)*
    ansa—loop, as of certain nerves
    ansa cervicalis—a nerve loop in the neck

2. DIGIT-, "finger," "toe" *(digitus)*
    digital—pertaining to a finger or toe
    digitate—having parts arranged like the fingers in a hand; with
        fingers
    digitipartite—having leaves divided in a handlike pattern
    digitule—any small, fingerlike process
    sexdigitate—with six fingers or toes
    impardigitate—having an uneven number of fingers or toes

3. FORMIC-, "ant" *(formica)*
    formic acid—a colorless acid which occurs in ants and some
        plants
    formicide—a substance used for destroying ants
    formication—an abnormal sensation of insects crawling on the
        skin; paresthesia

4. HAUST-, "to draw out," "to drink"

haustellum—a proboscis adapted for sucking

haustrum—one of the pouches or sacculations in the intestines

haustorium—an organ of certain parasitic protozoa by which they attach themselves to the host

5. MENT-, "mind" *(mens)*

mentation—the mechanism of thought; mental activity

menticide—the murder of the mind; a metaphorical term for the systematic attempt to break down a person's mental organization, to destroy his standards of values and ideals and induce radically different behavior patterns; approximately synonymous with brainwashing

mentalism—the doctrine that there is a distinct group of conscious or mental phenomena not reducible to physical phenomena

6. NERV-, "nerve," "vein of insect wing or leaf" *(nervus)*
(gen.) enervating

innervation—nerve distribution; vital nerve force

laterinerved—with lateral veins

rectinerved—with veins or nerves straight

trinervate—having three veins or ribs running from the bast to the margin of a leaf

nervure—one of the riblike structures which support membranous wings of insects; the branches of the tracheal system; a leaf vein

abnerval—away from a nerve; denoting the direction of an electric current passing through muscle fibers away from point of entrance of the nerve

7. PECTOR-, "breast" *(pectus)*

pectoral—pertaining to the chest; in the chest region

mediopectoral—applies to the middle part of the sternum

pectoriloquy—exaggerated bronchophony, in which there is distinct transmission of articulate speech in addition to increased intensity of the voice sounds

8. PIL-, "hair" *(pilus)*
(gen.) caterpillar

neuropile—in ganglia, as of the earthworm, a network of processes, as of ociation, motor and sensory neurons *piliferous*—bearing or producing hair

pilose—hairy, downy

pilomotor—nonmyelinated muscle fibers which cause movement of hair follicles

pilimiction—the passing of urine containing hairlike filaments

pilocystic—pertaining to encysted tumors containing hair and fat

9. PISC-, "fish" *(piscis)*

piscine—of, relating to, having the characteristics of fish

Piscidia—a genus of shrubs named for the fact that the leaves and bark poison fish when thrown into the water

piscivorous—fish-eating

10. PRESS-, "to press"

(gen.) depression, impression, repress, oppression

adpressed—closely applied to the surface

depressomotor—any nerve which lowers muscular activity

obcompressed—flattened in a vertical direction

pressoreceptor—a nerve ending located in the wall of the carotid sinus and aortic arch which is sensitive to stretching induced by changes of blood pressure within the vessels or direct pressure from without

11. ROD-, ROS-, "to gnaw"

corrosive—a substance which destroys organic tissue by chemical means or by inflammation

erosion—an eating, gnawing or wearing away

12. SEB-, "grease," "tallow" *(sebum)*

sebum—the secretion of the sebaceous glands of the skin

sebaceous—pertaining to sebum; secreting sebum

sebiparous—secreting fatty matter

dyssebacia—the plugging of the sebaceous glands, especially around the nose, with a dry, yellowish material

seborrhea—a functional disease of the sebaceous glands, characterized by an excessive secretion or disturbed quality of sebum

13. SENS-, SENT-, "to feel," "to perceive"

(gen.) sentence, presentiment, sensual, consent, assent, dissent

sensile—capable of affecting a sense

sentient—cells that are sensitive and perceptive

sensiferous—receiving or conveying sense impressions

consensual—applies to involuntary action correlated with voluntary action

sensilla—a small sense organ

pressosensitive—stimulated by change in blood pressure, as nerve endings in the carotid sinus

14. SOL-, "sun" *(sol)*

insolation—exposure to the sun's rays

solarization—the application of solar or electric light for therapeutic purposes

Solasteridae—a family of starfishes, typically brightly colored and having numerous arms

15. SOMN-, "sleep" *(somnus)*

hypersomnia—excessive sleepiness

somnifacient—a medicine producing sleep; a hypnotic

somnifugous—driving away sleep

16. SQUAM-, "scale" *(squama)*

squamous—applies to simple epithelium of flat, nucleated cells; scaly or pavement epithelium

esquamate—having no scales

squamiferous—bearing scales

squamulate—having minute scales

parietosquamosal—pertaining to the parietal bone and the squamous portion of the temporal bone

17. TER(R)-, "earth" *(terra)*

(gen.) terrestrial, interment, territory, Mediterranean, terrier, subterranean

terraneous—applies to land vegetation

terricolous—living in the earth

Terramycin—trademark for oxytetracycline

18. UTER-, "womb" *(uterus)*

utricle or *utriculus*—an air bladder of aquatic plants; the membranous sac of the ear labyrinth

Utricularia—a genus of aquatic plants having saclike ascidia that serve as animal traps

uterogestation—the part of the gestation period passed in the uterus *uterismus*—uterine contraction of a spasmodic and painful character

19. VACU-, "empty" *(vacuus)*

vacuole—one of the spaces in cell protoplasm containing air, sap or partially digested food

vacuome—the vacuolar system of a single cell

vacuolisation—the formation of vacuoles

20. VAS-, "vessel" *(vas)*
(gen.) vase

vascular—consisting of or containing vessels adapted for transmission or circulation of fluid

ideovascular—pertaining to circulatory changes induced by a mental image

vasodilation—relaxing or enlarging the vessels

vasifactive—producing new blood vessels

cardiovascular—pertaining to the heart and blood vessels

vasoneurosis—a psychoneurosis which partially expresses itself by disturbance of the vasomotor system; angioneurosis

EXERCISE

List the prefixes, bases and suffixes and give their meanings.

1. *amentia*—subnormal mental development; especially congenital intellectual incapacity

2. *dementia*—deterioration or loss of the intellectual faculties, the reasoning power, etc.

3. *haustellate*—having a proboscis adapted for sucking

4. *insomnia*—the inability to sleep

5. *formicarium*—an ants' nest, particularly an artificial arrangement for purposes of study

6. *haustorium*—an outgrowth of the stem, root or hyphae of certain parasitic plants which serves to draw food from the host plant, such as a sucker

7. *sensorium*—the seat of sensation or consciousness; the entire nervous system with sense organs

8. *terrarium*—a vivarium for terrestrial animals; a fully enclosed,

predominantly glass container for indoor cultivation of moisture-loving plants

9. *solarium*—a room for exposure of the body to sunlight

10. *piscicolous*—living within fishes, as certain parasites

11. *tentorium*—a chitinous framework supporting the brain of insects; a transverse fold of dura mater, ossified in some mammals, between the cerebellum and occipital lobes of brain

12. *squamella*—a small scale or bract

13. *squamelliform*—resembling a squamella

14. *pilosebaceous*—relating to the hair and the sebaceous glands

15. *pilonidal*—pertaining to or containing an accumulation of hairs in a cyst

16. *intrauterine*—within the uterus

17. *epilate*—to remove hair by the roots by the use of forceps, chemical means or roentgen therapy

18. *evacuate*—to empty, especially the bowels

19. *erose*—having an irregularly notched margin; applies to a leaf or a bacterial colony

20. *expectoration*—ejection of material from the mouth

21. *expectorant*—a remedy that promotes or modifies expectoration

22. *vasopressin*—a hormone of the posterior lobe of the pituitary gland which stimulates plain muscle by constricting arteries and raising blood pressure

23. *enervose*—having no veins; applies to certain leaves

24. *extravasation*—the passing of a body fluid from its proper place, as blood into surrounding tissues after rupture of a vessel

25. *digitinervate*—having veins radiating from the base, like fingers of a hand, with usually five or seven veins; applies to leaves

26. *appressorium*—an adhesive disk, as of a haustorium or sucker

27. *ansate*—having a handle; handle-shaped; loop-shaped; ansiform

MORE WORDS TO WORK WITH

acardionervia	formicivorous	sebolith
ansiform	genupectoral	solar
denervation	haustration	solstice
depilatory	haustus niger	somnambulism
depressant	hypersensitivity	somniloquism
desquamation	insensibility	somnolent
digitalis	interdigitation	squamation
digitigrade	mental	tectorium
exhaust	nervule	terrigerous
express	pisciculture	vacuum
extrasensory	pisciform	vasculum
extrauterine	retro-uterine	vasodentine
Formica	rodent	

LESSON 31.   Latin Suffixes VIII

Learn the following suffixes and their meanings.

1. *-itude,* "quality of," "state of" *(-itudo)*

LONG-, "long"	+ *-itude*	longitude
MULT-, "many"	+ *-itude*	multitude
GRAT-, "grateful"	+ *-itude*	gratitude

2. *-ity (-ety, -ty),* "quality of," "state of" *(-itas)*

GRAV-, "heavy"	+ *-ity*	gravity
DEXTER-, "right"	+ *-ity*	dexterity
BREV-, "short"	+ *-ity*	brevity

3. *-ance, -ancy; -ence, -ency,* "quality of being," "state of being" *(-antia, -entia)*

This suffix is actually a combination of *-ant, -ent,* indicating the present participle (Lesson 27), and *-y,* "quality of" (Lesson 30). Similarly *-(u)lence,* "state or quality of being full of," as in *virulence,* is a combination of *-(u)lent,* "full of" (Lesson 26) and *-y,* "quality of."

VIGIL-, "to watch"	+ *-ance*	vigilance
HESIT-, "to stick"	+ *-ancy*	hesitancy

e- + LOQU-, "to speak"		+ *-ence*	eloquence
in- + NOC-, "to harm"		+ *-ence*	innocence
FLU-, "to flow"		+ *-ency*	fluency

4. *-or,* "he who," "that which" *(-or)*

MOT-, "to move"		+ *-or*	motor
VICT-, "to conquer"		+ *-or*	victor
in- + CIS-, "to cut"		+ *-or*	incisor

NEW BASES

Learn the following bases and their meanings.

1. ADIP-, "fat" *(adeps)*

    adipocellulose—cellulose with a large amount of suberin, as cork tissue (suberin—a waxy substance developed in a thickened cell wall

    adipoleucocyte—a leukocyte containing fat droplets or wax, as in insects

    adipocele—a true hernia with hernial sac, containing only fatty tissue, also called lipocele

    adipopexis—fixation of fats; storage of fats

    adiposis—corpulence, obesity; excessive accumulation of fat in the body, local or general

    adiposogenital dystrophy—a combination of obesity and retarded development of sex glands resulting from impaired function of pituitary and hypothalamus

2. CALL-, "hard skin" *(callus)*

    callous—pertaining to an area of hardened and thickened skin, a callus

    corpus *callosum*—a structure of white matter in the brain

    procallus—the organized blood clot which forms in an early stage of repair of a fractured bone

3. CRE-, CRESC-, CRET-, "to grow"
    (gen.) increment, concrete, crescent, cescendo

    concrescence—a growing together of the roots of two teeth; a process by which the formative embryonic cells of the germ ring converge and fuse at the blastopore

    accretion—growth by external addition of new matter

    intercrescence—a growing into each other, as of tissue

concrement—concretion; a calculus; a union of parts normally separate, as fingers

4. FA-, FAT-, "to speak"
(gen.) affable, ineffable, fable, preface

confabulation—the fabrication of ready answers and fluent recitals of fictitious occurrences; generally, a component of the amnestic syndrome

infant—a child, usually up to two years; in Latin, literally "without speech"

5. FLU-, FLUX-, "to flow"; FLUVI-, "river" *(fluvius)*
(gen.) influence, fluency, influx, flux

confluent—running together; the opposite of discrete; in anatomy, coalesced or blended; applied to two or more bones originally separate

fluviatile—growing in or near streams; inhabiting and developing in streams (applies to certain insect larvae); caused by rivers (applies to deposits)

fluvioterrestrial—found in streams and in the land beside them

effluvium—body odor; that which emanates from an animal body, especially an ill-smelling emanation

ossifluence—osteolysis; resorption of bone; degeneration of bone

reflux—a return flow, as in a reflux condenser, which returns the condensate to the original fluid

afflux—flow of blood or other fluid to a part

6. FOSS-, "ditch," "trench," "to dig" *(fossa)*

fossa—a pit or trenchlike depression

fossette—a small pit; a socket containing the base of the antennule in arthropods

fossula—a small fossa; small pit

fossorial—adapted for digging; applies to the claws and feet of animals

fossiform—having the form of a fossa

7. MAGN-, "large," "great" *(magnus)*
(gen.) magnate, magnanimous, magniloquent

magnify—cause to appear larger

magniscope—a variety of chromophotograph

8. MAMM-, "breast" *(mamma)*

mammillary—nipple-shaped; pertaining to the nipple; shaped like a breast

mammiferous—developing mammae; milk-secreting; mammalian

mammillitis—inflammation of the mamilla, or nipple

mamelon—one of three elevations on the incisal edge of a recently erupted or little-worn incisor tooth

mammose—with teat-shaped processes

mammotropin—prolactin

9. MORT-, "death" *(mors)*
    (gen.) immortal, mortuary, mortgage, amortize, mortician

    abmortal—flowing away from the dead or dying toward the living tissue; applied to electric currents generated in an injured organ, as a muscle

    mortal—liable to death; causing death

    mortality—the quality of being mortal; the death rate

10. NOC-, NOX-, "harm" *(noxa)*

    anociassociation—an anesthetizing procedure whereby surgical shock, fear and postoperative neuroses are minimized greatly by excluding most of the painful and harmful stimuli

    nocifensor—efferent fibers which release chemical substances at their terminals, thus stimulating pain endings

    nociperception—perception of pain by the central nervous system

11. PAT-, "to spread or lie open"

    patent—open, exposed

    patulent—spread open; expanding

    patella—the kneecap or elbow cap

    prepatent period—the period in parasitic disease between the introduction of the organism and its demonstration in the body

12. PET-, PETIT-, "to seek"
    (gen.) petition, repetition, petulant, impetuous, competition

    impetigo—an acute inflammatory disease of the skin

    rectipetality—the tendency to rectilinear growth; autotropism

    acropetal—ascending; applies to leaves, flowers or roots developing successively from an axis so that the youngest arise at the apex

calcipete—a calcicole; a calciphil plant

13. PROPRI-, "one's own" *(proprius)*

(gen.) appropriate, expropriate, impropriety

propriogenic—applies to effectors other than muscles, or organs which are both receptors and effectors

propriospinal—pertaining wholly to the spinal cord; applies to fibers

proprietary—any chemical, drug or similar preparation used in the treatment of disease, if such an article is protected against free competition, or process of manufacture, by secrecy, patent, copyright or other means

proprium—those aspects of personality, collectively, that seem peculiarly one's own, which make for individuality and inward unity

14. SEC-, SEG-, SECT-, "to cut"

resection—the operation of cutting out, as the removal of a segment or section of an organ

palmatisect—palmate, with divisions nearly to the base

exsection—excision

transection—a section made across the long axis of a part, as transection of the spinal cord

sectorial—formed or adapted for cutting, as certain teeth

secondont—furnished with teeth adapted for cutting

15. SED- (-SID-), SESS-, "to sit," "to settle"

(gen.) reside, president, assiduous, session, insidious

insessorial—adapted for perching

obsession—an idea or emotion that persists in an individual's mind in spite of any conscious attempt to remove it

residual—pertaining to that which cannot be evacuated or discharged, as residual air in the lungs, residual urine in the bladder

16. SET-, "bristle" *(seta)*

seta—any bristlelike structure, as the sporophore of liverworts and mosses

setiger—a segment or process bearing bristles

setula—a fine bristle

setobranchia—a tuft of setae attached to gills of certain decapods

unisetose—bearing one bristle

setation—a covering or growth of setae

17. TRACT-, "to draw," "to drag"
(gen.) tractor, attractive, detract

traction—the act of drawing or pulling

distractile—widely separate; usually applies to long-stalked anthers

tractellum—a flagellum of forward end of Mastigophora, or of zoospores, with circumductory motion

protract—to extend in time; in anatomy, to extend or protrude a part of the body, as the tongue or mandible; to draw forward

cephalotractor—obstetric forceps

18. TUBER-, "swelling" *(tuber)*

tuber—a thickened, fleshy, underground stem with surface buds; a rounded protuberance

tubercle—a small nodule; a rounded prominence on the bone; a lesion produced by the tubercle bacillus

tubercular—characterized by the presence of small nodules or tubercles; often used erroneously to denote state of having tuberculosis

tuberiform—resembling or shaped like a tuber

tuberculoma—a conglomerate, caseous tubercle, usually solitary, which has attained such a size as to suggest the appearance of a tumor

tuberin—a simple protein of the globular type which occurs in potatoes

19. VEH-, VECT-, "to carry"
(gen.) vehement

advehent—afferent; carrying to an organ

revehent—applies to vessels carrying blood back from excretory organs

convection—a transmission or carrying, as of heat

vection—the conveyance of disease germs from the sick to the well

20. VIT-, "life" *(vita)*

vitalism—the theory that the activities of a living organism are under the guidance of an agency which has none of the attributes of matter or energy *intravital*—occurring during life, as intravital staining of cells

supravital staining—a method whereby cells may be stained and studied in the living state

EXERCISE

List the prefixes, bases and suffixes and give their meanings.

1. *adiposity* or *adiposis*—corpulence, obesity
2. *callosity*—a circumscribed area of thickened skin due to friction or pressure
3. *inappetence*—loss of appetite or desire
4. *potency*—having power; effectiveness
5. *excrescence*—an abnormal outgrowth upon the body
6. *retractor*—a surgical instrument for holding back the edges of a wound to give access to deeper parts or regions
7. *circumfluence*—in Protozoa, ingestion by protoplasm flowing toward food and surrounding it after contact
8. *vector*—a carrier, as many invertebrate hosts, of pathogenic organisms
9. *cutisector*—an instrument for removing bits of the skin
10. *natimortality*—proportion of stillbirths to the general birth rate
11. *protuberance*—a knoblike, projecting part
12. *tuberosity*—a protuberance on a bone
13. *sedentary*—not free-living; applies to animals attached by a base to some substratum; not migratory
14. *magnitude*—spacial quality or size; number representing the brightness of a celestial body
15. *sessile*—sitting directly on a base without support, stalk, pedicel or peduncle; attached, stationary
16. *setaceous*—bristlelike; set with bristles
17. *infanticide*—the murder of an infant
18. *proprioceptor*—a receptor located in a muscle tendon, joint or vestibular apparatus whose reflex function is locomotor or postural
19. *mammillated*—covered with nipplelike protuberances

20. *sectile*—capable of being cut

21. *nociceptor*—a receptor for painful stimuli

22. *patulous*—expanded; open

23. *fossulet*—a long, narrow depression

24. *vitality*—the condition of being alive

25. *cerebripetal*—afferent; transmitting or transmitted from the periphery to the brain

MORE WORDS TO WORK WITH

abstraction
accrescent
adipocere
antivivisection
appetite
bisect
centripetal
contractile
diffluence
devitalize
dissect
effluent
extract
fossil
infantilism

influenza
innocent
innocuous
insect
insectivorous
magnification
mammal
mammary
mortification
noxious
obnoxious
postmortem
prepatellar
propriate
prosector

retractile
secant
section
sedation
sedimentation
segment
setuliform
setirostral
subcallosal
subsidiary
tuberculosis
tuberculous
vehicle
vitamin

LESSON 32.   Latin Suffixes IX

Learn the following suffixes and their meanings.

1. *-ion*, "act of," "state of," "result of the act of" *(-io)*

ACT-, "to do"	+ *-ion*	action
com- + MOT-, "to move"	+ *-ion*	commotion
in- + CIS-, "to cut"	+ *-ion*	incision

2. *-ure,* "act of," "result of the act of" *(-ura)*

RUPT-, "to break"	+ *-ure*	rupture
CAPT-, "to seize"	+ *-ure*	capture

FRACT-, "to break"	+ -ure	fracture

3. *-us,* "act of," "result of the act of" *(-us)*

pro- + SPECT-, "to look"	+ -us	prospectus
con- + SENS-, "to feel"	+ -us	consensus
im- + PET-, "to seek"	+ -us	impetus

4. *-or,* "state of," "result of the act of" *(-or)*

TUM-, "to swell"	+ -or	tumor
PALL-, "to be pale"	+ -or	pallor
ERR-, "to wander"	+ -or	error

NEW BASES

Learn the following bases and their meanings.

1. CAV-, "hollow" *(cavus)*

   cavicorn—hollow-horned; applies to certain ruminants

   saxicavous—applies to rock-borers, as some molluscs; lithophagous

   intercavitary—within a cavity

   cavitoma—a series of changes in cotton fiber involving loss of strength and resulting from the activities of microorganisms

   portocaval or *portacaval*—pertaining to the portal vein and the inferior vena cava

   cavernous—having hollow spaces

2. COCT-, "to cook," "to boil"

   concoction—preparation made by combining different crude ingredients

   coctostable or *coctostabile*—able to withstand the temperature of boiling water without change

   coctoprecipitin—a precipitin produced in an animal by immunization with a boiled antigen, such as serum protein

3. CUT-, CUSS-, "to shake," "to strike"

   concussion—shock; the state of being shaken; a severe shaking or jarring of a part

   percussion—the act of firmly tapping the surface of the body with a finger or a small hammer to elicit sounds or vibratory sensations of diagnostic value *repercussion*—a driving in, or dispersion of, a tumor or eruption

4. DOL-, "to feel pain," "to cause pain"
(gen.) dolorous, Dolores, doleful, condolence

dolorogenic—possessing the quality of pain; causing or arousing pain

indolent—sluggish; usually applied to slowness in healing or growing, as an indolent ulcer; in medicine, causing little or no pain, as an indolent tumor

doloriferous—obsolete term for that which produces pain

5. EBURN-, "ivory" *(ebur, eburnus)*

eburneous—ivory white; white more or less tinged with yellow

eburnitis—increased hardness and density of the tooth enamel

eburnean—resembling ivory in color

6. FENESTR-, "window," "opening" *(fenestra)*
(gen.) defenestration

fenestrate—having small perforations or transparent spots (applies to insect wings); having numerous perforations (applies to leaves and dissepiments)

fenestrule—small opening between the branches of a polyzoan colony

craniofenestria—congenital bony defect involving the total thickness of the skull; lacuna skull

Fenestella—a genus of bryozoans whose colonies form lacelike patterns

7. GLUTIN-, "glue" *(gluten)*

glutinous—viscid, gluelike

agglutinin—an antibody occurring in a normal or immune serum which, when added to a suspension of its homologous, particulate antigen, causes the antigen elements to adhere to one another, resulting in clumps

agglutinogen—an antigen which, when injected into the animal body, stimulates the formation of a specific agglutinin

heteroagglutinin—an agglutinin of normal blood having the property of agglutinating foreign cells, including the blood corpuscles of other species of animals *gluten*—a mixture of proteins found in the seeds of cereals, which confers the property of toughness to dough

8. HI-, HIAT-, "to stand open"

dehiscence—the spontaneous opening of an organ or structure along certain lines in a definite direction

indehiscent—not splitting at maturity; applies to certain fruits

hiatus—a space or opening

9. I-, IT-, "to go"
(gen.) initial, sedition, ambitious, exit, obituary

concomitant—accompanying

ambitus—the outer edge or margin; outline of an echinoid shell viewed from the apical pole

abient—tending away from the source of stimulus

adient—tending toward the source of stimulus

10. LAMIN-, "thin plate" *(lamina);* LAMELL-, dimin. *(lamella)*

lamella—a plate or layer

lamination—arrangement in plates or layers; an operation in embryostomy consisting in cutting the skull in slices

lamellicorn—having antenna joints expanded into flattened plates

lamellirostral—having the inner edge of the bill bearing lamellalike ridges

laminiplantar—having scales of metatarsus meeting behind in a smooth ridge

laminectomy—surgical removal of one or more neural laminas of the vertebrae

lamellule—a small lamella

Laminaria—genus of kelp with smooth stipe and flat blade

11. LAT-, "broad," "wide" *(latus)*
(gen.) dilation

Vasodilan—tradename for a vasodilator for symptomatic relief in peripheral vascular diseases and cerebrovascular insufficiency

latiplantar—having the hind tarsal surface rounded

latisquamate—broad-scaled

12. LIG-, "to bind"
(gen.) obligation, oblige

ligament—a band of tough, flexible connective tissue

bicolligate—with two stretches of webbing on the foot

ligature—a cord or thread for tying vessels; the act of tying or binding

ligation—the operation of tying vessels with a ligature

alligation—the act of attaching or the state of being attached

13. MEAT-, "to go," "to pass"

meatus—an opening or passage

suprameatal—applies to triangle and spine over external acoustic meatus

meatitis—inflammation of the wall of a meatus

14. MIT(T)-, MIS(S)-, "to send," "to let go"
(gen.) commit, remittance, transmission, demise, remiss

emissary—any venous channel through the skull connecting the venous sinuses with the diploic veins and veins of the scalp

intromission—insertion, the act of putting in, the introduction of one body into another

15. PLEX-, "to interweave," "to braid"
(gen.) complexion

plexus—a network of interlacing nerves or anastomosing blood vessels or lymphatics

complex—in psychiatry, a group of ideas with strong emotional tone which have been transferred to the unconscious; a combination of symptoms or related factors

implex—endoplica or infolding of integument for muscle attachment in insects

plexiform—resembling a plexus or network

plexodont—having molar teeth with complicated crown patterns and multiple roots

16. PUNG-, PUNCT-, "to prick," "point" *(punctum)*
(gen.) compunction, punctuate, punctilious

punctual—relating to a point

punctate—dotted; full of minute points

punctulate—covered with very small dots or holes

punctiform—having the nature or qualities of a point; seeming to be located at a point, as a punctiform sensation; in bacteriology, very minute colonies *pungent*—ending in a rigid and sharp point

puncturation—the act or process of puncturing; the form or arrangement of punctures

17. RIG-, "to be stiff"

rigid—stiff or hard

rigescent—becoming rigid

rigiditas—stiffness, rigidity

18. RUB(R)-, "red" *(ruber)*

bilirubin—a reddish-yellow pigment of bile and blood

helicorubin—a red pigment of the gut of pulmonate gastropods

rubiginose—of a brownish-red tint; rust-colored

rubrospinal—applies to the descending tract or fasciculus of axons of the red nucleus in the ventrolateral column of the spinal cord

rubefacient—causing redness of the skin

rubella—German measles

rubescence—the state or quality of redness; a flushed or blushing countenance

erubescent—blushing red

19. SCRIB-, SCRIPT-, "to write"

(gen.) describe, prescribe, subscribe, conscription

circumscript—a marginal sphincter when sharply defined, as in sea anemones

superscription—the R$_x$ at the beginning of a prescription

inscription—the body or main part of a prescription; contains the ingredients and amounts to be used

subscription—the part of prescription containing directions to the pharmacist, indicating how the ingredients are to be mixed and prepared

20. VOLV-, VOLUT-, "to roll," "to turn"

(gen.) involve, revolution, devolve, volute

revolute—rolled backward, with the margin rolled toward lower side

involute—applies to leaves having the edges rolled inward at each side and to shells which are closely coiled

involucrum—in Hydromedusae, a protective cup into which nematocysts can be spirally retracted *obvolute*—overlapping; vernation when half of one leaf is wrapped round half of a similar leaf; half-equitant

obvolvent—bent downward and inward; applies to wings, elytra of insect

volvulus—a twisting of the bowel upon itself so as to occlude the lumen

EXERCISE

List the prefixes, bases and suffixes and give their meanings.

1. *decoction*—in pharmacology, a liquid preparation obtained by boiling medicinal vegetable substances in water

2. *dolor*—pain

3. *coitus*—sexual union between persons of opposite sexes

4. *eburnation*—an increase in the density of tooth or bone following some pathologic change

5. *succussion*—a shaking, especially of the individual, from side to side for the purpose of determining the presence of fluid in a cavity or hollow organ of the body

6. *delamination*—separation or splitting into layers, as in the dividing of cells to form new layers

7. *fenestration*—the presence of fenestrae or openings in a structure; an operation to create a permanently mobile window in the lateral semicircular canal, performed in cases of deafness caused by stapedial impediment of sound waves

8. *convolution*—a fold, twist or coil of any organ, especially any one of the prominent convex parts of the brain

9. *dilatation*—the state of being stretched; enlargement, as of a hollow part or organ

10. *plexure*—the act or process of weaving together

11. *obligate*—constrained, bound; not facultative, as an obligate anaerobe, which can live only as an anaerobe

12. *acupuncture*—puncture of the tissues with long, fine needles; used for centuries for relief of neuralgic pain or the release of fluid

13. *introitus*—an opening or orifice

14. *agglutination*—a joining together; an aggregation of suspended particles

15. *puncturation*—the act or process of puncturing or state of) being punctured; form or arrangement of punctures

16. *hiatal*—pertaining to a hiatus

17. *circumscription*—the state of being circumscribed; enclosed within narrow limits by an encircling boundary

18. *permeable*—affording passage; pervious

19. *sudoresis*—excessive sweating

20. *commissure*—strands of nerve fibers uniting, as structures in the two sides of the brain or spinal cords; the point of union of structures such as the lips and eyelids

21. *pruritus*—itching, an uncomfortable sensation due to irritation of a peripheral sensory nerve

22. *rubor*—redness due to inflammation

23. *rigor*—chill

24. *calorifacient*—heat-producing, usually applied to foods

25. *cavitation*—the formation of a cavity or cavities, as in tuberculosis of the lungs

26. *decubitus*—the recumbent or horizontal posture

27. *decubitus* ulcer—a bedsore

MORE WORDS TO WORK WITH

aditus	hiant	puncture
cavity	impermeable	remission
cerebellorubral	intermittent	rigidity
concave	intralamellar	rigorous
discutient	latirostral	rubeola
deglutinate	latitude	tic doloureux
dolorimeter	multilaminate	transcription
duplex	obligate	transient
ebur dentis	ordinopunctate	transitory
evolution	planoconcave	vasoligation
fenestellid	prescribe	voluble

LESSON 33.   Latin Suffixes X

Learn the following suffixes and their meanings.

1.   *-men, -min-,* "result of," "means of," "act of" *(-men)*

Various connective vowels appear before this suffix.

SPEC-, "to look at"	+ -(i)*men*		specimen
REG-, "to rule"	+ -(i)*men*		regimen
ACU-, "to sharpen"	+ *-men*		acumen
ACU-	+ *-min*	+ *-ate*	acuminate

2. A.   *-ment,* "result of," "means of," "act of"

Various connective vowels appear before this suffix.

LIG-, "to bind"	+ -(a)*ment*	ligament
FER-, "to boil"	+ *-ment*	ferment
ex- + CRE-, "to separate"	+ *-ment*	excrement

B.   *-mentum,* same meanings as *-ment*

MO(V)-, "to move" + *-mentum*	momentum

3. A.   *-ble, -bul,* "result of the act of," "means of," "place for"

FA-, "to speak"	+ *-ble*		fable
STA-, "to stand"	+ *-ble*		stable
MAND-, "to chew"	+ -(i)*ble*		mandible
MAND-	+ -(i)*bul*	+ *-ar*	mandibular

B.   *-bula, -bulum,* same meanings as *-ble, -bul*

PA(SC)-, "to feed" + *-bulum*	pabulum
in- + FUND-, "to pour" + -(i)*bulum*	infundibulum

4. A.   *-cle, -cul-,* "result of the act of," "means of"

SPECT-, "to look"	+ -(a)*cle*		spectacle
re- + CEPT-, "to take"	+ -(a)*cle*		receptacle
ob- + STA-, "to stand"	+ *-cle*		obstacle
TENT-, "to hold"	+ -(a)*cle*		tentacle
TENT-	+ -(a)*cul*	+ *-ar*	tentacular

B.   *-culum,* same meanings as *-cle, -cul-*

CURR-, "to run" + -(i)*culum*	curriculum
VIN(C)-, "to bind" + *-culum*	vinculum
TENT-, "to hold" + -(a)*culum*	tentaculum

5.   *-crum, -cr-,* "result of the act of," "means of"

FUL(C)-, "to prop up"	+ *-crum*		fulcrum
SIMUL-, "like"	+ *-(a)crum*		simulacrum
in- + VOLV-, "to roll"	+ *-crum*		involucrum
in- + VOLV-	+ *-cr-*	+ *-al*	involucral

6.   *-trum, -tr-,* "result of the act of," "means of"

SPEC-, "to look"	+ *-trum*		spectrum
ROS-, "to gnaw"	+ *-trum*		rostrum
CLAUS-, "to close"	+ *-trum*		claustrum
CLAUS-	+ *-tr-*	+ *-(o)phobia*	claustrophobia

NEW BASES

Learn the following bases and their meanings.

1. AG-, ACT-, "to do," "to drive," "to act"
(gen.) action, agile, transact, inactivity

    reagent—any substance involved in a chemical reaction

    abreaction—in psychoanalysis, the mental process by which repressed, emotionally charged material is freed and forgotten memories are brought to consciousness and relived with appropriate emotional release; catharsis

    cutireaction—a local skin reaction following the inoculation with or the application of extracts of pathogenic organisms

2. ALB-, "white" *(albus)*
(gen.) album

    albicant—tending to become white

    alburnum—sapwood or splint wood, i.e., the soft, white substance between the inner bark and true wood

    albiduria—passage of very pale, almost colorless urine

    albifaction—the act or process of blanching or rendering white

    albumin—a protein substance found in nearly every animal and some vegetable tissue

    noctalbuminuria—albumin in the night urine only

    Albugo—a genus of fungi causing the white rusts

3. CER-, "wax" *(cera)*

    adipocere—a waxlike substance which results from the decom-

position of dead animal tissues at suitable temperatures in the presence of moisture and in the absence
of air, as under earth or water

cereous—made of wax

cerosis—morbid condition of a membrane in which it seems to
consist of waxlike scales

ceraceous—waxy

ceriferous—wax-bearing; waxy

ceroid—a yellow-to-brown pigment found especially in the
liver in cirrhosis

4. FIL-, "thread" *(filum)*
(gen.) file, enfilade

filigerous—with threadlike outgrowths or flagella

filoplume—a delicate, hairlike feather with a long axis and a
few free barbs at the apex

filopodia—a threadlike pseudopodia found on some protozoa

filariasis—a diseased state due to the presence of nematode
worms of the super family Filarioidea

filipuncture—a method of treating aneurism by inserting wire
threads, hair or the like to promote coagulation

filaceous—rare word for that which consists of threads or
threadlike fibers or parts

5. FOR-, "to bore," "to pierce"

Foraminifera—an order of protozoans with calcarious shells
with minute openings for pseudopodia

foraminule—a minute foramen

transforation—the act of perforating the fetal skull

6. FOVE-, "pit" *(fovea)*

fovea—a small pit, fossa or depression; a small hollow at a leaf
base

foveate—pitted

foveiform—like a fovea

7. FUNG-, "mushroom," "fungus" *(fungus)*

fungistatic—inhibiting or preventing the growth of fungus

fungosity—fungous excrescence; fungous quality

fungivorous—fungus-eating animals and plants

8. GLOMER-, "ball of yarn" *(glomus)*

conglomeration—that which is made up of parts from various sources

glomerular—network of capillary blood vessels

glomus—a fold of the mesothelium containing a ball of blood vessels

glomerulus—the tuft of capillary loops projecting into the lumen of a renal corpuscle

glome or *glomerulus*—one of the two rounded prominences which form the backward prolongations of the frog of a horse's hoof

9. HAL-, HALIT-, "to breathe"

rehalation—the inhalation of air which has been inspired previously; sometimes used in anesthesia

inhalant—one who inhales; that which is inhaled

halitosis—the state of having offensive breath

10. MUC-, "mucus" *(mucus)*

mucific—mucus-secreting

mucigen or *mucinogen*—the substance of granules in cells of mucous membrane

mucocutaneous—pertaining to skin and mucous membrane

ovomucin—a glycoprotein from egg white

11. NUTRI-, NUTRIT-, "to nourish"

nutricism—a relationship of two animals with all the benefit to one partner

nutrient—that which affords nutrition

nutrilite—a substance which, in small amounts, functions in the nutrition of microorganisms

12. PALP-, "to touch," "to stroke"

palpation—the laying of the hand on a part of the body or the manipulation of a part for the purpose of ascertaining its condition or the condition of underlying organs

palpocil—a stiff, sensory filament attached to sense cells of Hydromedusae

palpus—feelers of Insecta

palpimacula—the sensory area on the labial palps of certain insects

impalpable—not capable of being felt; imperceptible to touch *palpitation*—any heart action of which the patient is conscious

13.   SEP-, SEPT-, "to separate," "wall" *(septum)*

septum—a partition; a dividing wall between two spaces or cavities

latiseptate—having a broad septum in the silicula

eseptate—not supplied with septa

septicidal—dividing through the middle of the ovary septa; dehiscing at the septum

septectomy—excision of part of the nasal septum

14.   SPIR-, "to breathe"
(gen.) spirit, conspire

aspirator—a negative pressure apparatus for withdrawing liquids from cavities

transpiration—exhalation of vapor through pores or stomata

suspiration—a sigh; the act of sighing

spirometer—an instrument for measuring the vital capacity or volumes of inhaled and exhaled air

15.   STRU-, STRUCT-, "to construct," "to build"
(gen.) obstruct, destruction, misconstrue, superstructure

obstruent—obstructing; tending to obstruct

ultrastructure—arrangement of ultramicroscopic particles

metastructure—ultramicroscopic organization

destrudo—the expression of the hypothesized death instinct

16.   TERMIN-, "end," "boundary" *(terminus)*
(gen.) interminable

abterminal—going from the end inward

atterminal—toward the terminal

indeterminate growth—growth of stem, branch or shoot not limited or stopped by growth of a terminal bud

paraterminal—near a terminal

17.   UMBR-, "shade," "shadow" *(umbra)*
(gen.) umbrella, umbrage, adumbrate

exumbral—pertaining to the rounded upper surface of a jelly fish

obumbrate—with some structure overhanging the parts so as partially to conceal them *subumbrella*—the concave inner surface of the medusoid bell

umbel—an arrangement of flowers or of polyps springing from a common center and forming a flat or rounded cluster

umbellule—a small or secondary umbel

umbellulate—arranged in umbels

umbraculum—any umbrellalike structure

Umbridae—a family of small, bottom-dwelling fresh-water fishes

18. UNGU-, "nail" (of finger or toe) *(unguis)*

unguiferate—having nails, claws or hooklike processes

unguitractor—a sclerite of an insect pretarsus that is partially invaginated in the tarsus

Unguiculata—Mammalia with nails or claws as distinguished from hoofed mammals and cetaceans

polyungia—the occurrence of supernumerary nails on fingers or toes; polyonychia

ungulus—diminutive of unguis hoof in Ungulata

19. VEL-, "veil," "covering" *(velum)*

velum—a membrane or structure similar to a veil

velar—situated near a velum

veliger—second stage in larval life of certain molluscs when the head bears a velum

velarium—the velum of certain Cubomedusae

velamen—a veil or membrane; a specialized, corky epidermis on aerial roots

20. VISCER-, "entrails" *(viscus)*

viscerosensory—relating to sensation in the viscera

viscerotrophic—pertaining to trophic changes induced by visceral conditions

viscerotonia—behavior counterpart of endomorphy of the somatotype characterized by sociability, relaxation and love of food

EXERCISE

List the prefixes, bases and suffixes and give their meanings.

1. *palpacle*—the tentacle of a dactylozooid or the palpon of Siphonophora

2. *exalbuminous*—without albumen; applies to seeds without endosperm or perisperm; exendospermous

3. *dissepiment*—the partition found in some compound ovaries, as in corals

4. *ceruminous*—pertaining to the cerumen, the wax of the ear

5. *spiracle*—the branchial passage between the mandibular and hyoid arches in fishes; the lateral branchial opening in tadpoles; the respiratory aperture behind the eye of skates, rays, etc.

6. *foramen*—the opening through coats of ovule; any small perforation

7. *umbraculiferous*—bearing an umbrella

8. *instrumentation*—the use of instruments in treating a patient

9. *perforatorium*—the acrosome; the body at the apex of the spermatozoon

10. *velaminous*—having a velamen; applies to roots

11. *agminate*—gathered into clumps or clusters

12. *nutriment*—nutritious material

13. *fungation*—the act of growing up rapidly, like a fungus, as certain pathologic growths

14. *filamentous*—composed of long, threadlike structures

15. *agglomerate*—grouped or clustered

16. *halitus*—a vapor, as that expired by the lungs

17. *coterminous*—having the same or coincident boundaries

18. *muculent*—rare term for that which is rich in mucus

19. *ambulacrum*—the locomotor tube foot of echinoderms

20. *foveolate*—having regular, small depressions

21. *excrementitious*—pertaining to excrement; fecal

22. *evisceration*—removal of internal organs

23. *subacuminate*—somewhat tapering

24. *subungual*—under a nail, claw or hoof; hyponychial

25. *duramen*—the hard, darker central region of a tree stem; the heartwood

26. *retinaculum*—a small, glandular mass to which an orchid pol-

linium adheres at dehiscence; a fibrous band which holds parts closely together; a minute, hooked prominence holding the egg sac in position in cirripedes, etc.

MORE WORDS TO WORK WITH

agitate
albino
biforous
cerolite
ceromancy
coagulate
dealbate
exhale
expiration
exterminate
filiform
foveation
fungicolous

glomerulonephritis
glomerulosclerosis
hyperactivity
imperforate
inhalator
inspiration
mucilage
mucin
mucopurulent
mucous
nutrition
pedipalp
perivisceral
react

reconstruction
respiratory
septifragal
sphygmopalpitation
terminate
terminology
umbraticolous
unguirostral
Ungulata
velamentum
velation
visceromotor
viscerotome

LESSON 34.   Latin Verb Suffixes

In addition to the verbal suffix -*ate*, which was treated in Lesson 12, Part I, there are also a number of other English verbal suffixes derived from Latin. Learn the following suffixes and their meanings.

1. -*fy*, "to make," "to cause"

    This is actually a form of the base FAC-, "to make."

    | TERR-, "frightened" | + -(i)*fy* | terrify |
    | LIQU-, "liquid" | + -(e)*fy* | liquefy |
    | PAC-, "peace" | + -(i)*fy* | pacify |

    Note that the adjective ending corresponding to -*fy* is -*fic*, "making," "causing."

    | TERR-, "frightened" | + -(i)*fic* | terrific |
    | PAC-, "peace" | + -(i)*fic* | pacific |

2. -*igate, -egate*, "to make," "to drive"

This is actually a form of the base AG-, "to do," "to drive."

MIT-, "soft"	+ -igate	mitigate
FUM-, "smoke"	+ -igate	fumigate
NAV-, "ship"	+ -igate	navigate
VARI-, "varied"	+ -egate	variegate

3. -esce, "to begin," "to be somewhat"

ex- + FERV-, "to bubble"	+ -esce		effervesce
con- + VAL-, "to be strong"	+ -esce		convalesce
ARBOR-, "tree"	+ -esce	+ -ent	arborescent

NEW BASES

Learn the following bases and their meanings.

1. CAUL-, "stem," "stalk" (caulis)

    caulicolous—applies to fungi growing on plant stems

    cauliflory—condition of having flowers arising from axillary buds on the main stem or older branches

    cauline—pertaining to a stem; applies to leaves growing on the upper portion of a stem

    caulocarpous—with a fruit-bearing stem

    caulome—the stem structure of a plant as a whole

    chylocaulous—with fleshy stems

    diplocaulescent—with secondary stems

    filicauline—with a threadlike stem

2. FLAV-, "yellow" (flavus)

    flavin—one of a group of yellow pigments isolated from various plant and animal sources

    riboflavin—a constituent of the vitamin B complex

    flavokinase—an enzyme that catalyzes the phosphorylation of riboflavin

    flavedo—yellowness of the skin

    biliflavin—a yellow coloring matter derivable from biliverdin

3. FLOCC-, "tuft, as of wool" (floccus)

    floccus—a tuft of wooly hairs on a plant

    flocculence—adhesion in small flakes, as of a precipitate

    floccose—covered with woollike tufts; applies to bacterial growths *flocculation*—coagulation or coalescence of finely divided or colloidal particles into larger particles, which precipitate

4. LABI-, LABR-, "lip" *(labium; labrum)*

labium—lip; liplike structure

labellum—the lower petal of an orchid; the small lobe beneath the labium in insects

bilabe—surgical instrument for removing foreign bodies from the urinary bladder through the urethra

labiogression—location of the anterior teeth in front of their normal position

labialism—the tendency to pronounce articulate sounds as if they were labial consonants, as *b, p, m*

labret—an ornament worn by some primitive people in a perforation of the lip

labrum—the upper or anterior lip of insects

5. LAT-, "to bear," "to carry"
   (gen.) relate, elated, translate

ablation—removal of a part by amputation, excision, etc.

sublation—removal; ablation

6. LEV-, "light" (in weight) *(levis)*
   (gen.) levity, lever

levator—that which elevates or raises

levitation—illusion of suspension of a body in the air performed by magicians; the subjective sense of floating or rising into the air without support, as in dreams or certain mental disorders

elevator—an instrument for lifting a part or for extracting the roots of teeth

7. LIGN-, "wood" *(lignum)*

ligneous—woody, of the nature of wood

lignivorous—wood-eating; applies to various insects

lignin—a complex substance which, associated with cellulose, causes the thickening of plant cell walls, and so forms wood

pyroligneous—pertaining to the destructive distillation of wood

lignite—a variety of coal intermediate between peat and

bituminous coal; applies especially when the texture of original wood is visible

8. LIQU-, "to be liquid"

colliquation—the breakdown of tissue, usually necrotic, so that it becomes liquefied

liquefaction—the change to a fluid form, usually of a solid tissue to a fluid or semifluid state

liquor—any of certain medicinal solutions, usually including aqueous solutions of nonvolatile substances; a British designation for any liquid

9. LUMIN-, "light" *(lumen)*

lumen—the cavity of a tubular part of an organ; the central cavity of a plant cell

luminosity—the property of emitting light

luminiferous—conveying or bearing light

sonoluminescence—the emission of light by various liquids when traversed by high-frequency sound or ultrasonic waves

triboluminescence—luminescence produced by friction

transillumination—illumination of an object by transmitted light; illumination of the paranasal sinuses by means of a light placed in the patient's mouth

10. MAN(U)-, "hand" *(manus)*

(gen.) manufacture, manuscript, emancipate, manicure

bimanous—having two hands; applies to certain primates

manubrium—a handlelike part, like the handle part of the malleus of the ear

manuduction—operation performed by the hands in surgical and obstetric practice

11. NIGR-, "black" *(niger)*

denigration—the act or process of rendering black

nigrometer—an instrument for measuring the intensity of black in pigments

nigrosine—any one of several dark blue or black aniline dyes

nigricant—blackish

12. OSS-, "bone" *(os)*

dermo-ossification—a bone formed in the skin

ossicle—any small bone

ossicular—pertaining to ossicles

ossifluence or *osteolysis*—resorption of bone; degeneration of bone

osselet—a hard nodule on the inner aspect of the horse's knee

perosseous—through bone

deossification—the absorption of bony material; the deprivation of the bony character of any part

13. PROXIM-, "near," "nearest"(*proximus*, "nearest the body")

proximal—in dentistry, surface of a tooth next to the adjacent tooth

cytoproximal—denoting that portion of a nerve fiber near its cyton

interproximal—in dentistry, between two adjacent teeth, as the interproximal space

proximolabial—pertaining to proximal and labial surfaces of a tooth

proximate—nearest, immediate, as proximate cause

14. SINISTR-, "left" *(sinister)*
(gen.) sinister

sinistrorse—applies to a spiral twining toward the left

sinistrogyration—turning or twisting to the left, as plane of polarization or a movement of the eye

sinistrotorsion—a twisting or turning toward the left

sinistrin—a levorotatory polysaccharide

15. SPIN-, "thorn," "spine" *(spina)*

infraspinous—beneath the spine of the scapula

spinulate—covered with spines

spinulation—a defensive spiny covering; the state of being spinulate

spinose—bearing many spines

spinocellular—pertaining to, or like, prickle cells

spination—distribution and arrangement of spines, as on an insect

16. STIP-, STIPIT-, "stalk" *(stipes)*

stipule—one of two membranes or foliaceous processes developed at the base of a leaf petiole

bistipulate—provided with two stipules

stipel—an outgrowth of leaflets resembling the stipule of a leafbase

stipitate—stalked

labiostipes—a portion of the basal part of insect labium

17. STRAT-, "layer" *(stratum)*

bistratose—with cells arranged in two layers

stratiform—applies to fibrocartilage coating osseous grooves

substratose—slightly or indistinctly stratified

stratosphere—the atmosphere above the tropopause, where temperature changes are small, and winds are essentially horizontal

stratigraphy—sectional radiography

18. TUM-, "to swell"

tumescent—swollen, enlarged

detumescence—subsidence of a swelling; subsidence of erectosexual organs following orgasm

tumefaction—a swelling, the act of swelling

tumentia—vasomotor disturbance characterized by irregular swellings, as in the legs and arms

19. VARI-, "varied," "changing," "spotted" *(varius)*

(gen.) various, invariable, variety

variole—a small pitlike marking found on various parts in insects; a foveola

variate—the variable quantity in variation; a character variable in quality or magnitude

varicella—chickenpox

varicelliform—characterized by vesicles resembling those of chickenpox

20. VENTR-, "belly" *(venter)*

(gen.) ventriloquism

biventer—having two bellies, as a muscle

biventral—applies to muscles of the biventer type; digastric

ventricle—a cavity or chamber, as of the heart or brain

ventral—pertaining to the belly; referring to the anterior aspect of the body

dorsiventral—pertaining to structures which stretch from dorsal to ventral surface

ventrad—toward the lower, or abdominal, surface

venter—abdomen; lower abdominal surface; protuberance, as
of muscle; a smooth concave surface

eventration—protrusion of abdominal viscera through the abdominal wall, as in ventral hernia

ventriculitis—inflammation of ependymal lining of the ven-
tricles of the brain; ependymitis

ventrose—having a belly or swelling like a belly; potbellied

EXERCISE

List the prefixes, bases and suffixes and give their meanings.

1. *acaulescent*—having a shortened stem
2. *spinulescent*—tending to be spiny
3. *efflorescence*—blossoming, time of flowering; bloom; spontaneous conversion of a crystalline substance into
   powder by loss of its water of crystallization; the
   eruption of an exanthematous disease
4. *nigrescent*—nearly black; blackish
5. *bioluminescence*—light production, as in many groups of animals, bacteria and fungi
6. *flavescent*—becoming yellow
7. *carnification*—alteration of tissue so that it resembles skeletal
   muscle in color and consistency; sometimes this affects the lungs
8. *variegated*—marked with different colors
9. *liquefaction*—conversion of material into liquid form
10. *ossify*—to turn into bone
11. *alleviation*—the modification of symptoms; lessening of pain
12. *lignescent*—developing the characteristics of woody tissue
13. *intumescence*—a swelling of any character whatever, as an
    increase of the volume of any organ or part of the
    body
14. *deliquescence*—the process of liquefaction by absorption of
    water from the atmosphere
15. *ramification*—the act or state of branching; a branch
16. *stratify*—to arrange in layers

17. *ingravescence*—an increase in weight or severity

18. *mortification*—old term for gangrene

19. *oblate*—flattened or depressed at poles

20. *exstipulate*—without stipules

21. *floccillation*—aimless picking and plucking at the bedclothes seen in delirious states, fevers and exhaustion; carphology

22. *dextromanual*—right-handed

23. *labiatiflorous*—having the corolla divided into two liplike portions

24. *sinistration*—a turning to the left; development of the dominance of the right side of the cerebral hemisphere in lefthanded persons; opposite of dextralization

25. *ventricumbent*—prone

26. *approximation*—the act or process of bringing together

MORE WORDS TO WORK WITH

ambisinistral	liquation	sinistrad
bilabiate	liquesce	sinistraural
Caulobacter	manipulate	stipellate
cerebrospinal	manual	subflavous
elevate	nigrities	substratum
illative	ossein	tumid
illuminate	osseous	tumor
labelloid	paraflocculus	variola
labiodental	proximad	ventral
labral	proximity	ventricose
lignicolous	sclerocauly	ventriduction

LESSON 35.   Latin Nouns

In this lesson we will treat Latin nouns which have found their way into English in unaltered form. You are already familiar with some of these words and with several of their different forms and endings: antenna, antennae; syllabus, syllabi; fungus, fungi; stratum, strata; genus, genera; appendix, appendices. These words have Latin endings, indicating *number, case, gender* and *declension*.

Number is a grammatical term referring simply to whether a word is singular or plural. In Latin, different endings are used to indicate the plural forms, just as in English, where *s* is generally used for this purpose.

Case is a grammatical term which refers to the way in which a noun is used in a sentence—whether it is the subject (nominative case), direct object (accusative case) or the possessor of something (genitive case). The various cases are indicated in Latin by different endings. We have something of this in English with our use of the forms *I* and *me*, as well as with the forms *who, whom* and *whose*, although our terminology is different (subjective, objective and possessive).

In studying Latin phrases, we will be interested mainly in the nominative and genitive forms, as in phrases like "right auricle of the heart," or "chamber of the eye." If a Latin word occurs by itself or as the subject of a phrase, it will be in the nominative case. The "of" relationship is indicated by the genitive case.

Gender is a grammatical term for sex. English uses a very simple system known as natural gender: male persons and animals are masculine, female persons and animals are feminine, and inanimate objects are neuter. Latin and most European languages make use of what is known as grammatical gender; i.e., it follows no natural system. Male persons and animals are masculine; female persons and animals are feminine, but some inanimate objects are masculine, some feminine and some neuter. Thus, in Latin, *vertebra* and *species* are feminine; *stratum* and *genus* are neuter; *musculus* and *oculus* ("eye") are masculine, but *cornea* is feminine. Knowledge of gender is important primarily in connection with adjectives, which must agree in gender with the noun they modify; thus, one finds *vertebra longa*, but *musculus longus*.

Declension denotes class. Latin nouns have been grouped into five declensions or classes with different sets of endings. Thus all first declension nouns have the same set of endings and so on. First and second declension nouns are presented below.

A. FIRST DECLENSION NOUNS

First declension nouns are for our purposes always feminine and have the following set of endings, which indicates their case and number.

sing.		plur.	
nom.	-a	-ae	
gen.	-ae	-arum	

Examples:

nom.	lingua ("tongue")	linguae ("tongues")
gen.	linguae ("of the tongue")	linguarum ("of the tongues")

There are no definite or indefinite articles in Latin, so *lingua* may be translated "tongue," "a tongue," or "the tongue," whichever seems more appropriate.

Translate the following phrases. Be sure to translate the genitive case by the preposition "of."

1. aqua camphorae
2. venae oculi
3. arcus costarum
4. agitator caudae
5. fistula corneae
6. decursus fibrarum (cerebralium)

B. SECOND DECLENSION NOUNS

There are two types of second declension nouns: those having the nominative singular ending in *-us,* which are masculine, and those having the nominative singular ending *-um,* which are neuter.

	sing.	plur.	sing.	plur.
nom.	-us	-i	-um	-a
gen.	-i	-orum	-i	-orum

Examples:

nom.	nervus	nervi	labium	labia
gen.	nervi	nervorum	labii	laborium

A few second declension masculine nouns have a nominative singular ending in *-er,* for example, *cancer,* but the rest of their endings follow the regular pattern.

Translate the following Latin phrases. Adjectives in parentheses may be omitted.

1. camera oculi
2. lobi cerebri
3. cervix uteri
4. flexor digitorum
5. pruritus ani
6. extensor digiti

7. defluvium capillorum

8. rigiditas articulorum

9. bursae musculi (longissimi) dorsi

10. nuclei nervi (facialis)

11. vena (obliqua) strii (sinistri)

12. lingula cerebelli

13. septum atriorum

14. vertex cranii

15. ligamentum colli costae

16. ansae nervorum (spinalium)

NEW BASES

Learn the following numerical bases and their meanings.

1. SEMI-, "half," "partly"
    semiplume—a feather with ordinary shaft but downy web
    semilunar—half-moon-shaped
    semicaudate—with a rudimentary tail

2. UN-, "one" *(unus)*
    (gen.) unique, uniform, unanimity
    unifoliate—with one leaf
    unilocular—one-celled; with one compartment
    uniparous—producing one offspring at a birth
    unipotent—cells which can develop into cells of one kind only
    unistrate—having only one layer

3. PRIM-, "first" *(primus)*
    (gen.) primary, prime, primrose, primitive
    primite—the first of any pair of individuals of a catenoid colony in pseudoconjugation of Gregarinida
    primibrach—in crinoids, all brachials up to and including the first axillary
    Primates—the highest order of the vertebrate class Mammalia; includes man, apes, monkeys and lemurs
    primigravida—a woman who is pregnant for the first time

4. SESQUI-, "one and one-half times"
    (gen.) sesquicentennial, sesquipedalianism
    sesquichloride—a compound of chlorine and another element containing three parts of chlorine and two of the other element
    sesquioxide—a compound of three parts of oxygen and two of another element

sesquidiploid—a triploid produced by a cross between tetraploid and diploid parents

5. DU-, "two" (duo)
(gen.) duet, dual, duplicate
duplicident—with two pairs of incisors in upper jaw, one behind the other
duodenal—pertaining to the duodenum (*duodenum*—that portion of the small intestine next to the pyloric end of
the stomach
duplicature—a circular fold near the base of protrusible portion of polyzoan polypide
conduplicate—applies to cotyledons folded to embrace the
radicle; applies to vernation when one half of leaf is
folded upon the other

6. BI-, BIN-, "two," "twice"
binate—growing in pairs
binary fission—reproduction by division of a cell in two approximately equal parts
bifid—forked, opening with a median cleft; divided nearly to
the middle line
bicipital—applies to biceps and to a rib with dorsal tuberculum
and ventral capitulum
bidenticulate—with two small teeth or toothlike processes
bistratose—with cells arranged in two layers
biventral muscle—muscle with two bellies separated by a
median tendon; digastric muscle

7. SECOND-, SECUND-, "second," "following" *(secundus)*
(gen.) secondary
secund—arranged on one side; applies to flowers or leaves on a
stem
secundiflorous—having flowers on one side of stem only
secundines—fetal membranes collectively; afterbirth
secundigravida—a woman pregnant the second time

8. TRI-, "three"
(gen.) tricycle, triangle, trivial, trident
tricostate—with three ribs
tridentate—having three toothlike divisions
trifid—cleft to form three lobes

9. TERTI-, "third"; TERN-, "three each"; TER-, "three times"

tertial or *tertiary*—applies to roots produced by secondary roots; applies to wing feather of humerus

tertiary—third; pertaining to third stage of a disease

ternate or *ternary*—arranged in threes; having three leaflets to a leaf; trifoliolate

ternatopinnate—having three pinnate leaves to each compound leaf

tertian—recurring every other day, as a tertian fever

tervalent or *trivalent*—having a valence of three; triple; used of chromosomes when three are present and associated in synapsis

ternary—consisting or based on three; pertaining to a crystal system in which three-sided forms occur; an alloy with three elements

10. QUADR(U)-, "four"

(gen.) quadrangle, quadruple, quadroon

quadrivalent—pertaining to association of four chromosomes

quadrijugate—applies to pinnate leaf having four pairs of leaflets

quadruped—a four-footed animal

11. QUART-, "fourth"; QUATERN-, "four each"

(gen.) quart, quarter

quaternary—applies to flower symmetry when there are four parts in a whorl

quaternate—in sets of four; applies to leaves growing in fours from one point

quartan—recurring every three days, as on first, fourth and seventh day

12. QUINQUE-, "five"

quinquetubercular—applies to molar teeth with five tubercles

quinquecostate—having five ribs on the leaf

quinquepartite—divided into five parts

13. QUINT-, "fifth"; QUIN-, "five each"

quinate—applies to five leaflets growing from one point

quinary—applies to flower symmetry in which there are five parts to a whorl *quintuplet*—one of five children born at one birth

14. SEX-, "six"; SEXT-, "sixth"
    (gen.) sextet, sexagenarian
    sexfid—cleft into six, as a calyx
    sextant—a maximum angle of sixty degrees
    Sexostiatae—group of spiders marked by six cardiac ostia

15. SEPT-, SEPTEM-, "seven"; SEPTIM-, "seventh"
    (gen.) September, septuagenarian, Septuagint
    septimal—based on the number seven
    septempartite—divided into seven parts
    septuplet—one of seven children born at one birth

16. OCT-, "eight"; OCTAV-, "eighth"
    (gen.) octet, octoroon, October, octogenarian, octave, octavo
    octant—one of eight cells formed by division of fertilized ovule
        in plants
    octane—the eighth member of the paraffin or marsh gas series
    octavalent—having a valence of eight

17. NOVEM-, "nine"; NON-, "ninth"
    (gen.) November, nonagenarian
    nonipara—woman who has had nine live births
    nonillion—ten to the thirtieth power
    nonan—having an exacerbation every ninth day

18. DECEM-, "ten"; DEC-, DECIM-, "tenth"
    (gen.) decimate, December
    deciliter—one-tenth of a liter
    decipara—a woman who has borne ten children
    decemfid—cleft into ten parts

19. CENT-, "hundred," "hundredth"
    (gen.) centennial, century, centurion, bicentennial
    centipede—elongated, segmented arthropods with many legs
    centinormal—having one-hundredth of normal strength
    centimeter—one-hundredth of a meter

20. MIL(L)-, "thousand," "thousandth"
    (gen.) millennium, mil, mile
    millimicron—one thousandth of a micron

millipede—myriopods constituting the class Diplopoda having numerous segments and legs

millimeter—one-thousandth of a meter

EXERCISE

List the prefixes, bases and suffixes and give their meanings.

1. *uniforate*—having only one opening
2. *semiligneous*—partially lignified; with stem woody only near the base
3. *primiparous*—pertaining to a woman bearing or giving birth to her first child
4. *bilocellate*—divided into two compartments
5. *duplicity*—the condition of being double
6. *quinquefid*—cleft into five parts
7. *bicolligate*—with two stretches of webbing on the foot
8. *octoradiate*—having eight rays or arms
9. *tricipital*—having three heads or insertions, as triceps
10. *decemjugate*—with ten pairs of leaflets
11. *quadrimaculate*—having four spots
12. *duodecimal*—of or relating to twelve or twelfths
13. *sexdigitate*—with six fingers or toes
14. *milliliter*—one-thousandth of a liter
15. *septifolious*—with seven leaves or leaflets
16. *binovular*—pertaining to two ova; dizygotic
17. *decempartite*—ten-lobed; divided into ten lobes
18. *unisetose*—bearing one bristle
19. *unicameral*—having only one cavity or chamber
20. *tricrural*—with three branches
21. *quadrumanous*—having hind feet, as well as front feet, constructed like hands, as most Primates except man
22. *bilateral*—having or relating to two sides
23. *sesquihora*—an hour and one-half

MORE WORDS TO WORK WITH

biped	million	semiovate
bisect	novemdecillion	septisyllabic
centiliter	octal	sesquisulfide
decemfoliate	octillion	sexangular
decibel	percent	sexidigital
decile	primine	sextigravida
decillion	quadrate	sextuplicate
decimal	quadrifoliate	trilacunar
decinormal	quadrilocular	triseptate
duipara	quartile	triternate
duodecimal	quinquelocular	unicorn
milligram	quintillion	uniflorous
millihenry	secundine	unilateral

LESSON 36.   Latin Third Declension Nouns

The third declension comprises masculine, feminine and neuter nouns. The endings are as follows:

	Masc. and Fem.		Neut.	
	sing.	plur.	sing.	plur.
nom.	—	*-es*	—	*-a (-ia)*
gen.	*-is*	*-um (-ium)*	*-is*	*-um (-ium)*

Examples:

nom.	radix	radices	foramen	foramina
gen.	radicis	radicum	foraminis	foraminum

There are three difficulties in connection with the third declension which are not encountered with the first two declensions.

1. There is usually a difference between the form of the nominative singular and the form of the base of the word which is used for the other cases and for English derivatives. This is not just a difference in endings, but in the spelling of the word, and this difference has a number of variants. It can be seen in some Latin words with which you are familiar, for example, *genus,* which has the plural *genera,* and *index* with the plural *indices,* as well as in other Latin words of the third declension, as, for instance, *caput* (gen., *capitis*), *adipositas* (gen., *adi-*

positatis) and *mons* (gen., *montis*). This difference in form accounts for instances in previous lessons when some of the bases differed from the actual Latin word found in parentheses.

2. There is no one ending for the nominative singular of the third declension as there is for the first two. *Cartilage, adipositas, flexor* and *radix* are all nominative singular. The endings in the other cases, however, are the same for all nouns of the third declension.

3. There is often no way of distinguishing gender in the third declension by means of endings. *Appendix* is feminine, while *fornix* is masculine.

Despite these problems, however, all is not chaos, and the third declension can to some extent be systematized. There are certain large groups of third declension nouns of similar form in the nominative singular and with similar differences between the nominative singular and the base used in the other cases. These patterns are listed below in the nominative singular and genitive singular, along with examples.

A. Masculine Nouns

> *-or, -oris:*   tumor, tumoris; flexor, flexoris

B. Feminine Nouns

> *-io, -ionis:*   articulatio, articulationis; impressio, impressionis
>
> *-itas, -itatis:*   extremitas, extremitatis; fragilitas, fragilitatis

C. Masculine and Feminine Nouns

> *-ix* or *-ex, -icis:*   radix, radicis; fornix, fornicis; index, indicis
>
> *-x, -cis:*   nux, nucis; calx, calcis
>
> *-o, -inis:*   margo, marginis; longitudo, longitudinis
>
> *-is, -is:*   pelvis, pelvis; cutis, cutis
>
> *-ns, -ntis:*   dens, dentis; pons, pontis; mons, montis

D. Neuter Nouns

> *-men, -minis:*   foramen, foraminis; lumen, luminis
>
> *-us, -eris* or *-oris:*   corpus, corporis; genus, generis; viscus, visceris

By no means can all third declension nouns be classified according to the above system, as, for example, *crus, cruris,* but it works for the majority of them.

Give the genitive singular of each of the following nominative singular words.

1. unguis	9. pollex
2. lotio	10. latitudo
3. rigiditas	11. sudamen
4. arrector	12. fons
5. basis	13. acumen
6. dolor	14. naris
7. falx	15. impetigo
8. regio	

Translate the following. Words in parentheses may be omitted.

1. rigor mortis
2. venae cordis (anteriores)
3. incisura apicis cordis
4. dorsum pedis
5. foramen apicis dentis
6. fragilitas ossium
7. ligamenta (collateralia) articulationum digitorum (manus)
8. musculus rectus abdominis
9. fissura auris (congenita)
10. musculus longus capitis
11. compressor naris
12. extensor indicis
13. arrectores pilorum
14. retinacula cutis
15. ligamenta basium
16. flores sulfuri
17. radix unguis

NEW BASES

Learn the following bases and their meanings.

1. ARC(U)-, "bow," "arch" *(arcus)*
   (gen.) arcade

   arciferous—applies to the pectoral arch of toads

   arciform—shaped like an arch or a bow

   arcualia—small, cartilaginous pieces, dorsal and ventral, fused or free, on the vertebral column of fishes

   arcatura—a condition of horses marked by the undue outward curvature of the forelegs

2. CALCAR-, "spur" *(calcar)*

   calcarine—a fissure extending to the hypocampal gyrus on the medial surface of the cerebral hemisphere

   calcarate—having a spur or spurlike point

   calcarium or *calcar*—a spurlike prominence, as a clawlike process on the leg or wing of a bird that is not the termination of a digit

3. CING-, CINCT-, "to bind," "to gird"
   (gen.) precinct, succinct

   cingulum—a girdle; the waist

   subcingulum—the lower lip part of the cingulum of rotifers

   cingulectomy—the surgical removal of the cingulate gyrus (in the brain)

4. CLIV-, "slope" *(clivus)*
   (gen.) proclivity

   declive—a lower or descending part

   clivus—a slope

   postclival—the fissure behind the clivus of the cerebellum

5. CUSPID-, "point" *(cuspis)*

   cusp—a pointed or rounded eminence on or near the masticating surface of a tooth; that which is designed to occlude in the sulcus of a tooth; one of the pointed flaps or leaflets making up a heart valve

   bicuspid—having two cusps, as bicuspid teeth, or as the mitral valve of the heart

   multicuspid—with several cusps or tubercles; applies to molar teeth

quadricuspid—having four cusps

6. FASCI-, "band" *(fascia)*
    fascia—an ensheathing band of connective tissue
    fasciola—a narrow color-band
    fasciole—a ciliated band on certain echinoids used for sweep-
    ing water over surrounding parts
    fascitis—inflammation of a fascia
    fasciodesis—the suturing of a tendon to a fascia

7. FERR-, "iron" *(ferrum)*
    ferrihemoglobin—hemoglobin in which the iron is normally in
    a ferrous state
    ferrotherapy—treatment of disease by use of chalybeates
    ferruginous—having the color of iron rust

8. FLAGELL-, "whip," "whiplike appendage" *(flagellum)*
    paraflagellum—a subsidiary flagellum
    hemoflagellate—any protozoan flagellate living in the blood of
    its host
    Flagellaria—a genus of herbs with leaves terminating in a
    tendril

9. GLABR-, "smooth" *(glaber)*
    glabrous or *glabrate*—with a smooth, even surface; devoid of
    hairs
    glabella—the space on forehead between the supercilliary
    ridges
    glabificin—an antibody which renders bacteria smooth

10. LIEN-, "spleen" *(lien)*
    lienal—pertaining to the spleen; applies to an artery, vein or
    nerve plexus
    gastrolienal—pertaining to the stomach and spleen
    lienotoxin—a cytotoxin with specific effect on spleen cells

11. LONG-, "long" *(longus)*
    longicorn—having long antenna, as some beetles
    longirostrine—having a long jaw
    longimanous—long-handed

12. NAS-, "nose" *(nasus)*
    nasion—the middle point of the nasofrontal suture

nasute—having a well-developed proboscis; member of a caste of soldier termites with snoutlike processes

nasicorn—bearing a horn or horns on the nose

13. NUC-, "nut" *(nux)*

nucellus—parenchymatous tissue between the ovule and its inner integument

nuculanium—a fleshy fruit, as a grape

mononucleosis—a condition of the blood or tissues in which there is an above-normal increase in the number of large, mononuclear leukocytes or monocytes

nucleolin—the substance of which the nucleus is formed

nucleic acids—one of a group of compounds found in nuclei and cytoplasm

nuclease—an enzyme capable of splitting nucleic acids

14. OS-, OR-, "mouth" *(os)*

aborad—tending aborally; situated or directed away from the mouth

osculum—an excurrent opening in a sponge

deorality—the shifting of instinctual activity away from gratification through oral expression

osculant—closely adherent; intermediate in character between two groups

osculation—anastomosis of vessels; kissing

osculometer—a gradual series of circular arcs for determining by superposition the curvature at any point on a curve

15. PALLI-, "mantle," "covering" *(pallium)*

pallial—pertaining to mantle of a mollusc; pertaining to the cerebral cortex

branchiopallial—pertaining to the gill and mantle of molluscs

neopallium—the cerebral cortex

16. PRON-, "inclined," "face down" *(pronus)*

prone—lying with the face downward

pronator—a muscle that produces pronation

17. SAC(C)-, "bag," "sac" *(saccus)*

saccate—pouched

sacellus—a one-seeded, indehiscent pericap enclosed within a hardened calyx *ovisac*—old term for an ovarian follicle

18. SIN(U)-, "curve," "hollow," "cavity" *(sinus)*
     (gen.) insinuate
     sinuate—winding; tortuous; having a wavy margin
     sinusoid—a minute blood space in organ tissue
     perisinuous—surrounding a sinus

19. STA-, STAT-, "to stand"
     (gen.) circumstance, extant, instant, status, substance
     distolabial—relating to the distal and labial surfaces of the teeth
     distoversion—the tilting of a tooth so that the crown moves distally
     instance—in psychoanalysis, the dominance or perseverance of one kind of mental function in comparison to others
     stabile—stationary; immobile, maintaining a fixed position
     stable—compound which is unlikely to break down or dissolve

20. VITR-, "glass" *(vitrum)*
     vitrella—a crystalline cone cell of an invertebrate eye
     vitreodentine—a very hard variety of dentine
     vitrescence—the condition of becoming hard and transparent like glass
     vitrina or *vitreous*—the transparent, gelatinlike substance filling the globe of the eye
     Vitrina—a genus of land snails having a thin, translucent shell

EXERCISE

List the prefixes, bases and suffixes and give their meanings.

1. *vitrification*—the act or process of making glass; the glassy condition of cells or organisms which have been instantly frozen

2. *sacculation*—the state or process of being sacculated; divided into small sacs; the formation of small sacs

3. *palliopedal*—pertaining to the molluscan mantle and foot

4. *distad*—toward or at a position away from the center or from the point of attachment

5. *declivous*—sloping downward

6. *sinupalliate*—in molluscs, having a well-developed siphon, and so an indented pallial line

7. *exflagellation*—the formation of actively motile flagella in the microgametocyte

8. *palliative*—that which affords relief but not cure

9. *lienculus* or *lienunculus*—a detached part of the spleen; accessory spleen

10. *pronation*—the condition of being prone; the act of placing in a prone position; the turning of the palm of the hand downward

11. *glabrescent*—glabrous or becoming glabrous

12. *enucleate*—to remove an organ or a tumor in its entirety, as an eye from the socket; literally translates as "to take out the kernels"

13. *Fasciola*—a genus of trematode flukes

14. *fascioliasis*—infestation with the *Fasciola hepatica;* normally occurs in sheep and other herbivorous animals

15. *longipedate*—long-footed

16. *arcuate*—arched, curved, bow-shaped

17. *hypoferremia*—a diminished or abnormally low iron level in the blood

18. *nucivorous*—nut-eating

19. *cincture*—a girdle or belt

20. *tricuspidate*—having three points; applies to leaves

21. *postnasal*—situated behind the nose

22. *inosculation*—the joining of blood vessels by direct communication; the uniting by small openings

23. *circumoral*—around or near the mouth

24. *subcalcarine*—under the calcarine fissure in the brain

25. *flagellomania*—sexual excitement from whipping or being whipped

MORE WORDS TO WORK WITH

adnasal	arc	cingulate
aerosinusitis	barosinusitis	coctostable
aflagellar	biflagellate	cuspule

MORE WORDS TO WORK WITH *(Continued)*

declivity	instability	oral
distal	in vitro	orifice
ecalcarate	lienitis	palliate
elongate	lienomalacia	prone
fasciolicide	longevity	pronograde
ferric	longitude	sacciform
ferroconcrete	nasal	saccular
ferromagnetism	nuciamentaceous	sinuous
flagellula	nuciferous	sinus
frigostable	nuclear	stature
glabellad	nucleolate	vitritis
infranasal	orad	vitropression

LESSON 37.   Latin Fourth and Fifth Declension Nouns

Endings of fourth declension nouns are as follows. Almost all nouns in this declension are masculine; a few of them are neuter.

	Masc.		Neut.	
	sing.	plur.	sing.	plur.
nom.	*-us*	*-us*	*-u*	*-ua*
gen.	*-us*	*-uum*	*-us* or *-u*	*-uum*

Examples:

nom.	ductus	ductus	cornu	cornua
gen.	ductus	ductuum	cornu(s)	cornuum

It is difficult to distinguish this class of noun from the second declension masculine ending in *-us*, as, for example, *stimulus,* but fortunately there are not too many nouns of this class, and they usually appear in the nominative singular, where they do not differ from the second declension form.

A number of fourth declension nouns are formed on the base of verbs. These are nouns which make use of the suffix *-us*, "act of," "result of the act of" (see Lesson 32).

AUDIT-, "to hear"   + *-us*   auditus, "sense of hearing"

pro- + CESS-, "to go"	+ -*us*	processus, "process"	
CREPIT-, "to crackle"	+ -*us*	crepitus, "crackling"	

Translate the following phrases. Adjectives in parentheses may be omitted.

1. ductus lacrimales
2. ligamenta collateralia articulationum digitorum manus
3. genu internum radicis nervi (facialis)
4. septum sinuun (frontalium)
5. arteria genu (suprema)
6. ligamenta (cruciata) genu
7. processus articulares
8. apertura externa aqueductus vestibuli
9. cervix cornu

Fifth declension nouns are, for all practical purposes, always feminine. Their endings are as follows.

	sing.	plur.
nom.	-*es*	-*es*
gen.	-*ei*	-*erum*

Examples:

nom.	scabies	scabies
gen.	scabiei	scabierum

Translate the following phrases.

1. facies dorsalis
2. arteria transversa faciei
3. facies articulares inferiores

NEW BASES

Learn the following bases and their meanings.

1. CALC-, CALCANE-, "heel" *(calx; calcaneus)*
   calcaneal—pertaining to the heel bone

calcaneocavus—a type of talipes (talipes—a deformity of the foot)

calcaneus—the heel bone

2. CERVIC-, "neck" *(cervix)*

buccocervical—pertaining to the cheek and the neck; also pertaining to the buccal surface and neck of a tooth

cervicobrachialgia—condition in which pain extends from cervical region to arms or fingers

endocervicitis—inflammation of the lining membrane of the cervix uteri

cervicum—the flexible intersegmental region joining the insect head and thorax

3. CORP-, CORPUS-, CORPOR-, "body" *(corpus)*

(gen.) corporal, incorporeal, corps

incorporation—the process of intimately mixing the particles of different bodies into a practically homogeneous mass

corpuscle—a small, rounded body; an encapsulated sensory nerve end-organ; an old term for blood cell

4. COX-, "hip," "hip joint" *(coxa)*

coxa—the proximal joint of the leg of an insect

intercoxal—between coxae

epicoxite—a small process at the end of the toothed part of the coxa in insects

coxopodite—the proximal part of the protopodite of the crustacean limb

coxosternum—plates formed by fusion of the coxites and sternum

5. FIBUL-, "clasp," "outer bone of the leg" *(fibula)*

fibula—the slender bone at the outer part of the leg

infibulation—the act of clasping or fastening a ring or frame to the genital organs to prevent copulation

parafibular—pertaining to an accessory element outside the fibula

6. FREN-, "rein," "bridle" *(frenum)*

frenum—a fold of integument at the junction of the mantle and body of Cirripedia

frenate—having a frenum

frenulum—a fold of membrane, as a process on hindwing of Lepidoptera for attachment to forewing

7. FURC-, "fork" *(furca)*

   trifurcate—with three forks or branches

   furciferous—bearing a forked appendage, as some insects

   furcula—a forked process or structure

   furculum—any furcula, but especially the wishbone

   furcasternum—the forked poststernite or sternellum in many insects

8. FUS-, "spindle" *(fusus)*

   fuseau—a spindle-shaped structure

   fusula—the minute tubes of a spinneret

   Fusobacterium—a genus of spindle-shaped bacteria

9. FUSC-, "dark," "brown," "tawny" *(fuscus)*

   fuscous—grayish-brown

   subfuscous—somewhat fuscous; dusky

   fuscin—a brown pigment in the retinal epithelium

   obfuscation—mental confusion

10. GEMM-, "bud" *(gemma)*

    (gen.) gem

    gemmation—budding

    gemmule—a small bud

    gemmulation—the formation of gemmules

    gemmiparous—reproducing by bud formation

11. GEN(U)-, "knee" *(genu)*

    (gen.) genuflect

    genu—a kneelike bend in an organ or part; the anterior end of the corpus collosum

    geniculum—a sharp bend in a nerve

    genupectoral—pertaining to the knee-chest posture

12. GERM-, GERMIN-, "sprout," "bud," "germ" *(germen)*

    (gen.) germane

    germiduct—the oviduct of a trematode

    germigen—the ovary of a trematode

    dysgerminoma—a tumor of an ovary

    germicide—an agent that kills germs

    ovigerm—a cell which produces or develops into an ovum

13. **MAL(E)-, "bad"** *(malus)*
(gen.) malefactor, malevolent, malfeasance, malediction
malinger—to pretend to be ill
malocclusion—any deviation from normal occlusion of the teeth
malpractice—improper medical treatment through carelessness, ignorance or intent

14. **NAR-, "nostril"** *(naris)*
naricorn—the horny part of the nostrils in Turbinares
nariform—shaped like nostrils
internarial—situated between the nostrils
narica—the brown coati

15. **PAPILL-, "nipple"** *(papilla)*
epapillate—not having papillae
papilliform—like a papilla in shape
papillose—bearing papillae

16. **PECTIN-, "comb"** *(pecten)*
pectinella—a comblike membranella of some infusoria
pectineal—applies to the process of the pubis of birds
pinnatopectinate—pinnate with pectinate lobes

17. **PINN-, PENN-, "feather," "wing," "fin"** *(pinna; penna)*
(gen.) pen, pinnacle
bipenniform—feather-shaped, with sides of vein of equal size
brevipennate—with short wings
pennaceous—penniform; like a plume or feather
bipinnate—having leaflets growing in pairs or paired stems
pinnule—a secondary leaflet of a bipinnate or pinnately compound leaf
bipinnatific—with leaves segmented, and then segments again divided
pinnatisect—with leaves lobed almost to base or midrib
pinnatodentate—pinnate with toothed lobes
Pinnipedia—a suborder including seals and walruses

18. **PULMO(N)-, "lung"** *(pulmo)*
gastropulmonary—pertaining to the stomach and lungs
pulmogastric—pertaining to the lungs and stomach

pulmobranchia—a gill-like organ adapted to air-breathing conditions; a lung book, as of spiders

19. RAD-, RAS-, "to scrape"
(gen.) eraser

radula—a short and broad strip of membrane with longitudinal rows of chitinous teeth found in the mouth of most gastropods

raduliform—like a radula, or flexible file

rasorial—adapted for scratching or scraping, as fowls

rastellus—a group of teeth in arachnid chelicera

erasion—the surgical removal of tissue by scraping

20. VAGIN-, "sheath" *(vagina)*

vagina—a sheath; the canal from the vulvar opening to the cervix uteri

vaginicoline—living in the vagina, as an animalcule

evagination—outpouching of a layer or part

EXERCISE

List the prefixes, bases and suffixes and give their meanings.

1. *invagination*—the act of ensheathing or becoming ensheathed; the process of burrowing or infolding to form a hollow space within a previously solid structure, as the invagination of the nasal mucosa within a bone of the skull to form a paranasal sinus

2. *pinninervate*—with veins disposed like parts of a feather

3. *bifurcate*—to divide into two branches

4. *pinnatifid*—applies to leaves lobed halfway to the midrib

5. *subgeniculate*—somewhat bent

6. *fibulocalcaneal*—pertaining to the fibula and calcaneus

7. *gemmiparity*—the state of reproducing by bud formation

8. *calcaneodynia*—pain in the heel

9. *infuscate*—tinged to appear dark, as insect wings

10. *hysterofrenic*—capable of checking an attack of hysteria

11. *gemmaceous*—pertaining to buds

12. *intragemmal*—within a taste bud

13. *corpulence*—obesity

14. *cervicodynia*—cramp or neuralgia of the neck

15. *cellipetal*—moving toward a cell

16. *cervicovaginitis*—an inflammation involving the cervix uteri and vagina

17. *subpectinate*—tending to be comblike in structure

18. *fusocellular*—consisting of spindle-shaped cells

19. *abradant*—an agent which scrapes or rubs off the external layers of a part; an abrasive

20. *coxalgia*—disease of the hip

21. *papilloma*—a neoplastic growth of epithelium

22. *cardiopulmonary*—pertaining to the heart and lungs

23. *malinterdigitation*—abnormal occlusion of the teeth

24. *antenarial*—situated in front of the nostrils

25. *corrasible*—erasable

26. *corassin*—the wearing away of rocks in stream

MORE WORDS TO WORK WITH

bilifuscin	gemmiferous	papillitis
bipectinate	geniculate	papillomatosis
cervicectomy	germarium	petit mal
corpse	germinate	pinnigrade
coxitis	haemofuscin	pulmonary
extracorporeal	malaise	pulmotor
fibular	malaria	rasion
frenotomy	mal de mer	vaginate
furcate	malignant	vaginipennate
furcellate	malposition	vaginula
fusiform	narial	vanilla
fusospirillar	papillary	

LESSON 38.   Latin First and Second Declension Adjectives

Adjectives agree with the noun they modify in *case, number* and *gender*. Adjectives do not have a particular gender of their own, but take on the gender of the noun with which they are used. Unlike English, Latin adjectives are usually placed after the noun; e.g., musculus longus.

One type of adjective combines the endings of both the first and second declensions. In other words, it can have the -a set of endings, the -us set of endings or the -um set. It has the -a set when used with feminine nouns, the -us set with masculine nouns and the -um set with neuter nouns. Note that if the case and number of the noun change, the case and number of the adjective likewise change: bursa longa, bursae longae, bursum longarum. Similarly, musculus longus, musculi longi, etc.; dorsum longum, dorsi longi, dorsa longa, etc. When this type of adjective is used with first or second declension nouns, there is no problem; the adjective has the same ending as the noun, as can be seen from the examples. Translate the following phrases.

1.   atrium cordis dextrum

2.   ligamentum carpi transversum

3.   musculus longus colli

4.   bursae subcutaneae

5.   palatum durum

6.   musculus flexor digiti quinti

The difficulty arises from the fact that adjectives do not necessarily agree with nouns in declension. Thus, one finds the first and second declension type of adjective used not only with first and second declension nouns, but also with third, fourth and fifth declension nouns, and in such instances noun and adjective will not have identical endings. Each adjectival ending is determined by the gender and case of the noun it modifies, e.g., dura mater, genu corporis callosi.

Use the correct form of the word *albus* to modify each of the following nouns. Example: extensor albus.

1.   putamen

2.   flexor

3.   corona

4.   ramus

5.   impressio

6. facies
7. flexibilitas

Translate the following phrases.

1. dermatitis factitia
2. cor adiposum
3. cornu cutaneum
4. ductus biliferi
5. corpus luteum
6. lac fermentum
7. pes arcuatus
8. pars flaccida
9. calx chlorinata
10. dermatitis calorica
11. flexibilitas cerea
12. corpus adiposum buccae
13. dermatitis exfoliativa
14. filum durae matris spinalis

As with second declension masculine nouns, a few first and second declension adjectives have a nominative singular ending in -*er*, e.g., *dexter, sinister,* although the other endings are regular. Another termination of adjectives is -*issimus* or -*rimus,* the superlative ending, which is to be found in such phrases as musculus latissimus colli, musculus longissimus dorsi and pulsus celerrimus.

NEW BASES

Learn the following bases and their meanings.

1. FACI- (-FICI-), "face," "surface" *(facies)*
    bifacial—applies to leaves with distinct upper and lower surfaces
    dentofacial—pertaining to both the teeth and the face
    coronofacial—relating to the crown of the head and the face
    interface—a surface which forms the boundary between two faces or systems

demifacet—part of a parapophysis facet when divided between centra of two adjacent vertebrae

superficies—the outer surface

2. FRUG-, FRUCT-, "fruit" *(frux)*

fructification—fruit formation

fructose—fruit sugar

fructescence—the period of maturing of fruit

3. GEMIN-, "twin," "paired" *(geminus)*; GEMELL-, diminutive form of "twin" *(gemellus)*

(gen.) Gemini

geminate—growing in pairs; paired

bigeminate—doubly paired; twin-forked

bigeminy—the condition of occurring in pairs; in cardiology, a premature beat coupled with each normal beat

4. GEN-, GENIT-, "to produce," "to beget"; GENER-, "race," "kind" *(genus)*

(gen.) progenitor, congenial, ingenious, degenerate

congener—a person, animal, plant or thing allied by origin, nature or function to another

genital—pertaining to the reproductive organs

generic—pertaining to a genus; general

5. GINGIV-, "the gums" *(gingiva)*

gingiva—the gums

gingivosis—a disease of the gums of poorly nourished children

labiogingival—pertaining to the lips and gums

6. INCUD-, "anvil" *(incus)*

incus—the middle arc of the chain of ossicles in the ear, so named from its resemblance to an anvil

incudate—relating to the incus; also applies to a type of rotifer mastax with large and hooked rami and reduced mallei

incudectomy—surgical removal of the incus

7. LUTE-, "yellow," "corpus luteum" *(luteus)*

corpus luteum—the yellow endocrine body formed in the ovary at the site of a ruptured Graafian follicle

luteal—pertaining to the corpus luteum

lutein—a yellow chemical isolated from egg yolk

luteoma—an ovarian tumor made up of cells resembling those seen in the corpus luteum

urolutein—a yellow pigment sometimes found in urine

lutescent—becoming yellow

luteofuscous—any of several dark, grayish colors averaging orange-yellow in hue

8. MALLE-, "hammer" *(malleus)*

malleate—hammer-shaped

submalleate—somewhat hammer-shaped

malleolar—the vestigial fibula in ruminants

malleoramate—applies to a type of trophi with looped manubrium and toothed incus in the rotifer gizzard

malleation—a spasmodic action of the hands, consisting of continuously striking any nearby object

malleus—one of the ossicles of the internal ear having the shape of a hammer

malleotomy—incision of or division of the malleus

9. NOD-, "knot" *(nodus)*

node—the knob or joint of a stem at which the leaves arise; an aggregation of specialized cardiac cells; any small rounded organ, knob or protuberance

binodal—having two nodes, as the stem of a plant

noduliferous—bearing nodules; applies to roots of leguminous plants

trichonodosis—a pseudoknotting and fraying of the hair associated with thinning and breaking of the hair shaft

10. OLE-, "oil" *(oleum)*

oleiferous—producing oil

oleosome—a plastid in a plant cell which forms or helps to form oil globules; elaioplast

olein—a fat which is liquid at ordinary temperatures, found in animal and vegetable tissues

oleophobic—lack of strong affinity for oils

oleocellosis—a spotting of citrus fruits by oil liberated from the oil glands of the rind

oleocyst—a diverticulum of the nectocalyx in various Calycophora that contains oil

11. ORB-, ORBIT-, "circle," "cavity of the eye" *(orbita)*
orbitomalar—pertaining to orbit and malar bone
orbiculate—nearly circular in outline; applies to leaves
orbitale—the lowest point on the inferior margin of the orbit
Orbicella—genus of star corals

12. PALPEBR-, "eyelid" *(palpebra)*
palpebra—either of the two movable folds that protect the eyeball
palpebrate—furnished with eyelids; to wink
palpebral—pertaining to the eyelid

13. PEL(L)-, PULS-, "to push," "to drive," "to beat"
(gen.) repel, expulsion, impulsive, propellant
pulsellum—a flagellum situated at the posterior end of the protozoan body
impulsion—the act of driving or urging onward, either mentally or physically
pulsatile—pulsating, throbbing
pulsion—the act of pushing forward
retropulsion—a driving or turning back, as of the fetal head; a running backward; a form of walking sometimes seen in Parkinsonism

14. PLUR-, "more," "many" *(plus)*
(gen.) plurality
pluriparity—the condition of having born several children
plurivorous—living upon several hosts, as fungus
plurilocular—having more than one compartment or loculus

15. SCAND- (-SCEND-), SCANS-, "to climb"
(gen.) descend, transcend
scansorius—the small, anterior gluteal muscle
scandent—climbing in any manner
Scansores—an order of birds having two toes before and two behind, such as parrots

16. SCOP-, "broom," "brush" *(scopa)*
scopate—having a tuft of hair like a brush
scopulate—like a brush
Scoparius—a species of shrub commonly called broom-tops

17. SOLV-, SOLUT-, "to loosen," "to dissolve"
    (gen.) insolvent, resolution, dissolute
    absolute—free from admixture
    solute—the dissolved substance in a solution
    solvent—that component of a homogeneous mixture which is in
        excess; a liquid which dissolves another substance
        with no change in chemical composition; a liquid
        which reacts chemically to bring a solid into solution

18. STRI-, "furrow," "groove" *(stria)*
    stria- a streak or a line; a narrow, bandlike structure
    striature—striation, state of being striated; arrangement of
        striae
    striatum—striped or grooved

19. TEND-, TENS-, TENT-, "to stretch"; TENDIN-, "tendon"
                                                        (tendo)
    (gen.) tendency, extend, extent, attention, tense
    tension—the act of stretching; the state of being stretched or
        strained
    distension—a state of dilatation
    tensor—a muscle that serves to make a part tense

20. VELL-, VULS-, "to tear"
    avulsion—the forcible tearing or wrenching away of a part, as
        a polyp or a limb
    divulsor—an instrument for forcible dilatation of a part or of
        stricture in any organ
    revulsion or *revellent*—the drawing, by irritation, of blood from
        a distant part of the body

EXERCISE

List the prefixes, bases and suffixes and give their meanings.

1. *lateropulsion*—a tendency to move to one side in forward
    locomotion
2. *palpebration*—the act of winking; nictitation
3. *pluriseptate*—with multiple septa
4. *exorbitism*—abnormal protrusion of the eyeball from the orbit
5. *malleable*—capable of being beaten or rolled into thin sheets

6. *liposoluble*—soluble in fats

7. *luteinization*—the formation of corpus luteum

8. *corticostriate*—pertaining to nerve fibers arising in the cerebral cortex and terminating in the corpus striatum

9. *nodose*—characterized by nodes; jointed or swollen at intervals

10. *nodosity*—the state of being nodose

11. *facet*—a small plane surface, especially on a bone or a hard body

12. *dissolution*—separation of a compound into its elements

13. *tendon*—a band of dense, fibrous tissue forming the termination of a muscle

14. *tergeminate*—thrice-forked with thin leaflets

15. *compulsive*—pertaining to an act performed on irresistible impulse

16. *congenital*—present from birth

17. *gingivostomatitis*—inflammation of both gingivae and oral mucosa

18. *iridoavulsion*—avulsion of the iris

19. *incudomalleal*—relating to the incus and the malleus

20. *scansorial*—formed or adapted for climbing; habitually climbing

21. *avulsion*—the forcing, tearing or plucking away of a part

22. *infructescence*—an inflorescence matured into a fruit

23. *scopuliform*—resembling a small brush

24. *frugivorous*—fruit-eating

25. *extensor*—a muscle that extends or stretches a limb or part

26. *oleiferous*—producing oil

MORE WORDS TO WORK WITH

anteorbital	fructosuria	incudal
ascend	geminiflorous	indigenous
convulsion	genocide	intensification
dissolution	gingivalgia	internodal
facioplegia	gingivitis	luteotrophin
fructiferous	hypertension	malleable

MORE WORDS TO WORK WITH (Continued)

mallet
miscegenation
nodular
oleaginous
palpebritis
petroleum
plural
plurigravida

pluripartite
progeny
pulsation
regenerate
scopulite
soluble
striated
striola

subtend
subtentorial
superficial
tendinoplasty
tendinous
tensile
urogenital

LESSON 39.   Latin Third Declension Adjectives

The second type of adjective is that of the third declension; there are no fourth or fifth declension adjectives. The endings of most third declension adjectives are as follows.

	Masc. and Fem.	Neuter	Masc. and Fem.	Neuter
	sing.		plur.	
nom.	*-is*	*-e*	*-es*	*-ia*
gen.	*-is*	*-is*	*-ium*	*-ium*

Examples:

nom.	dorsalis	dorsale	dorsales	dorsalia
gen.	dorsalis	dorsalis	dorsalium	dorsalium

A few adjectives, however, have the nominative singular for all three genders in *-ens* (the present participle); e.g., *paralysis agitans.* The genitive of these is *-entis,* and the other forms are regular. Likewise, the comparative forms of adjectives in the nominative is -(i)*or* for masculine and feminine, -(i)*us* for neuter, e.g., *inferior, inferius; minor, minus.*

Use the correct form of dorsalis to modify each of the following nouns. Example: musculus dorsalis

1. labium

2. corona

3. sudamen

4. digitus

5. facies

6. folium

7. extremitas

8. impressio

9. flexor

Translate the following phrases.

1. adductor brevis
2. ductus semicircularos
3. filum terminale
4. os frontale
5. incisura anterior auris
6. cornu inferius
7. musculi subcostales
8. arteriae recurrentes
9. digitus annularis
10. nervus abducens
11. foramen occipitale magnum
12. venae comitantes
13. arteria dorsalis
14. fissura longitudinalis cerebri
15. musculus cervicalis ascendens
16. musculi intercostales externi

NEW BASES

Learn the following bases and their meanings.

1. ALVEOL-, "cavity," "hollow" *(alveolus)*

   alveolus—the bony socket of a tooth; the air cell of a lung; a cavity, depression or pit cell

   alveolation—the formation of alveoli

   alveolingual—pertaining to the lingual aspects of the alveolar process

   labialveolar—pertaining to the lip and alveolar process of the maxilla and/or mandible

2. ATRI-, "entrance hall," "room" *(atrium)*

   atrium—the first chamber of the heart; the tympanic cavity of the ear below the malleus

   atriocoelomic—connecting atrium and coelom

   interatrial—the groove separating the two atria of the heart

   sinoatrial—pertaining to a region between the atrium and sinus

3. AX-, "axis" *(axis)*
    abaxile—not situated in the line of the axis
    axiate—in reference to a definite axis
    adaxial—turned toward the axis
    axilemma—the sheath surrounding axial cylinders in medullated nerve fibers
    axopodium—a pseudopodium with axial filament

4. BARB-, "beard" *(barba)*
    (gen.) barber
    barbate—bearded; having hair tufts
    barbicel—a small process on a feather barbule
    barbula—the row of teeth in the peristome of certain mosses

5. BIL-, "bile" *(bilis)*
    bilicyanin—a blue pigment resulting from oxidation of biliverdin
    urobilin—a brown pigment of urine
    bilirubinemia—the presence in the blood of bilirubin, the principle pigment of bile

6. BRACTE-, "thin plate" *(bractea)*
    tribracteate—with three bracts; applies to a floral leaf
    bracteole—a secondary bract at the base of a flower
    bracteolate—having a bracteole
    bracteose—with many bracts

7. BURS-, "bag," "pouch" *(bursa)*
    (gen.) bursar, disburse, reimburse
    bursicle—a pouchlike receptacle
    bursiculate—shaped like a small pouch or purse
    bursa—a small sac filled with liquid interposed between parts that move upon one another

8. CLAV-, "club" *(clava)*
    clavate—club-shaped; thickened at one end
    clavellate—diminutive of clavate
    obclavate—club-shaped and attached at the thicker end

9. EGO-, "I"
    alteregoism—an altruistic feeling for only those who are in the same situation as oneself
    egomania—abnormal self-esteem

superego—the subdivision of the psyche which acts as the conscience of unconscious

egoism—the view that self-interest is basis of motivation and morality

egopathy—hostility deriving from the effort to exalt one's own ego by pushing others down

10. ILE-, "ileum" *(ileum)*

ileum—the last division of the small intestine

ileac—pertaining to the ileum

ileocolic—pertaining to the ileum and the colon

11. ILI-, "flank," "hip" *(ilium)*

iliocaudal—connecting the ilium and tail; applies to muscle

sacroiliac—pertaining to the ilium and sacrum

iliopsoas—pertaining to the ilium and the loin

12. LENT-, "lentil," "lens" *(lens)*

caudatolenticular—applies to the caudate and lenticular nuclei of the corpus striatum

lenticil—a ventilating pore in angiosperm stem or roots

lenticulate—lens-shaped

lentigerous—furnished with a lens

lentiginose—freckled; speckled; bearing many small dots

13. PILE-, "cap" *(pileus)*

pileus—one of the cerebellar hemispheres; the membrane which sometimes covers a child's head at birth

pileated—crested; applies to birds

pileolated—furnished with a small cap or caps

14. SPIC-, "point," "spike" *(spica)*

interspicular—occurring between spicules

spicule or *spicula*—a small, spike-shaped bone; a needlelike body

spicate—spiked

spiculum—the dart of a snail

15. UNC-, UNCIN-, "hook" *(uncus; uncinus)*

aduncate—crooked; bent in the form of a hook

unciform—shaped like a hook or barb

unciferous—bearing hooks or hooklike processes

Uncinula—a genus of mildew with hooked appendages

EXERCISE

List the prefixes, bases and suffixes and give their meanings.

1. *bursolith*—a calculus formed within a bursa
2. *subclavate*—somewhat club-shaped
3. *axon*—the efferent process of a nerve cell
4. *axopetal* or *axipetal*—pertaining to nerve impulses transmitted along an axon toward the cell body
5. *egotic*—pertaining to the ego; pertaining to enjoyment of personal pleasures, such as those of body or status; less derogatory in its implications than egotistic or egoistic
6. *barbellate*—with stiff, hooked, hairlike bristles
7. *ileitis*—inflammation of the ileum
8. *pileorrhiza*—a root-covering
9. *iliopagus*—conjoined twins united in the iliac region
10. *subaduncate*—somewhat crooked
11. *circumlental*—surrounding a lens
12. *atriopore*—the opening of the atrial cavity in Cephalochorda
13. *spiculiferous*—furnished with or protected by spicules
14. *axoneme*—a thread of the strand forming an infusorian stalk; an axial filament of a flagellum
15. *atrioventricular*—pertaining to an atrium and a ventricle of the heart
16. *clavicorn*—having club-shaped antennae
17. *ebracteate*—without bracts
18. *spicosity*—the condition of having spikes
19. *interalveolar*—among alveoli, applies to cell islets
20. *myobilin*—a brown pigment excreted in feces in conditions associated with rapid atrophy or destruction of muscle tissue
21. *egomorphous*—tending to read into the actions of others what one wants to find there

MORE WORDS TO WORK WITH

atrium cordis
aveolitis
axil
axiolite
axostyle
barb
Barbet
biliary

bracteody
bursectomy
bursitis
cholecystoileostomy
clavola
egocentric
egotism
ileectomy

ileocolic
iliocostal
iliopectineal
microlentia
pileum
spiculiferous
subunicate

LESSON 40.   Latin Phrases

Translate the following.

1. corrugator supercilii
2. columna fornicis
3. genu internum radicis nervi facialis
4. radix arcus vertebrae
5. musculus obliquus capitis inferior
6. rigiditas cadaverica
7. camera anterior oculi
8. cartilago alaris major
9. morbus coxae senilis
10. cervix columnae posterioris (griseae)
11. depressor alae nasi
12. bursae subcutaneae digitorum dorsales
13. corrugator cutis ani
14. musculus depressor radialis nasi
15. extensor carpi radialis accessorius
16. labia oris
17. digitus minimus
18. linea alba
19. foramen ovale

20. sulcus frontalis inferior
21. facies articulares superiores
22. crista colli costae
23. os uteri internum
24. levator labii superioris
25. frenulum valvulae coli

NEW BASES

Learn the following bases and their meanings.

1. CAN-, "white," "gray" *(canus)*; CAND-, "to be glowing white"
   (gen.) candid, candidate, candor
   incandescent—glowing with heat and light
   canities—grayness or whiteness of the hair
   canescent—grayish

2. CLAV-, "key," "collarbone" *(clavis)*
   (gen.) enclave, exclave
   clavicle—collarbone
   subclavian—under the clavicle
   clavicular—pertaining to the clavicle

3. CLIN-, "to slope," "to lean" (This base is KLIN- in Greek.)
   clinocephaly—congenital flatness or concavity of the vertex of the head
   syncline—a trough of stratified rock in which the beds dip toward each other
   patroclinus—inherited from the father

4. CREN-, "notch" *(crena)*
   crenate—scalloped or notched
   crenation—the creation of abnormal notching in the edge of an erythrocyte
   subcrenate—tending to have rounded scallops

5. FAV-, "honeycomb" *(favus)*
   favella—a conceptacle of certain red algae
   faveolate—honeycombed or alveolate
   favus—a distinctive type of tinea capitis characterized by the formation of honeycomblike mats

6. FRONT-, "forehead," "front" *(frons)*
    frontad—toward the frontal aspect
    frontonasal—pertaining to the frontal sinus and the nose

7. FRUTIC-, "shrub" *(frutex)*
    frutex—a shrub
    frutescent—shrublike
    fruticulose—like a small shrub

8. INGUIN-, "groin" *(inguen)*
    inguinal—in the region of the groin
    exinguinal—occurring outside the groin
    inguinodynia—pain in the groin

9. LAN-, "wool" *(lana)*
    lanolin—hydrous wool fat
    lanuginous—covered with down
    lanopalmic acid—a fatty acid present in wool fat

10. LOB-, "lobe" *(lobus)*
    lobotomy—incision into a lobe
    lobule—a small lobe or subdivision of a lobe
    lobular—pertaining to a lobule

11. LUMB-, "loin" *(lumbus)*
    lumbar—pertaining to the loins
    lumbago—pain in the lumbar region
    lumbocostal—pertaining to the loins and rib

12. NUD-, "naked" *(nudus)*
    nudism—in psychiatry, a morbid tendency to remove clothing; the practice of the nudist cult
    nudibranchiate—having gills not covered by a protective shell or membrane
    nudicaudate—having a tail not covered by hair or fur

13. PAR-, "equal" *(par)*
    parivincular—applies to the bivalve hinge ligament attached to nymphae
    paripinnate—pinnate without a terminal leaflet
    disparate—not situated alike

14. TEMPOR-, "the temples" *(tempora,* pl.)
    temporal—pertaining to the temple

infratemporal—below the temporal fossa

parietotemporal—pertaining to the parietal and temporal bones or lobes

15. VITELL-, "yolk of an egg" *(vitellus)*

vitellus—a yolk; the yolk of the egg of the common fowl

vitellarium—an accessory genital gland found in tapeworms which secretes the yolk or albumin for the fertilized egg

vitelloduct—the duct which conveys vitellus from the yolk gland into the oviduct

EXERCISE

List the prefixes, bases and suffixes and give their meanings.

1. *suffruticose*—somewhat shrubby
2. *prefrontal*—in the anterior part of the frontal lobe
3. *infraclavicular*—beneath a clavicle
4. *ilioinguinal*—pertaining to the iliac and inguinal regions
5. *reclinate*—curved downward from the apex to the base
6. *dorsolumbar*—pertaining to the back and the loins
7. *lanoceric* acid—an acid in wool fat
8. *lanulous*—covered with short, fine hair
9. *canescent*—grayish
10. *disparity*—difference, inequality
11. *bicrenate*—doubly crenate
12. *bilobate*—having two lobes
13. *imparidigitate*—having an odd number of digits
14. *favose*—honeycombed; alveolate
15. *incanous*—hoary, white
16. *nudiflorous*—having flowers without glands or hairs
17. *lipovitellin*—a lipoprotein in egg yolk
18. *vitellolutein*—the yellow pigment from lutein
19. *frontotemporal*—pertaining to the frontal and temporal bones

MORE WORDS TO WORK WITH

adfrontal
anticlinal
autoclave
candle
clavicula
clavicularium
comparable
crenellation
crenocyte
crenulated
declination
denudation
favid

frontogenesis
frontolysis
fruticetum
impar
inclination
inguino-abdominal
interclavicular
interfrontal
intravitelline
lanasteral
lanolated
lanose
lobiped

lobopodium
lubocostal
lumbarization
monoclinic
multilobulate
nudiped
ovovitellin
parity
recline
subinguinal
suffrutex
temporopontine
vitellophag

FURTHER REFERENCES

GENERAL SCIENTIFIC LANGUAGE

Andrews, Edmund. *A History of Scientific English*. Peterboro, N.H.: William Bauhan, Inc., 1947.

Brown, Roland W. *Composition of Scientific Words*. Washington, D.C.: Smithsonian Institution Press, 1954.

Flood, W. E. *Scientific Words: Their Structure and Meaning*. New York: Duell, Sloan, and Pearce, 1960.

Hough, John N. *Scientific Terminology*. New York: Holt, Rinehart, and Winston, 1953.

Nybakken, Oscar E. *Greek and Latin in Scientific Terminology*. Ames: Iowa State University Press, 1959.

Savory, Theodore H. *The Language of Science*. London: Andre Deutsch, 1953.

GENERAL MEDICAL LANGUAGE

Agard, Walter R. and Howe, Herbert M. *Medical Greek and Latin at a Glance*. 3rd ed. New York: Hoeber-Harper, 1955.

Bollo, Louise E. *Introduction to Medicine and Medical Terminology*. Philadelphia: W. B. Saunders Co., 1961.

Cooper, John W. and McLaren, Alexander C. *Latin for Pharmaceutical Students*. 5th ed. London: Pitman, 1950.

Dorland, William A. N. *Dorland's Illustrated Medical Dictionary*. 24th ed. Philadelphia: W. B. Saunders Co., 1965.

———. *Dorland's Pocket Medical Dictionary*. 21st ed. Philadelphia: W. B. Saunders Co., 1965.

Frenay, Sister Mary Agnes Clare. *Understanding Medical Terminology*. 3rd ed. St. Louis, Mo.: Catholic Hospital Association, 1964.

Harnet, Jessie M. *Medical Terminology Made Easy*. Chicago: Physicians' Record Co., 1951.

Hoerr, N. L. and Osol, A. *Blakiston's New Gould Medical Dictionary*. 2nd ed. New York: McGraw-Hill, 1956.

———. *Blakiston's Illustrated Pocket Medical Dictionary*. 2nd ed. New York: McGraw-Hill, 1960.

Jaeger, Edmund C. *A Source-Book of Medical Terms*. Springfield, Ill.: Charles C. Thomas, 1953.

MacNalty, Sir Arthur S. *Butterworth's Medical Dictionary*. London: Butterworth, 1965.

Parr, John A. *Parr's Concise Medical Encyclopedia.* Amsterdam: Elsevier, 1965.

Pepper, Oliver H. *Medical Etymology.* Philadelphia: W. B. Saunders Co., 1949.

Roberts, Ffrangcon. *Medical Terms: Their Origin and Construction.* 4th ed. London: William Heinemann Medical Books, Ltd., 1966.

Schmidt, J. E. *Reversicon: A Medical Word Finder.* Springfield, Ill.: Charles C. Thomas, 1958.

————. *Dictionary of Medical Slang.* Springfield, Ill.: Charles C. Thomas, 1959.

Skinner, Henry Alan. *The Origin of Medical Terms.* 2nd ed. Baltimore: Williams and Wilkins, 1961.

Smith, G. I. and Davis, P. E. *Medical Terminology: A Programmed Text.* New York: John Wiley and Sons, Inc., 1963.

Stedman, Thomas L. *Stedman's Medical Dictionary.* 21st ed. Baltimore: Williams and Wilkins, 1966.

Taber, Clarence W. *Cyclopedic Medical Dictionary.* 9th ed. Philadelphia: F. A. Davis Co., 1964.

Taylor, Norman B. and Taylor, A. E. *The Putnam Medical Dictionary.* New York: G. P. Putnam's Sons, 1961.

Thompson, William. *A. R. Black's Medical Dictionary.* 6th ed. London: Black, 1965.

Wain, Harry. *The Story Behind the Word.* Springfield, Ill.: Charles C. Thomas, 1958.

LANGUAGE FOR SPECIALIZED SUBJECTS

American Psychiatric Association. *A Psychiatric Glossary.* 2nd ed. Washington, D.C.: American Psychiatric Association, 1964.

Ainsworth, G. C. *Ainsworth's and Bisby's Dictionary of the Fungi.* 5th ed. Kew Surrey: English Commonwealth Mycological Institute, 1961.

Atkinson, Thomas G. *Oculo-Refractive Cyclopedia and Dictionary.* 3rd ed. Chicago: Professional Press, 1944.

Bennett, Harry. *Concise Chemical and Technical Dictionary.* 2nd ed. New York: Chemical Press Co., 1962.

Carpenter, J. Richard. *An Ecological Glossary.* New York: Hafner, 1962.

Carter, G. B. *A Dictionary of Midwifery and Public Health.* 2nd ed. London: Faber and Faber, 1963.

Denton, George B. *The Vocabulary of Dentistry and Oral Science.* Chicago: American Dental Association, 1958.

Dobson, Jessie. *Anatomical Eponyms.* 2nd ed. Edinburgh: Livingstone, 1962.

Etter, Lewis E. *Glossary of Words and Phrases Used in Radiology and Nuclear Medicine.* Springfield, Ill.: Charles C. Thomas, 1960.

English, Horace B. and English, Ava C. *A Comprehensive Dictionary of Psychological and Psychoanalytical Terms.* New York: McKay, 1965.

Featherly, Henry. *Taxonomic Terminology of the Higher Plants.* New York: Hafner, 1954.

Goldman, Max R. *Ophthalmic Glossary.* Pittsburgh: Rimbach, 1952.

Gould, Julius and Kolb, William L. *A Dictionary of the Social Sciences*. New York: Free Press of Glencoe (MacMillan), 1964.

Grant, J. *Hackh's Chemical Dictionary*. 4th ed. London: McGraw-Hill, 1964.

Henderson, I. F. and Henderson, W. D. *A Dictionary of Scientific Terms*. 7th ed. Princeton, N.J.: D. Van Nostrand Co., 1960. Also 8th ed. under title *A Dictionary of Biological Terms*. Edinburgh and London: Oliver and Boyd, 1963.

Hinsie, Leland E. and Campbell, Robert J. *Psychiatric Dictionary*. 3rd ed. New York: Oxford University Press, 1960.

Honig, T. M. *The Van Nostrand Chemist's Dictionary*. Princeton, N.J.: D. Van Nostrand Co., 1962.

Jacobs, Morris B. *A Dictionary of Microbiology*. Princeton, N.J.: D. Van Nostrand Co., 1957.

Jaeger, Edmund C. *A Biologist's Handbook of Pronunciations*. Springfield, Ill.: Charles C. Thomas, 1960.

———. *A Source-Book of Biological Names and Terms*. 3rd ed. Springfield, Ill.: Charles C. Thomas, 1962.

Kamenetz, Herman L. *Physiatric Dictionary: A Glossary of Physical Medicine and Rehabilitation*. Springfield, Ill.: Charles C. Thomas, 1965.

Karel, Leonard and Roach, Elizabeth S. *A Dictionary of Antibiosis*. New York: Columbia University Press, 1951.

Kupper, William H. *Dictionary of Psychiatry and Psychology*. Paterson, N.J.: Colt Press, 1953.

Leftwich, A. W. *A Dictionary of Zoology*. Princeton, N.J.: D. Van Nostrand Co., 1963.

Robbins, Samuel D. *Dictionary of Speech Pathology and Therapy*. Cambridge, Mass.: Sci-Art Publishers, 1963.

Rose, Arthur and Rose, Elizabeth. *The Condensed Chemical Dictionary*. 6th ed. New York: Reinhold, 1961.

Savory, Theodore H. *Latin and Greek for Biologists*. London: University of London Press, 1946.

Snell, Walter H. and Dick, Esther A. *A Glossary of Mycology*. Cambridge, Mass.; Harvard University Press, 1957.

Stearn, William T. *Botanical Latin: History, Grammar, Syntax, Terminology, and Vocabulary*. New York: Hafner, 1966.

Taber, Clarence W. and Castallo, Mario A. *A. Taber's Dictionary of Gynecology and Obstetrics*. Philadelphia: Davis, 1944.

Warren, Howard C. *Dictionary of Psychology*. Boston: Houghton Mifflin, 1934.

Winick, Charles. *Dictionary of Anthropology*. Totowa, N.J.: Littlefield, Adams, and Co., 1968.

INDEX TO BASES

Greek bases appear in **BOLDFACE** type; Latin bases are in *ITALICS*. All page numbers refer to places in which bases first are presented.

D

H

I

X

XANTH-, "yellow," 93
XEN-, "host," "stranger,"
  "foreigner," 137
XER-, "dry," 99
XYL-, "wood," 152

Z

ZO-, "animal," "living being,"
  23
ZYG-, "yoke," 108
ZYM-, "ferment," "enzyme,"
  144